CROSS-CLASS FAMILIES

Cross-class Families

A Study of Wives' Occupational Superiority

SUSAN McRAE

CLARENDON PRESS · OXFORD

1986

Oxford University Press, Walton Street, Oxford OX2 6DP
Oxford New York Toronto
Delhi Bombay Calcutta Madras Karachi
Kuala Lumpur Singapore Hong Kong Tokyo
Nairobi Dar es Salaam Cape Town
Melbourne Auckland
and associated companies in
Beirut Berlin Ibadan Nicosia

Oxford is a trade mark of Oxford University Press

Published in the United States
by Oxford University Press, New York

British Library Cataloguing in Publication Data
McRae, Susan
Cross-class families: a study of wives'
occupational superiority.
1. Marriage   2. Interpersonal relations
3. Wives—Employment
I. Title
306.8'72   HQ734
ISBN 0-19-827264-2
ISBN 0-19-827263-4 Pbk

60 036 41 22 6

Set by Spire Print Services, Ltd., Salisbury
Printed in Great Britain
at the University Printing House, Oxford
by David Stanford
Printer to the University

For Alan

Acknowledgements

Many people helped me in the creation of this book. First and foremost are the families themselves: the thirty women and twenty-six men who generously gave me time and information. Without them the book would not exist; I am both indebted and grateful to them all. I trust I have represented their views faithfully, and hope they will forgive me any differences in interpretation which might exist between us. My thanks also go to the various personnel managers, union representatives, nursing officers, supervisors, and head teachers who helped me locate these families. A tedious process was alleviated through their kind co-operation.

This book is an amended version of my doctoral thesis. My thesis supervisor, Mr John Goldthorpe, guided and encouraged me throughout the four years needed to complete the work. His insights and criticisms helped make the thesis better than I originally thought possible. To him go many thanks. I owe a debt also to Dr Anthony Heath, who helped me get started on this research project. Although we came to differ somewhat in the final analysis, his understanding and friendship in the beginning were very important.

Finally, I must acknowledge the financial support given to me for three years by the Association of Commonwealth Universities and, in my final year, by the Social Sciences and Humanities Research Council of Canada. Their support, although generous, was not always enough, however. And when it was not, my sister Nancy came to my rescue. To her goes the last word and my heartfelt gratitude.

S.M.

Nuffield College
Oxford
March, 1985

Contents

List of Tables

Abbreviations

ASTMS	Association of Scientific, Technical, and Managerial Staffs
BL	British Leyland
BR	British Rail
BT	British Telecom
HNC	Higher National Certificate
MLSO	Medical Laboratory Scientific Officer
NORC	National Opinion Research Centre
RG	Registrar-General
SEG	Socio-economic group
SEI	Socio-economic Index
SRN	State-registered nurse
WES	Women and Employment Survey

1

Introduction

This book is about cross-class families. A cross-class family is one in which both husband and wife undertake paid employment but at very different levels in the occupational structure. For example, a scientist may be married to an office clerk, a teacher to an electrician or a nurse to a lorry driver. All of these may be called cross-class families. This categorization assumes that the majority of people in modern capitalist society derive their class position from their relationship to the occupational structure. As a result of this, and because of the complexity of the modern occupational structure, several variations of cross-class families potentially exist. The most interesting variation for sociological analysis, however, is the cross-class family in which the wife holds a higher level occupation than her husband. Such families invite study if for no other reason than they seem, at first glance at least, to fly in the face of social convention and practice. The most dramatic instance of this family is one in which the *wife* is employed at a professional level and her husband as a manual worker: the cross-class family *par excellence* and, as such, the subject of this work.

Very little is known about cross-class families. Until recently their existence was obscured by the exclusion of women from social class analysis. Attempts to rectify this exclusion have led to a continuing debate over the place of women in stratification analysis, one result of which has been to reveal the existence of families who may be neither working class nor middle class but rather what has come to be called cross-class.[1] Women have generally been excluded from class analysis by the conventional practice within sociology of assigning entire families to class positions on the basis of the occupation of the family 'head'—that is, on the basis of the occupation of the husband. An increase in the labour force participation of women, and especially of married women, led to this conventional practice being called into question. From 1881 until 1951, the labour force participation rates of all women remained constant at about 35%. By the census year 1961, however, this participation had begun to increase, climbing by 1971 to 43%, and by 1981 to 47%. For married women, the change has been more dramatic. In 1911, the labour force participation rate of married women was less than 10%. By 1951 this figure began to increase such that by 1971 it stood at 42%, and by 1981 had reached nearly 50%. During these years, then, the involvement of wives in paid employment changed from only one in ten working outside the home to one in two.[2] In light of this increased employment, critics argue, should not married women be regarded in class terms as more than passive beneficiaries of their husband's occupational attainments? Should they not be seen as co-determiners at least of their class fates? And as such, should they not occupy places of their own in the analysis of class stratification?

The reasons behind the exclusion of married women from unique places in stratification analysis are now quite familiar.[3] In brief, many mainstream sociologists have continued to rely upon husbands' occupations as proxies for the class positions of entire families on the grounds that it is the family, and not the individual, which is the unit of class analysis. And, because of the pattern of wives' employment, this family unit is best represented by the occupation of the male breadwinner. In conventional terms, women remain 'largely peripheral to the class system' and thus, despite their increased labour force participation, are not fundamental to class analysis. Against this conventional approach are those who point out, firstly, that such practice renders women invisible by obscuring the nature of wives' contributions to family resources and class fate through their own occupational positions, educational backgrounds, and economic rewards (Garnsey, 1978); and secondly, that in many familes wives have occupations which may be said to be of a different, and higher, social class than the occupations of their husbands. Assuming that the family's class is determined by the male 'head of household' alone distorts the class position of these families (Acker, 1973; Britten and Heath, 1983) and, as a result, conceals the existence of cross-class families.[4]

Quite clearly, the labour force participation of married women underlies the arguments of both sides to this debate. Because cross-class families were revealed to exist as a direct result of this debate, and—more importantly—because the question of which families are to be regarded as cross-class forms part of this debate, an examination of the participation of married women in paid employment is pertinent. As noted above, the labour force participation of wives has increased dramatically. As might be expected, however, this employment does not follow the same pattern as that of men. Women continue to bear almost complete responsibility for both child-care and housework, and this responsibility is reflected in their patterns of employment. For example, unlike men the majority of married women in paid employment work on a part-time basis. In fact, virtually all of the increase in female labour force participation has come through the increase in women's part-time employment, with the rate of participation of women in full-time employment remaining constant around 30% since 1951. Part-time employment has, however, increased fourfold (Joshi *et al*., 1983: 34). Moreover, nine out of ten of these part-time workers are married women (*General Household Survey 1979*, 1981: Table 5.10. In 1981 more than one-fifth of married women in employment worked 16 hours or less each week, while more than one-half worked 30 hours or less. Only about 40% of married women worked 35 or more hours weekly. Unmarried women and men, however, predominately work full time. In 1981, 73% of unmarried women (including single, divorced, and widowed) and 90% of men in employment worked 35 or more hours each week (*Labour Force Survey 1981*, 1982: Table 4.9, p. 17). Marriage, and the responsibilities of marriage, clearly put wives in a different relationship to the labour force than that experienced by other women and husbands. Part-time employment for women means, moreover, lower rates of pay and fewer opportunities for promotion. The recent Department of Employment survey, *Women and Employment: A Lifetime Perspective* (WES) (Martin and Roberts, 1984), includes over 4,000 married women, of whom 27% were in full-time work and 33% in part-time work. Taking into account the differences in hours worked, the survey found that, on average, part-time women workers earned only £1.60 per hour in comparison with £1.90 per hour for full-time women workers. More than half of the part-time workers surveyed earned less than £1.50 per hour (1984: 46). Furthermore, this survey found that only 16% of part-time women workers believed promotion possibilities existed with their present employers, while nearly 70% reported that no opportunities existed for additional job training. These figures contrast with those for full-time women workers: 41% believed promotion was possible; 46% had opportunities for additional training (1984: 51–2). And as part-time workers, married women are often subject to different legal rights and employment benefits than those which

accrue to full-time employees. Under National Insurance regulations, employers paying less than a specified weekly wage are
exempt from making contributions on behalf of their employees. In
addition, redundancy payments, maternity benefits, minimum
periods of notice, and legal rights against unfair dismissal do not
apply to those working 16 hours or less per week, unless the employee has been continuously employed by the same employer for
five years. Indications are that in 1979 30% of part-time workers in
manual occupations and 23% in non-manual occupations fell into
this unprotected category (Joseph, 1983: 168).

The pattern of married women's employment is not, of course,
constant over the years. Rather, such employment varies with
women's entry into the different stages of the family life cycle. For
the majority of women, motherhood continues to dictate the pattern
and timing of paid employment. Findings from the WES reveal that
marital status alone does not affect women's employment patterns;
rather, the presence of children and the age of the youngest child are
the crucial determinants. Table 1.1 reproduces in part data from the
WES. The table disaggregates women by year of first birth, and
shows the breakdown between working and not working as well as
between full-time and part-time employment. Clearly observed from
this table are the effects of children on mothers' employment. Less
than half of women's time since motherhood is spent in paid employment; at best, only about one-quarter of this time is spent in
full-time employment. Prior to motherhood, however, more than
80% of the time since marriage was spent in full-time paid work
(WES p. 133, Figure 9.9). Families, and family obligations, change
the nature of wives' labour force participation.

The location of women in the occupational structure also has a
bearing on the issue at hand. One of the strongest claims advanced
for the inclusion of married women in class analysis is the fact that a
significant number of wives appear to occupy positions in the occupational structure which are of a higher class than the positions held
by their husbands. Census data is used to demonstrate this potential
occupational disparity between spouses. Referring to those couples
who straddle the manual/non-manual boundary, that is, those couples whose jobs may perhaps have differing class-related attributes,
we find that more than one-third of the husbands in Classes IIIM
and IV, and one-quarter of husbands in Class V have wives in Class
IIINM.[5] In other words, between 25% and 35% of men in manual

Table 1.1 *Proportion of Time that Women with Children have spent Working and Not Working since Birth of First Child by Period of First Birth* (%)

	Period of First Birth					
	1940–4	1945–9	1950–4	1955–9	1960–4	1965–9
Working						
Full time	25	22	21	19	18	14
Part time	19	24	24	26	27	25
Total	44	46	45	45	45	39
Not Working						
Domestic reasons	52	49	51	53	53	59
Other reasons	4	5	4	2	2	2
Total	56	54	55	55	55	61
Base	111	366	449	502	628	635

Note: Other reasons for not working include looking for work, waiting to take up a job, illness.
Source: J. Martin and C. Roberts, *Women and Employment: A Lifetime Perspective*, Department of Employment, London, HMSO, 1984, Table 9.19, p. 132.

work have wives employed in routine white-collar work. Under the auspices of conventional sociology, all of these families would be categorized as 'working class' by virtue of the husbands' occupations. With the inclusion of married women in class analysis, however, they are families who might be better categorized as 'cross-class'. They are the families who, in many respects, form the focus of debate, for, if such a considerable number of families are miscategorized because of the omission of the wives' occupational positions and contributions to family resources and class fate, then much of the analysis of class stratification that has been done to date is potentially inadequate.

That such familes are indeed 'cross-class' is the position taken by Britten and Heath who argue that the 'cross-class family is a large and important category within the contemporary class structure which class theorists ignore at their peril' (1983: 60). Britten and Heath base their arguments upon acceptance (albeit, reluctant acceptance) of the manual/non-manual boundary as the line of cleavage between the working and the middle classes. In doing so, they confront the so-called Boundary Problem in sociology—that is, the question of where the line is to be drawn between the middle class and the working class. Traditionally, this line has been drawn at the manual/non-manual boundary for it is very nearly axiomatic in sociology that life chances, and thus class positions, vary significantly over this divide (Parkin, 1979: 11). However, it is also true, as Britten and Heath note, that the data which support this demarcation are overwhelmingly based upon the experiences of men in the occupational structure. In the case of women in the occupational world, it may well be that this traditional demarcation of class positions does not hold. Non-manual employment for women almost invariably means routine, low-level clerical or sales work and the like. Since the 1960s, women have comprised over 70% of the routine grade non-manual work force. Furthermore, it is this sector of the labour force specifically—the junior non-manual workers—which has called into question the cogency of the traditional boundary between the classes. Whatever doubts may exist about the degredation of employment conditions among male routine white-collar workers, however, few writers dispute that the market and work situations of their female counterparts rarely exceed those of male manual workers.[6] And if they in fact do not better the conditions confronting men in manual employment, there is little reason to assume that marriage between women in routine non-manual work and men in manual work are 'cross-class' at all: husbands and wives in these families will share the same class position.

That there is considerable doubt about the cogency of distinguishing between the middle and working classes on the basis of employment in manual or non-manual work with respect to women workers is known to Britten and Heath. They write:

The usual practice, then, of regarding the manual/non-manual divide as the major 'break' in the class structure separating the middle and working classes is thus called into question in the case of women's jobs. The woman in the lowest level of Class IIIN, that is, the female typist, shop assistant, or office machine operator, might be regarded as occupying what is essentially a proletarian position which has more in common (with regard to its economic conditions) with the manual occupations of Classes IV and V. The same argument might also be extended, although perhaps with less plausibility, to the female clerks and cashiers. (1983: 52)

Despite this understanding of the 'essentially proletarian' nature of much junior white-collar work, Britten and Heath consider the incumbents of such occupations to be in superior positions, in class terms, to men in manual work. Hence, they create a new stratum in the class structure—the cross-class family—comprising husbands in manual and wives in junior non-manual employment. In a later paper, membership in this new class stratum is restricted by the authors when they drop from consideration women in clearly proletarian jobs—the shop assistants (Heath and Britten, 1984). Cross-class families are now to be seen as created by marriage between women in office work—'numerically an extremely important group of women'—and men in manual occupations.[7] However, even this restricted categorization is potentially misleading, and carries with it the possibility of obscuring the actual class position of women in routine office work. The familes singled out by Heath and Britten as 'cross-class' are in fact unlikely to be so. The market and work situations confronting the wives in such families are more likely to resemble those confronting their husbands than to differ in more favourable directions. If the designation 'cross-class' is to have meaning conceptually, it must reflect marked differences relevant to class analysis between the occupational positions of husbands and wives. Heath and Britten's inclusion of women in office work lessens the conceptual clarity of this designation by neglecting the extent to which office work itself offers little in the way of class advantages to the women so employed. An examination of the market and work situations of women in junior non-manual work, drawing upon Heath and Britten and others, confirms that in regard to women's employment at least, non-manual work should not automatically be seen as in a superior position to the great bulk of manual work performed by men. And in doing so, this examination demonstrates that the designation 'cross-class', when applied to the families of men and women in these occupations is, in fact, misplaced.

Market Situation

With regard to market situation, the position of women in junior grade non-manual work may readily be shown as unlikely to be superior to that of men in manual employment.[8] Women have long been paid much less than men. In recent years, women workers in general have earned only 75% of men's wages. In comparing women

in junior non-manual work with men in manual jobs, however, this
income disparity increases. In 1981, female white-collar workers, in
routine positions, earned £77.50 per week on average in comparison
with an average gross weekly wage of £121.90 for male manual
workers. In other words, women so employed earned only 63.5% of the
wages gained by men in the manual occupations.[9] Heath and Britten
confirm the unfavourable position of women in these occupations:
'The position of female office workers in the class structure . . . in
market terms . . . is still subordinate to male manual workers
(1984: 481). The data these authors bring to bear on this issue support their contention: only in terms of sick pay do women in offices
fare better than the majority of male manual workers. In regard to
incomes and pensions—stronger measures of class position than sick
pay, one could argue—women in offices equal only the position of
unskilled male manual labourers, falling significantly behind both
skilled and semi-skilled male manual workers (1984: 478–9).

Between-sex income disparities are both considerable and persis-
tent, and are a reflection of the fact that women most often hold
positions at the bottom of the occupational hierarchy. Promotion
into well-paid positions, for women in routine white-collar occupations, is generally difficult to obtain. In fact, few studies exist about
the promotional possibilities available to such women. However,
data collected in 1980 by Crompton and Jones about the contemporary work situation of clerical employees indicate that the
domestic responsibilities of female clerical workers interfere with
their chances of occupational advancement:

> The bulk of the deskilled, routinized work in the modern office is carried out
> by women, most of whom will never be promoted. Some of the lack of
> promotion may be attributed to gender discrimination but by no means
> all . . . Women . . . do not acquire promotable qualities—notably formal,
> post-entry qualifications and long unbroken work experience; that they do
> not is largely explained by the fact that, for the majority of women, the
> demands of the domestic role—especially the responsibilities associated with
> childrearing—assume priority over those of the work role at key points in
> the individual's career. (1984: 243)

Crompton and Jones report that their findings generally confirm the
views of Stewart *et al.*, who suggest that women white-collar workers
are most usually hired to perform 'the most menial clerical tasks
with limited opportunities for promotion' (1980: 94). Furthermore,

security for women in these routine grade occupations is much more tenuous than either for men in similar occupations or for women in higher level white-collar employment. Recorded unemployment figures for 1981 show that the bulk of unemployment among women workers is found in the junior white-collar occupations. Fifty per cent of the unemployment among women workers was contributed by clerical and other junior non-manual occupations, while women employed in managerial and professional occupations comprised only 10% of the total recorded unemployment. In this, junior non-manual jobs held by women compare with craft and other manual jobs held by men. More than 80% of unemployment among males is found in the manual occupations. For both groups of workers job security is not a guaranteed feature of work-life (*Social Trends*, 13, 1983).

Work Situation

The market situation of female workers in routine white-collar work is thus quite unfavourable and, as such, may be assumed to reflect the work situations which these employees experience. It is more difficult, however, to make clear and definitive statements about work situation than is the case with market situation. This is so for two reasons. In the first instance, data about the work situations of those employed in clerical and routine grade non-manual work are very scarce, although theoretical speculations abound. In the second instance, it is implausible to speak about their work situation in general, as social relationships at work may be expected to vary considerably with the type and size of office in which such workers are located. It is, in fact, in assessing work situation that Silverman's words are most apt: 'If we are to advance from speculation, the pressing need would now seem to be the attempt to dismantle the notion that there exists a unitary occupational group of "white-collar workers" or "clerks"' (1968: 333). Such evidence as does exist, however, renders it possible to make certain limited statements which support the contention that for a great many, perhaps the majority of, women in junior non-manual employment, there is little in their working environment which would place them—in class terms—in positions of obvious superiority to men employed in manual work.

Work situation as outlined by Lockwood may be seen to comprise two elements—an individual's social relationship with his or her co-workers, and the same individual's place in the authority hierarchy and subsequent social relationships with management. In regard to the latter, being confined to low-paid low-level positions means being denied the opportunity to exercise authority and, as for manual workers, means spending the work-day in relationships of subordination to the managers and supervisors who fill the middle-class occupations above. This position in the hierarchy of authority could well mean that 'middle-class assimilation'—often assumed to accrue to those of working-class origin by virtue of their workplace proximity to management—will seldom occur. In large, bureaucratically organized offices, such as in the public sector which provides a considerable portion of jobs for women at this level, social and spatial segregation often exists between upper and lower levels of employees, as McNally notes:

The great majority of females employed in the lower grades of work are physically segregated from the environs of the executives . . . Where . . . there is a concentration of females engaged on principally mechanical tasks, they are often situated in a special work area at some distance from the executive suite. Routine grade clerical workers, on the whole, do not hold highly personal relationships with the management, and indeed they are not expected to. Their immediate boss is much more likely to be a female supervisor and their contact with executives may be minimal. (1979: 75)

In this, junior white-collar workers closely resemble manual workers who are also, by and large, socially and physically separated from management. Furthermore, the environs of large, bureaucratic public sector offices provide little in the way of support for the traditional belief in the identification of junior white-collar workers with the interests of the dominant class as a result of their employment side-by-side with representatives of this class. As Parkin notes, such identification is easier to effect in the private than in the public sector because

. . . not only is there usually no subordinate manual group physically present to inspire a sense of white-collar status elevation, but also the charms of management are likely to seem less alluring when the chain of command stretches ever upwards and out of sight into the amorphous and unlovely body of the state. (1979: 12)

In this work situation, junior non-manual workers take the place of the missing manual workers. They are the subordinate group: at the bottom of the authority hierarchy, they are there to perform specific tasks, rarely to be groomed for promotion, nor to be cultivated for their political views or for intellectual discourse. Such workers are, in effect, the 'working class' of the office.

The comparison of junior white-collar workers with manual workers is often based upon the spread of office mechanization and rationalization as both have a marked effect on the work situation of employees. The effects of rationalization are not sufficiently documented, though, to support the contention that the office is now, for junior grade employees, indistinguishable from the factory (cf. Mumford and Banks, 1967, Braverman, 1974: 326–48). In addition, many offices remain small friendly places, untouched by mechanization or rationalization. In these offices, it is likely that the work situation of clerical and lower grade employees is quite distinct from that of most manual workers. However, evidence does exist that it is specifically *women's* lower grade non-manual occupations which have been the most affected by rationalization, with the effect that it is this work which is now the most routinized (McNally, 1979; Crompton and Jones, 1984). In large offices at least, it is quite likely that the effects of technological change have degraded the position of female clerical employees. Thus it seems certain that in many cases, and in large offices especially, the work situations of junior white-collar workers have little to suggest in the way of superior conditions to those of many manual occupations. Heath and Britten argue otherwise, however, and suggest that for female office workers their '. . . work situation, to follow Lockwood's standard distinction, may be such to offer distinctive experiences that can form a different and independent basis of what might be called 'class behaviour' from those of manual male work' (1984: 481). As Heath and Britten bring little evidence beyond differences in party or class identification to support this contention, there seems little reason to ignore other evidence which does exist, and which suggests the opposite. Certainly, for women in these jobs a cleaner, more pleasant workplace and a lack of obligation to wear 'unflattering overalls and headgear' (McNally, 1979: 76) would not, in class terms, be sufficient to offset the effects of being situated on the lowest rungs of the hierarchy of authority as outlined. Moreover, this means that, for women employed in junior white-collar work and married to manual workers, there would be little in their putative 'middle-class' occupational environments to generate strong contrasts between their class position at work and their class position at home. Husbands and wives in such marriages would in fact share very similar work situations.[10]

And so, on both accounts—market and work situation—female junior white-collar workers cannot be deemed to rank higher in class position than men in manual occupations. There seems little reason, following Britten and Heath, to categorize marriages between such workers as cross-class. Although Britten and Heath do show some preliminary findings which suggest that such families differ slightly from families in which both spouses are employed in manual work,[11] in the absence of further research into the family lives of such couples it seems unlikely that a 'large and important category' in the class structure, hitherto obscured, has now been revealed.

Genuine Cross-class Families

The attention paid by Britten and Heath, among others, to the position of married women in the class structure has, however, revealed the existence of certain families in which there are potentially quite marked class differences in the occupational attainments of husband and wife. Census data show that nearly 10% of men in the manual occupations (Classes IIIM, IV, and V) are married to women in Classes I and II.[12] It is in this group of families, I suggest, that *genuine* cross-class families are to be found. Unlike wives employed in junior non-manual work, there can be little doubt that wives in professional and semi-professional work enjoy certain occupational advantages over their manually employed husbands. These advantages, moreover, place them unambiguously in different positions in the class structure. In the next chapter the differences between these two occupational groups are discussed fully, demonstrating that it is to marriages between men and women so occupied—that is, between men in manual work and women in higher level non-manual or professional work—that the designation 'cross-class' ought to be reserved. Under the aegis of conventional sociology, of course, these families would be categorized as 'working class' by virtue of the husbands' occupations. This study demonstrates that such categorization is misleading, and that when it is the wife who has the superior tie to the occupational structure, either through income, job security, or career prospects, then it is the wife who is 'head of household', at least in so far as this term is used in class analysis. Cross-class families are markedly different from other families in the class structure.

Such families are, of course, few in number. The Census indicates a population of approximately 10% within Britain as a whole. There are reasons to believe that this figure in fact overestimates the number of cross-class families in existence, as is discussed shortly. However, in spite of being a minority pattern within British society, cross-class families remain important for class analysis. Not only do they put into perspective other, putative cross-class families but also—and more importantly—they elucidate the processes of class within the family by reversing the normal relationship of husband and wife to the occupational structure. Should this pattern become more widespread through the continued entry of married women into paid employment, study of their lives today could well be of special importance to class theory in the future.

However, interesting as these familes are to the study of class, they are even more interesting simply as families. In Britain, as elsewhere, it is the norm for husbands, not wives, to form the most enduring and economically rewarding attachment to the labour force. It is the norm for families to derive their standing in the community from the occupational attainments of husbands. It is the norm for women to marry men, if not above them on the social scale, then at least of equal standing. In genuine cross-class families such as the ones to be examined here, however, such norms do not always hold. At first glance at least, cross-class families lead lives which run counter to many of the prevailing social conventions of our society. It is, moreover, as individuals who contravene social norms that the men and women of cross-class marriages have long been known in the pages of English literature. Although such marriages have remained outside the range of vision of most sociologists until quite recently, cross-class marriages—or *mésalliances*, as they have been called—did not escape the view of D. H. Lawrence, Henry James, Charles Dickens, and Thomas Hardy. Their visions, however, were often cruel and harsh, reflecting society's condemnation of those who dared marry, or love, outside their proper social sphere. Walter and Gertrude Morel, for example, in Lawrence's *Sons and Lovers*, lived a life of despair and hatred. The daughter of a 'good old burgher family, famous independents who had fought with Colonel Hutchinson', and herself a teacher, Gertrude Coppard married a miner, swayed by a romantic vision of his occupation:

This was a new tract of life suddenly opened before her. She realized the life of the miners, hundreds of them toiling below earth and coming up at evening. He seemed to her noble. He risked his life daily, and with gaiety. (1929: 11)

Their marriage, however, suffered for their differences, and happiness escaped them:

The pity was, she was too much his opposite. She could not be content with the little he might be; she would have him the much that he ought to be. So, in seeking to make him nobler than he could be, she destroyed him. She injured and hurt and scarred herself, but she lost none of her worth. (1929: 16)

Not all cross-class liasons come to marriage, however. Grace Melbury and Giles Winterborne, in Hardy's *The Woodlanders*, promised to each other since childhood, were prevented from marrying by Grace's acquiescence to the social ambitions of her father. The daughter of a timber merchant, Grace was convinced by her father's words:

I've noticed, and I've noticed it many times, that a woman takes her colour from the man she's walking with. The woman who looks an unquestionable lady when she's with a polished-up fellow, looks a tawdry imitation article when she's hobbing and nobbing with a homely blade. You sha'n't be treated like that for long, or at least your children sha'n't . . . if it costs me my life you shall marry well! Today has shown me that whatever a young woman's niceness she stands for nothing alone. You shall marry well! (1926: 106–7)

Grace had been educated at great expense by her father to a level far beyond her former lover who made his living as a cider-maker. Heeding her father, she turned from Giles and married above her station, to a doctor, the son of former land-owners. Moreover, as Mrs Fitzpiers, Grace initially little regrets having turned from the alliance her father so strongly opposed:

No—I could have never married him! she said, gently shaking her head. Dear father was right. It would have been too rough a life for me. And she looked at the rings of sapphire and opal upon her white and slender fingers that had been gifts from Fitzpiers. (1926: 223)

Rings of sapphire and opal were, however, to be of small comfort to Grace as she realized the cost of her acquiescence to social convention and social ambition. As her husband soon repented his 'cross-class' marriage and turned to the lady of the manor for solace, Grace came to understand that the differences which had separated her from her woodlander were artificial, meaningless—the products of a social order which valued position and place above goodness and love:

> She had made a discovery . . . she had looked into her heart, and found that her early interest in Giles Winterborne had become revitalized into luxuriant growth by her widening perceptions of what was great and little in life. His homeliness no longer offended her acquired tastes; his comparative want of so-called culture did not now jar on her intellect; his country dress even pleased her eye; his exterior roughness fascinated her. Having discovered by marriage how much that was humanly not great could co-exist with attainments of an exceptional order, there was revulsion in her sentiments from all that she had formerly clung to in this kind. Honesty, goodness, manliness, tenderness, devotion, for her only existed in their purity now in the breasts of unvarnished men; and here was one who had manifested such towards her from his youth up. (1926: 277)

Grace's discovery, however, came too late.

Sons and Lovers and *The Woodlanders* are only two of the many examples in literature of cross-class liaisons and, for those who enjoy such tales, the experiences of men and women in fictional *mésalliances* can add to an understanding of real-life individuals found living in apparently similar situations.[13] The modern-day cross-class family shares many of the same problems which confronted fictional couples in times past. Friends and relatives must be reconciled to their union; intellectual differences between spouses must be harmonized; husbands and wives must be valued for who they are rather than for what they do. And looking backwards in time can sometimes help in understanding the force of social norms upon families in our own society. For like the fictional couples in the pages of literature, modern-day cross-class families contravene many of the norms which govern the living together of men and women in marriage. Such families live in a society governed by male occupational dominance; a society which believes that husbands are the main breadwinners, while wives work only for 'pin-money'; which believes that wives complement, but rarely exceed, their husbands' achievements. The study of families who contravene these norms not only throws into sharper relief the patterns of interaction found in socially more 'normal' families, but also reveals the continuing strength of such conventions. When moreover, these norms are stripped away and, in many cases, replaced with their opposites, the family processes which act to sustain or hinder their development are laid bare.

In much of this study, then, cross-class families will be used to illustrate the consequences of deviation from male occupational dominance for family stability and harmony. Talcott Parsons suggests that such deviance will be a source of marital conflict, that joint participation by husband and wife in the labour force when they are equally in competition for occupational status will threaten conjugal stability:

> . . . this small conjugal unit can be a strongly solidary unit. This is facilitated by the prevalence of the pattern that normally only *one* of its members has an occupational role which is of determinate significance for the status of the family as a whole . . . the wife and mother is either exclusively a 'housewife' or at most has a 'job' rather than a 'career'. . . by confining the number of status-giving occupational roles of the members of the effective conjugal unit to one, it eliminates any competition for status as especially between husband and wife, which might be disruptive of the solidarity of marriage. So long as the lines of achievement are segregated and not directly comparable, there is less opportunity for jealousy, a sense of inferiority, etc. to develop. (1943: 192)

Cross-class families provide a clear test of Parsons' theories and so in what follows reference is made to him on several occasions. The initial chapters introduce the families and their work experiences; chapters 5 and 6 focus on work-related issues and their impact on family life; subsequent chapters take the readers into the domestic lives of cross-class families and out of the home into their wider social worlds. The aim throughout is to describe qualitatively the range of variation found in such families. Just as there is no one entity in modern society which may be called 'The Family', this study reveals that there is no one 'Cross-class Family'. Rather, there is a variety of such families, created as the individual men and women so married come to terms with the realities of their personal situations. These families share in common a unique position within society as a consequence of the spouses' occupational attainments. How they respond to their common position varies considerably from family to family. These responses, however, are in large measure shaped by the degree and kind of normative agreements between husband and wife. And where similar agreements hold, similar responses are found.

Notes

1. The debate over the position of women in social stratification analysis has produced a vast literature, for a review of which, see Acker, 1980.
2. Derived from Censuses of Population and British Labour Statistics: Historical Abstracts 1886–1968, quoted in Joseph, 1983. For 1981 figures, see OPCS, *Labour Force Survey 1981*, HMSO, 1982, p. 14. These figures, of course, refer to the proportion of women (or wives) in the labour force in any given year. In addition, it may be noted that virtually all married women will spend some of their married lives in the labour force.
3. The debate in question has been extremely well documented over the past decade, and for this reason I do not repeat it in full here. For a few of the better known quotations from mainstream sociology see Goldthorpe, 1980: 288; Giddens, 1973: 288; Parkin, 1972: 15.
4. For a full discussion of the 'other side' in this debate, see the following: Watson and Barth, 1964; Haug, 1973; Acker, 1973; Oakley, 1974; Ritter and Hargens, 1975; Garnsey, 1978; Philliber and Hiller, 1979; Heath, 1981; Allen, 1982; Britten and Heath, 1983; and others. For a summary of the arguments of these writers see Acker, 1973.
5. Figures in the text are taken from the following:

Social class of husband	Social class of wife (%)					
	I	II	IIINM	IIIM	IV	V
I	7	32	46	4	9	1
II	2	35	42	5	14	2
IIINM	0.7	16	54	17	18	4
IIIM	0.2	9	34	13	33	11
IV	0.1	8	27	11	39	14
V	(13)	6	19	12	41	23
All wives	1	16	36	10	28	9

( ) = Actual number.
$N = 499,314$.

Source: Devised from Table 52, Census 1971, Household Composition Tables (10% Sample) 1975, part 3. Quoted in Ivan Reid, *Social Class Differences in Britain*, 2nd Edition, 1981.

6. The inferior position of women in the labour market has been very well reported; so well, perhaps, that it may be taken as common knowledge. Some of the many sources include: Hakim, 1979; Routh, 1980; Rhee,

1968; Murgatroyd, 1982 on occupational segregation. McNally, 1979;
Routh, 1980; McIntosh, 1980 on income differences. Blackburn, 1967;
McNally, 1979; Heath, 1981; Crompton and Jones, 1982 on promotional prospects. Also see Westergaard and Resler, 1975 for an
overall discussion of women's position in the labour market.

7. Heath and Britten include marriages between men in manual work
and women in higher level non-manual or professional occupations in
the categorization 'cross-class family'. As will be seen in the text, I
agree entirely with this inclusion. Heath and Britten concentrate their
attentions on the numerically larger group of women in junior non-
manual work who are married to manual workers, however. It is only
with regard to this latter group that I find myself in disagreement with
these authors.

8. Market and work situation refer to David Lockwood's now classic
distinctions between the three aspects of class position: market situation or 'the economic position, narrowly conceived, consisting of
source and size of income, degree of job security, and opportunity of
upward occupational mobility'; work situation or 'the set of social relationships in which the individual is involved at work by virtue of his
position in the division of labour'; status situation or 'the position of
the individual in the hierarchy of prestige in the society at large'
(1958: 15). Status situation is not discussed in the text primarily because no major study of the status of occupations held by women has
been undertaken. It is known, however, that the non-manual jobs
normally done by women frequently rank lower than many manual
jobs when such jobs are assessed on the basis of men's tenure; see
Goldthorpe and Hope, 1974. In addition, it has been argued that the
status of 'female' has in itself a status-depressing effect; see Eichler,
1980.

9. See *New Earnings Survey 1981*. The average weekly wage for women in
junior non-manual work is calculated from Table 87, pp. D15–16. For
women's earnings relative to men's, see *Employment Gazette*, October
1980. In addition, men worked considerably longer hours for their
wages than did women: 46.2 hours on average as compared to only
36.5 hours on average for women. Source: *Employment Gazette*, February 1983, Table 5.6, p. S50.

10. Part of the work situation of employees is, of course, social relationships with co-workers. In this regard, the work situation of junior
non-manual workers from working-class origins *may* vary from that of
manual workers from working-class backgrounds in that the former
may interact socially with co-workers from 'middle-class' backgrounds
and thus assimilate different social norms and mores (see Heath, 1981
for a discussion of middle-class assimilation in the workplace). I do not
think, however, that the socializing which may occur in this manner is
sufficient to offset the effects of such workers' placement in the social
hierarchy of authority as discussed in the text.

11. In their 1983 paper, Britten and Heath find differences in family
income, educational qualifications of both spouses, family size and

voting behaviour. The last of these findings is, perhaps, the most interesting from the perspective of class analysis. The authors, however, provide little in the way of assurance that these voting differences are in fact indicative of class differences. Nor do they tell us why wives' occupations are more or less important as discriminators than, say, geographical location, housing tenure, or experiences of occupational mobility. In their 1984 paper, the authors again find differences in voting and fertility, arguing that women's occupations have a greater effect on these two aspects than do the occupations of their husbands. I do not dispute that Britten and Heath have introduced more detail into the class structure by the inclusion of women's occupations as a distinguishing variable. I would suggest, however, that the greater detail obtained in this manner does not necessarily imply the existence of a new class stratum, but instead illustrates the differences within presently found classes.

12. See note 5 above.
13. Cf. Henry James, *The Princess Casamassima*, London: Heron Books, n.d.; Charles Dickens, *Dombey and Son*, London: Collins, 1964.

2

Why Cross-class?

The most commonly accepted distinction between the middle class and the working class is participation in manual or non-manual employment. It is generally held that workers on either side of this boundary have different opportunities, different life chances. This dichotomy is not, however, based simply on whether a worker engages in physical labour, for as is abundantly clear, a great many 'middle class' occupations demand physical exertions. Rather, the manual/non-manual distinction symbolizes differing relationships to the division of labour, differing conditions of employment, and thus, differing positions in the hierarchy of reward and control. Therefore it is possible to argue, as in the previous chapter, that women in junior white-collar jobs, while nominally performing non-manual work, are actually in the same class position as the great bulk of manual workers. Quite the opposite is true, however, of women employed in higher level white-collar jobs and in professional occupations. Women located thus in the division of labour enjoy clear advantages which place them in a different, and more favourable, class position than that of manual workers.

An examination of the relationship of these women and of men in manual work to the division of labour shows why it is plausible to accept marriages between such individuals as cross-class and, in doing so, provides a foundation for the discussions of work and family life which follow. This examination will be undertaken through investigation of the differing conditions of employment confronting such workers, and by analysis of the varying economic, or market situations which attend the two sets of occupations. John Goldthorpe distinguishes between employees in the class structure on the basis of their varying functions and conditions of employment. In doing so, he delineates two distinct categories of employees:

... (a) those in subordinate positions who, via a labour contract, exchange more or less discrete amounts of labour for wages on a short-term basis and

(b) those in positions involving some exercise of authority or expertise, whose conditions of employment imply the exchange of 'service' for 'compensation' in a more diffuse and long-term fashion. (1983: 467)

It is possible to show that the husbands and wives in cross-class families correspond to these two types of employment. This may be done by illustrating the varying methods of payment, uses of time, and relationships between income and hours worked which are associated with their differing positions in the occupational structure.

One of the most readily apparent distinctions between manual and non-manual employees is the manner in which such workers are paid. In 1979, 77% of manual workers received their income in weekly cash packets. Although this represents a decrease from 89% of such workers in 1969, it remains considerably higher than the 34% of non-manual workers paid in this way.[1] Cash payments each week for the exact number of hours worked does more than simply give the worker immediate and tangible reward for his or her labours, rather it signifies a very specific relationship to the employer and to the division of labour itself. This relationship, moreover, differs significantly from that of employees paid monthly, by cheque, on the basis of an annual salary. As Willis points out in *Learning to Labour*:

... in middle class professions it is clear that the yearly salary is paid in exchange for the use of continuous and flexible services. Remuneration here is not based on the particular amount of time spent on the job and, of course, those 'on the staff' are expected to work overtime and at home for no extra cash. Such workers, their wages form makes clear, are being paid for what they are: for the use of their capacities, for their general potential . . . The social implications of the weekly wage packet are very different. The *general* capacity of labour power which is recognized by the salary form is here broken up into weekly lumps and riveted to a direct and regular award. Weekly wages, not yearly salaries, mark the giving of labour. The quantity of the wage packet is the quantitative passing of time. Its diminuation is loss of measured time, its increase 'overtime'. (1977: 131)

Willis captures an essential difference between manual workers and the rest of the labour force: each hour and, often, each minute worked by those in manual jobs is counted and paid for. For many, this is brought home by the act, each day, of clocking in and out. Lateness means minutes lost. Minutes lost mean less in the weekly pay packet. The employer purchases from such workers not expertise

nor authority but time—a specific amount of money for a specific
amount of time.

The relationship between time and money experienced by manual
workers is markedly different from that enjoyed by those employed
in higher level occupations who are, as Willis points out, paid for
what they are—for their expertise. Their annual salaries express a
relationship between employer and employee which is based on
trust (cf. Fox, 1974; Goldthorpe, 1982). The employer must delegate
to the employee both responsibility and freedom to perform the
required work tasks on trust, without recourse to constant supervision or coercion. The employee must develop a sense of loyalty to
the employer. Trust and loyalty are symbolized by an annual salary
tied not to the number of hours worked but to the value of the
employee's expertise. Thus, few employees at this level are paid
'overtime'. For many professions, such as, for example, teaching or
social work, the work that needs to be done simply needs to be done,
and if this work requires time at home, or time at night, then such is
the nature of the job. For others, excess demands on their working
time are compensated through afternoons off, or an extra day's holiday—these employees 'self-regulate' their hours of work so that, on
balance, they work a reasonable number of hours for the salary they
draw. In either case, 'overtime' payments are neither claimed nor
expected. Rather than measuring their working life in hours and
minutes and being paid accordingly, employees at this level have a
continuous, long-term relationship to their work and are recognized
as having such through their annually calculated salaries.

The differences inherent in the use of time between manual workers and those in professional employment may be clearly illustrated
by reference to the 1983 industrial dispute at the Cowley plant of
British Leyland (BL) in Oxford. Known as the 'washing-up' dispute, it concerned management's wish to dispense with the traditional 3-minute washing-up time allotted workers at the end of each
shift. The workers resented this encroachment upon their privileges
and a strike ensued, costing BL many millions of pounds in lost
revenues and the workers considerable loss of wages. In the end, the
workers returned to work and accepted a cash payment in exchange
for the forgone 3 minutes. Few readers would dispute, I am sure,
that such a situation developing among higher level non-manual
and professional employees is beyond the power of imagination.
Expertise and authority are purchased from such employees—not
minutes.

Unlike professional employees, then, manual workers often have a direct relationship between the number of hours they work and the amount of money they earn. As a result of this, they are subject to fluctuations in the economy to a much greater extent than are their salaried counterparts. When the economy is experiencing growth and there is a high demand for labour, manual workers can expect to augment their weekly earnings considerably through working over-time.[2] During periods of economic recession, however, this avenue is often closed and, indeed, manual workers may suffer loss of basic income through temporary plant closures and the institution of short-time working hours. From 1974 to 1981 the proportion of workers in manual occupations receiving overtime fell from 60% to 46% of all manual employees. The amount of overtime pay as a percentage of average gross earnings for all manual workers also fell from 16% to 12% in this period as a result of fewer extra hours being demanded by employers. In addition, the number of manual work-ers in manufacturing on short-time working hours fluctuated during this period, peaking in January 1981 at 13.7% (*Social Trends*, 13, 1983). As employees contracted to hourly paid working conditions, there is little manual workers can do to protect themselves from the economic fluctuations represented by these decreased demands for overtime. In contrast, only about 6% of women in higher level non-manual employment gained additional income through over-time in 1981. This extra income, moreover, represented only slightly more than 1% of total income earned (*New Earnings Survey 1981*, 1982: D80–1). Clearly, then, far fewer of these women would be subject to income fluctuation through loss of overtime opportunities, and such fluctuation as might exist would represent only a minor drain on income.

The relationship to the occupational structure of those in higher level white-collar and professional employment expressed by their method of payment and use of time is thus also associated with greater stability of income. Annual salaries as a source of income rather than the hourly wages accompanying manual work protect such employees from fluctuations in the economy and put them in a more advantageous position. This aspect of class position coexists with other elements of the market situation of professional em-ployees and higher level white-collar workers which distinguish them from the manually employed. Greater job security, for exam-ple, is associated with employment at the upper end of the occupa-tional hierarchy. Almost 80% of male unemployment occurs among the manually employed, while incumbents of professional and managerial occupations account for only 10% of unemployment among both men and women (*Social Trends*, 13, 1983: 61). This differential impact of unemployment is a reflection of the distinctive conditions of employment associated with managerial and professional occupations as outlined by Goldthorpe. Hired to exchange 'service' for 'compensation' on a 'diffuse and long-term basis', such employees are treated quite differently from manual workers during times of employee reductions. And while managerial and professional occupations are subject, like manual occupations, to recession and depression in the economy as a whole, differential treatment allows the incumbents of these occupations to remain outside unemployment statistics to a far greater extent than their manually employed counterparts. For example, in many cases the employers of managerial and professional workers will allow them sufficient time to secure new employment before being compelled to leave their present place of work (Sinfield, 1981: 128). In other situations, such as in the public sector, employment contracts secure the workers' positions within the organization, and the employing body undertakes a system of 'managed vacancies' to combat the need for staff reductions. In this system, vacancies which arise through retirement and other causes are held in limbo until such time as they are needed. In time of economic restraint, overstaffing in one area is reduced by the transfer of staff into a 'managed vacancy' in another area. In both illustrations the result is the same: men and women employed at this level are protected from unemployment. Thus, the imbalance in unemployment rates between managerial and professional workers and the manually employed is more than a reflection of the greater expertise or higher credentials that the former group bring to bear in the performance of their work. It is a reflection of the very nature of their relationship to the occupational structure—a relationship not shared by manual workers.

Historically, a third aspect of the market situation of workers has also favoured middle class, professional employees. The opportunity for upward occupational mobility has traditionally been seen as a prerogative of those engaged in non-manual work. Few organizations employing manual workers have a recognized hierarchy of positions through which a manually employed worker may progress out of manual work and into white-collar work. Thus, for most manual workers, advancement at work happens predominately as a matter of 'chance' and is often unsought and unexpected. Moreover, such advancement as occurs generally happens early in the worker's life, by age 25–9 or so; beyond the early thirties, a manual worker's chance of promotion out of manual work becomes slight (Westergaard and Resler, 1975; Goldthorpe, 1980). Unlike manual work, however, higher level white-collar and professional occupations are frequently located in bureaucratic organizations with recognized promotional hierarchies. Thus, individuals in these occupations may plan 'careers' and seek after specific objectives. While not all individuals so employed will achieve promotion, and many will be subject, in Giddens' terms, to 'career blocks',[3] employment in a bureaucratic hierarchy does mean that the opportunity to advance occupationally over the course of one's work-life exists in far greater measure for those employed above the level of manual work.

These differences in promotional possibilities and job security together with the varying conditions of employment outlined earlier are, I suggest, sufficient to accept marriages between men in manual work and women in professional or semi-professional employment as indeed cross-class. Although in many job-related aspects, such as number of days paid holiday and levels of income, the holders of these jobs are closer than they were formerly, the differences between them in their respective relationships to the occupational structure are such as to mark them as being in distinctive class positions. Women in such marriages will, on average, have greater job security, more chance for career advancement, and be paid in a manner which identifies them as long-term, trusted employees, than will their manually employed husbands. These job characteristics will frequently be associated with greater autonomy and authority than that normally allowed to manual workers. Moreover, the fact that the more advantaged position in the occupational structure is held by the wives in these families will often mean that the impact of work upon family life varies considerably from the impact of work upon other families in the class structure. In many respects cross-class families are unlike other families because of the diverse occupational attainments of the husbands and wives. In the following chapters, the differences in occupational conditions elaborated here will be discussed in relation to the domestic lives of cross-class families; first, however, the way in which appropriate families were located is briefly outlined.

The Selection of Cross-class Families

Cross-class families of the type described here are a small minority of British society. 1971 Census data indicate that approximately 10% of men in the manual classes are married to women in Classes I and II. In fact, there is reason to believe that the actual representation of cross-class families in the population is less than suggested by the Census. Using the criteria for accepting married couples as cross-class just outlined, that is, differing functions and conditions of employment and varying market situations, one could argue that the classifications used by the Registrar-General (RG) quite likely *overestimate* the number of familes actually in cross-class circumstances. For example, the RG's Social Class IIIM includes both self-employed manual workers, with and without employees, and foremen and supervisors of manual workers. Similarly, the RG's Social Class II includes housekeepers and matrons in hotels, schools, hostels and common lodging houses. Individuals employed in these occupations are likely to be in employment circumstances quite different from those experienced by the bulk of manual workers on the one hand, and women in higher level white-collar or professional occupations on the other. If we are unwilling to accept marriages between such individuals as cross-class—on the grounds that the contrasts in their conditions of employment will not usually be sufficiently marked as to constitute class differences—then nearly one-half of the 'cross-class' families appearing in the Census are 'lost'. The almost 10% of cross-class marriages among manual workers in the population at large becomes, by a more strict definition and categorization, only about 5%—a minority indeed.

One is, then, confronted with a tiny proportion of the population within which to find sufficient cross-class families for research. With such a small population, the aim must be to assemble a reasonable number of families from the few available. Simple random sampling techniques for locating these families would clearly be inappropriate. In the first instance, no sampling frame, or accurate and complete list of the entire population of cross-class families from which one might draw a sample, exists. Secondly, compilation of such a list would require financial resources beyond those of a single researcher. Moreover, should such a sampling frame come into existence, any randomly drawn sample of cross-class families taken from it would be, by virtue of their limited representation in society, spread over a geographical area too widely dispersed to be economically feasible. Instead of random sampling techniques, then, an alternative method of locating cross-class families must be devised. One way would be to contact as many women as possible employed in the relevant occupations in a specific area, and to filter through these women in hopes of finding those who are married to manual workers. In this way, provided there was nothing unusual about the chosen geographical area, one could reasonably expect to locate suitable families. Such, in fact, was the course of action undertaken.

Access to appropriate families was sought through the places of employment of the wives. This was done in hopes of finding as wide a variety of husbands' occupations as possible. The choice of wives' employers was restricted to the public sector because of prior knowledge of the over-representation of women in higher level employment in fields such as teaching, nursing, and social work. And further, the public sector offers more centralized location and ease of access to larger numbers of such women than would be possible in the private sector of the economy. Therefore, through the assistance of various individuals and organizations, 2,155 introductory questionnaires devised to elicit information about the respondent's education and occupation together with details about the occupations of her husband and parents were distributed to women employed as teachers, librarians, social workers, district nurses and health visitors, para-medical professionals, and higher level local government officers. Of the 2,155 questionnaires distributed, 603 (28%) responses were received, predominately from couples employed in occupations of the same social class. Eighty one per cent of replies were received from women with husbands in the same or higher occupational position as themselves; 24 replies, or 4.2%, came from women in the strictly defined category of cross-class families.

In the event of contacting these 24 families for personal interviews, three families were unable to participate in interviews for various personal reasons. This left only 21 strictly defined cross-class families. As the aim was to assemble a reasonable number of families, it was thought that 21 was insufficient. Restricted from seeking new families from the population at large by financial considerations, I decided to relax the strict definition of what it means to be a cross-class family but to do so within very specific limits. Therefore, the following nine families were added: (1) two families in which the husbands are employed as foremen of manual workers were accepted by virtue of the social distance between the occupations of the husbands and their wives, both of whom are employed as Head Teachers; (2) three families in which the wives are employed in senior clerical/supervisory positions (socio-economic group SEG 5.2, RG's Social Class IIINM)) were accepted because of the seniority of their positions at work; (3) two families in which the husbands are nominally self-employed were accepted by reason of the fact that both men have worked for the same companies for the past several years; (4) one family in which the husband is self-employed was accepted by virtue of the same reason for accepting the foremen—the degree of social distance between his occupation as hire-car driver and that of his wife as Deputy Head Teacher; (5) one family which has ceased to operate in the cross-class pattern was accepted—a former factory worker, the husband has left active employment to care for the children while his wife continues her career as an architect. Thus expanded, the study now encompassed thirty families. In most of the families included 'after the fact', the circumstances and conditions of employment of the spouses are such that little difference exists between them and the more strictly defined cross-class families. This suggests that the 'strict definition' of a cross-class family may be too strict. Relaxation of this definition to include manually employed men in supervisory or self-employed circumstances (SEGs 8 and 12) and women in senior clerical positions (SEG 5.2) would bring the percentage of cross-class families in the population as a whole closer to 10% than to the 5% suggested earlier. Even with such a relaxed definition, however, cross-class families remain a minority pattern in British society.[4] (See Appendix 1 for further discussion of the research methods).

The thirty families thus located include a wide variety of husbands' occupations ranging from a very unskilled printer's helper to highly skilled telecommunications engineers. The wives' occupations are much less disparate and are over-represented by teachers. Some variety, however, does exist in the jobs held by the wives. The thirty couples who form the basis of the research are listed in Table 2.1 (the names given to these couples are not, of course, their real names).

Table 2.1. *Couples who form the Basis of the Research*

Name	Wife's occupation	Husband's occupation
Barnes	Polytechnic lecturer	Lorry driver
Paton	District nurse	Agricultural fitter
Young	Librarian	Telecommunications engineer
Peterson	Teacher	Electrician
Allan	Teacher	Electrician
Creighton	Deputy Head	Foreman welder (redundant)
Fielding	Teacher	Fireman
Henderson	Health visitor	Printer
Aston	Teacher	Garage driver
White	Teacher	Printer
Henley	Teacher	Printer's helper
Parker	Teacher	Farm worker
James	Teacher	Forklift driver
Ashcroft	Computer programmer	Milk roundsman
Roberts	Librarian	Car mechanic (unemployed)
Leonard	Senior Secretary and clerical supervisor	Heating and ventilating fitter
Thompson	Senior secretary	Train driver
Norton	Training officer	Kitchen helper
Harvey	Head librarian	Telecommunications engineer
Everett	Senior records officer	Heating and ventilating fitter
Mason	Teacher	Jointer (self-employed)
Meredith	Administrative officer	Heating and ventilating fitter
Light	Deputy Head	Hire-car driver, (self-employed)
Miller	Deputy Head	Service engineer (plumber)
Jason	MLSO	Turner machinist
Abbot	Head Teacher	Sawmill foreman
French	Teacher	HGV driver (redundant)
Stone	Architect	Former factory worker
Smith	Teacher	Telecommunications engineer
Unger	MLSO	Roof tiler (self-employed)

Note: MLSO = Medical Laboratory Scientific Officer.

Interviewing Cross-class Families

With the exception of four husbands who chose otherwise (Leonard, Unger, Harvey and Mason) all of the above participated in personal interviews. Each family was visited briefly prior to interviewing so that the issues to be covered and the format to be followed could be

discussed. During the actual interviews, each husband and wife was
met and spoken with individually. This approach was taken in order
to gain maximum freedom of conversation. As the husbands and
wives were asked virtually identical questions, it also allowed a type
of check on the validity of the information being offered. As it turned
out, there was very little discrepancy between the spouses' reports.
Most often the interviews occurred at night and in the home of the
respondent. Almost invariably, the spouse who was not being
interviewed that evening went out for several hours leaving the other
to speak freely. The majority of interviews were taperecorded and
lasted approximately 2 hours each.

The issues discussed in these interviews covered a wide range of
topics. The aim was to discover the nature of life in a cross-class
family from the perspective of those living in such circumstances. I
wanted to understand their lives as they saw and experienced them.
I was after—to quote Thomas—the respondent's 'definition of the
situation': how did they interpret the differences in occupational
achievement between themselves and their spouses? Did they view
themselves as being in different social classes? Did the higher status
of the wife's occupation matter to them as marriage partners? What
were the consequences inside the family of such different positions
outside the family? What were the consequences of these different
work roles on the family's relationships with others—friends,
relatives, work colleagues? Unfortunately, I was unable to interview
the children of these couples, something which would be worth while
as a study in its own right. I did, however, ask questions about such
children; specifically these centred on parental aspirations for their
children occupationally and, in the relevant cases, parental
satisfaction with their children's occupational choices. In all, the
aim was to gain an interpretive understanding of life in cross-class
families.

There is no way of knowing if the families interviewed here are
'representative' of some wider universe of cross-class families. The
way in which they are located for study means that there can be no
grounds for deciding that they are, or that they are not.
Furthermore, the theoretical considerations which went into the
choice of families carry the possibility that other combinations of
husbands' and wives' occupations might count as 'cross-class'.
However, if the group of families assembled here cannot be said to
exhaust *all* variations of cross-class families, it can be shown to

contain *a wide range* of such families. Moreover, the men and women of these families, as will be seen, manifest most of the problems and family situations one would a priori expect in families who deviate from some more socially normal 'traditional' family. The aim was to assemble a reasonable number of genuine cross-class families, and then to discover what it means to be such a family. The following chapters will decide if this aim has been successfully fulfilled.

It is not unusual, however, to seek information about family life from a small number of families. Bott (1957), in her now classic study of the relationship of families to their social environments, chose only twenty 'ordinary' families as the foundation of her research. Further, Rapoport and Rapoport (1976) selected and interviewed only sixteen families living in a 'dual-career' pattern. Both Bott and the Rapoports were as cautious as this study intends to be about making inferences from a small number of families to the population at large. The Rapoports do remind us, however, that:

It is important, as is often not recognized, not to assume that no extrapolations can be made because sometimes the *wrong* extrapolations are made from individual families to the larger society. We can see reflected in their experiences cultural contradictions, social–structural discontinuities or other deficiencies as well as certain positive cultural values. To point them out as societal issues is entirely legitimate. It would be erroneous methodologically, however, to suggest that because any given proportion of our families showed one or another pattern—say of men doing the cooking—that this was likely to be the proportion one would find if one drew a random sample of families representing the whole population. (1976: 29–30)

In the following, I will follow the lead suggested by Rapoport and Rapoport and attempt to relate the experiences of these cross-class families to the wider social context in which they are found. In doing so, however, it must be remembered that, like Bott's work, this study concerns only *some* families, not all families nor The Family. Thus, no empirical generalizations will be made to some wider universe of families. This does not mean, though, that the findings will be without interest in more general terms. As will be seen, the special relationship, via their occupational positions, that these husbands and wives have to the larger society illuminates the way in which society itself shapes family life. It is possible to see, through these thirty families, norms and modes of behaviour which exist on a much wider scale.

Notes

1. Tydeman, 1981: 428. Of course, the same employment relationship could be expressed by calculation of wages hourly and payment by monthly (or weekly) cheque. What is of importance is the linking of payment to the exact number of hours worked. Payment in cash is used to express this relationship.

2. The high incomes that many associate with manual work are often due to overtime work; of those receiving overtime pay since 1974, such additions to their pay packets have represented, on average, 23% of gross average earnings. Extra earnings for such workers, however, mean long working weeks—since 1974, between 9 and 10 hours beyond the basic work time. *Social Trends*, 13, 1983, p. 68. Also see Westergaard and Resler (1975: 84–5).

3. Giddens introduces the notion of career blocks in partial explanation of the rise of white-collar unions (1973: 191). He especially cites teachers as characteristic of occupations in which, once the given occupational position is attained, further advancement is strictly limited. This is no doubt quite true with respect to promotion out of teaching and into levels of administration such as Head Teacher or within the department of education itself. However, while still teachers, individuals can strive for positions as department head, pastoral head, and so on.

4. Support for including men employed as foremen in the category 'cross-class' comes from Stewart *et al.* who write:

   An examination of our data shows that foremen appear to maintain working-class lifestyles in terms of the neighbourhoods they live in and the types of leisure activities they engage in. While it would seem reasonable to rate foremen above manual workers in reputational terms, they probably remain members of the groups from which they are recruited (1980: 53).

3

The Families

In the course of investigating the work and personal worlds of cross-class families, I have had numerous opportunities to discuss my work with others, both inside and outside the realm of social scientific research. On these occasions, considerable surprise is often expressed that the men and women of these families are actually married to each other. Class homogamy is a common enough phenomenon that cross-class families appear quite unusual, perhaps even odd. In fact, the social backgrounds of the men and women in the majority of families reported here are really very similar: like does tend to marry like after all. This remains so even in the case of cross-class families because there are several routes through which individuals may travel before finding themselves as partners in a cross-class marriage. If the families are arranged into a rough typology on the basis of their social origins, using father's occupation as an indicator of such, we see not only the overwhelming similarity of class backgrounds among the respondents, but also the different types of cross-class families located for study. Of course, social origin measured by the occupation of each respondent's father is only one of many ways in which it is possible to group families together. It is chosen here in order to focus on the similarities in family backgrounds of the husbands and wives in this research: only in the so-called 'pure' cross-class family do the spouses have truly disparate origins. This 'pure' family type, as will be seen, is the minority of the families gathered for study.

The chapter presents all thirty couples within this typology; an explanation of each 'type' (Table 3.1) is accompanied by a brief exposition of the way in which each couple met and some few details about their family and work histories. In this way, the chapter provides a reference point for readers so that at any time in the following chapters they may easily check back and re-establish who each family is and how they came to be a cross-class family.

Table 3.1. *A Typology of Cross-class Families*

Type	Name	Number
One	The 'Pure' Cross-class Family	8
Two	The Occupationally 'Upwardly Mobile' Wife	16
Three	The Occupationally 'Downwardly Mobile' Husband	5
Four	The Disabled Husband	2

Note: The number of families listed here adds to 31 instead of the expected 30. One family contacted for interviews was unable to continue; they are included here in Type Four to illustrate the typology.

Type One: The 'Pure' Cross-class Family

This family type is the one which most readily comes to mind when thinking of cross-class families. Husband and wife come from truly disparate social backgrounds and each was established in their respective occupations or trained for these occupations prior to marriage. The wife is from a middle-class family; her father held a middle-class job, as did her mother if she in fact held paid employment. The wife continued her education beyond the minimum school-leaving age, in most cases obtaining either a university or college degree. The husband, on the other hand, comes from a working-class background and follows his father into a manual occupation. He did not continue in school beyond the minimum age but may have acquired a technical training or held an apprenticeship. Seven of the families located for research fulfil all of these conditions; the eighth, a second marriage for both spouses, will be seen to fall into this type by virtue of the wife's circumstances prior to remarriage.

The Allans: Teacher and Maintenance Electrician

As the daughter of a self-employed businessman and the son of a coal miner, Mr and Mrs Allan had very different advantages in their early lives. Mrs Allan attended grammar school and followed her mother into teaching, while Mr Allan only avoided going into the mines after leaving the local secondary modern by virtue of the strenuous efforts of his parents to find him an alternative source of employment. They succeeded and Mr Allan was apprenticed as an electrician. The Allans met at a public dance while Mrs Allan was on holiday with her parents in Mr Allan's home town. Once decided upon marriage, they determined to start life away from either of their childhood homes and so moved south to take advantage of the teaching position offered to Mrs Allan. Mr Allan, aged 41, and Mrs Allan, aged 39, are the parents of a 5-year old daughter.

The Barneses: Lecturer and Lorry driver

Mrs Barnes has her doctorate in economics and teaches in a poly-technic. Mr Barnes left school at age 15 with no certificates and has not continued his education in any way since that time. The son of a farm worker and a school caretaker, Mr Barnes has driven lorries for a large transport firm for the past 15 years. Until his marriage some 5 years ago, he drove very large vehicles for this firm but soon afterwards changed to smaller, less demanding trucks in order to reduce the 'carry-over' effect from work to home: two stressful jobs in one family caused tension and conflict. Mr and Mrs Barnes met in the local pub after Mrs Barnes had purchased a cottage in the small village where Mr Barnes has spent his lifetime. Both married for the second time, Mr and Mrs Barnes do not intend to have children although Mr Barnes maintains contact with his two teenaged children from his first marriage. Mr Barnes is 37 years old; Mrs Barnes, the daughter of a shop owner, is 42.

The Hendersons: Health Visitor and Printer

Marrying 'across class lines' is quite common in Mrs Henderson's family: her mother came from a family of white-collar workers and married a farm worker; her daughter is a senior secretary married to a carpenter; Mrs Henderson herself is a fully trained SRN working as a health visitor and is married to a printer. Although Mrs Henderson's father began as a farm worker, he went on to become a successful farmer, employing others to work for him. Mr Henderson, aged 48, is the son of a carpenter and an in-home tailor. He had completed an apprenticeship as a printer and was continuing his training in lithographics at night school when he met Mrs Henderson in the church to which both are devoted. Mrs Henderson, now aged 50, was at that time working as a nurse, which she continued to do until the birth of her first child. After a 10-year absence from the work force, Mrs Henderson resumed nursing in the mid-seventies and acquired extra training to become a health visitor. Recent pressure from her husband has meant that Mrs Henderson is now pursuing her career on a part-time basis. The Hendersons have three children, two of whom still live in the family home.

The Leonards: Senior Secretary and Heating and Ventilating Fitter

Before her marriage, Mrs Leonard thought about the differences between herself and her husband, recalling: 'I was surprised to marry a *worker*!' The daughter of a senior government officer, Mrs Leonard, aged 28, met her husband at a pub. At this time she was working in local government as personal secretary to a senior officer, having acquired a 2-year secretarial training at a technical college. Her husband, also aged 28, is the son of a factory worker and part-time clerk. He completed an apprenticeship as a heating and ventilating fitter and has worked for his present firm since entering the labour force. Mr Leonard declined participation in an interview. At present, Mrs Leonard supervises a staff of six and is responsible for work allocation, staff scheduling, the co-ordination of departmental routine as well as secretarial duties. Although encouraged by her employer to seek promotion, Mrs Leonard has no ambition in this direction and intends at some future date to withdraw from paid employment for an indefinite period to have and raise children.

The Whites: Teacher and Printer

The daughter of a scientific research technician and the son of a factory worker, Mr and Mrs White have been married for 15 years and have two school-age children. Mrs White left school initially with six 'O' levels and began work as a research technician in a university laboratory. While so employed, she was introduced by a cousin to her future husband, then working in an unskilled position in the printing department of a large factory. Mr White left school at age 16 with no certificates and was unable to complete the City and Guilds apprenticeship which would have qualified him for a more skilled job with this firm. While married, Mrs White returned to full-time education and acquired a teaching certificate. She is now employed as a part-time teacher. Mr White continued in an unskilled job for 2 years, finally acquiring on the job the skills which had first escaped him during his apprenticeship. For the next 20 years, Mr White continued his factory employment but in a skilled capacity. One month prior to interviews, Mr White, aged 38, was unexpectedly offered promotion out of manual work into a supervisory position. Mrs White, aged 33, does not consider her husband's job change to be a change in occupational status and neglected to mention his promotion during our interview.

The Harveys: Head Librarian and Telecommunications Engineer

Mrs Harvey, the daughter of a government officer, has a BA Honours in German, an Associate of Library Association certificate, and a postgraduate Certificate in Education. Aged 36, Mrs Harvey has moved out of active librarian work and is employed in local government library management, in charge of a staff of fourteen. Her husband, who declined participation in a personal interview, left school at age 15 without certificates and entered the Navy. Aged 41, Mr Harvey spent 9 years in the Navy as an ordinary seaman before obtaining work with his present firm 14 years ago. He is employed as a telecommunications engineer and obtained all of his training on the job. He intends to remain with this firm until retirement. Mrs Harvey is, however, seeking promotion and hopes to proceed into the ranks of upper management. Mr Harvey has been married before and is the father of a teenaged son. The Harveys, who do not intend to have any children of their own, met in a pub.

The Millers: Teacher and Service Engineer (Plumber)

The Millers met through friends when both were still in school: she was attending grammar school while he was at a local secondary modern. They met again when Mrs Miller was in college studying for her teacher's certificate and Mr Miller was doing his National Service, and married soon after Mrs Miller had completed her studies. The son of a maintenance foreman, Mr Miller left school before his fourteenth birthday to undertake an apprenticeship as a plumber. Aged 52, he is employed as a service engineer and has been with his present firm for more than 20 years. Because of continual changes in technology, Mr Miller has over the years supplemented his apprenticeship with a variety of upgrading and retraining courses. Mrs Miller, the daughter of a shop manager, is

presently acting Deputy Head of the school at which she has taught
for the past 25 years. Aged 49, she would like to assume the duties of
a Deputy Head on a permanent basis. The Millers have three grown
children.

The Jameses: Teacher and Forklift Driver

As the daughter of a coal miner, Mrs James originally comes from a
similar class background to that of her husband, the son of a factory
worker. In 1958, however, when a qualified teacher, Mrs James
married a university lecturer. Married for 20 years, she became the
mother of two daughters and taught on both a full-time and part-
time basis before divorcing. During her first marriage, Mrs James
upgraded her teaching qualifications, obtaining a Certificate in Special Education, and is now in charge of an experimental educational
programme. Aged 45, she has been remarried for 5 years and lives
with her teenage daughters and husband in the home she purchased
from her former husband. Mr James, aged 48, is employed as a
forklift driver in a large factory. He left school without certificates at
age 15 and has held his present job since 1955. In his spare time, Mr
James runs discos for private parties and it was at such a party in the
home of one of her friends that Mrs James met her second husband.

As mentioned earlier, these eight 'pure' cross-class families are composed of individuals with quite disparate social backgrounds. As
such, they are the minority of families collected together for
research. In the following three types of families, husbands and
wives share similar social origins although the routes they followed
in becoming cross-class families vary considerably.

Type Two: The Occupationally 'Upwardly Mobile' Wife

This family type is the most numerous of the families reported here.
In sixteen families, the wives have gained educational qualifications
or work experience leading to positions above those of their manually employed husbands. In these families, both come from
working-class backgrounds. Their fathers held manual jobs, as did
their mothers if they worked outside the home during marriage. The
husbands usually did not continue in school beyond the minimum
required age, but may have obtained technical training or completed
an apprenticeship. Half of the wives acquired further education

immediately after leaving school and were thus qualified at the time of their marriages. The other half did not continue with their education until later in married life, thus bringing themselves and their families into a cross-class family pattern sometime after marriage had occurred. These two groups will be presented separately.

(a) QUALIFICATIONS AT MARRIAGE

The Creightons: Deputy Head Teacher and Foreman Welder

The daughter of a maintenance electrician and the son of a railway signalman, the Creightons met at a village cricket match and have been married since 1950. They are the parents of two grown children. Active participation in employment came to an end in late 1982 for both Mr and Mrs Creighton, but in very different ways. Mrs Creighton was a qualified teacher when she married and continued teaching for 6 years before leaving active employment for 9 years to have and raise her children. She returned to teaching when the youngest child started school and was promoted through the school system until reaching the position of Deputy Head of a large comprehensive 10 years ago. After arguing with her Head about the matter for 3 years, she was finally allowed to take voluntary early retirement. She is now aged 58. Mr Creighton left school at age 14 with no qualifications. He began training as a welder and after 20 years was promoted to working-foreman. Ten years later, he was relieved of his welding duties and worked solely as foreman. In time, he was promoted again and put in charge of four welding departments. Company changes and the introduction of efficiency 'experts', however, resulted in Mr Creighton's demotion back to working-foreman, and in late 1982 he was forced to take 'voluntary' redundancy. At age 55 and much against his wish, Mr Creighton is now an unemployed welder.

The Parkers: Teacher and Farm Worker

The Parkers spent their years in junior school together and met again at age 16 when they formed a friendship which was to culminate in marriage 5 years later. Mrs Parker, aged 31, is the daughter of a butcher while her husband, also aged 31, is the son of a railway worker. Before marrying, Mrs Parker completed teacher training and obtained an Honours degree in Education. She is now Department Head, and the mother of a 3-year-old daughter. Mr Parker trained at an agricultural college and followed his maternal grandfather and uncle into farm work. The Parkers live in a tied cottage on a small privately owned farm where Mr Parker drives both tractor and combine.

The Youngs: Librarian and Telecommunications Engineer

The Youngs met at a pub through mutual friends soon after Mr Young had moved to Reading with his parents. Mrs Young, aged 28, works as a mobile librarian, travelling from village to village. Her father was a general labourer, while Mr Young is the son of a factory worker. In moving with his parents, Mr Young, aged 24, lost seniority with his present firm and is now working at a level below his skill capabilities. Leaving school at age 16, he completed a City and Guilds Apprenticeship and hopes, through continued training, to become a technical officer freed from manual work. At present the Youngs have no children.

The Patons: District Nurse and Agricultural Fitter

The Patons grew up in the same small town, went to the same schools, and after a 7-year wait to buy their own home married in 1978. At this time, Mrs Paton, the daughter of a stonemason, had been nursing for 4 years. In recent years, she obtained additional qualifications and is now a district nurse. Mr Paton, whose father was an electrician and mother a part-time factory worker, left school at age 15 without qualifications and undertook a 5-year apprenticeship. He has held his present job since completing this training, and is responsible for servicing and repairing new and used farm equipment. Mr Paton, aged 29, and Mrs Paton, aged 28, as yet have no children; should they decide to have a family, Mrs Paton will withdraw from paid employment for a limited period.

The Petersons: Teacher and Electrician

The daughter of a service engineer and the son of a gardener and a part-time cleaner, the Petersons met while Mrs Peterson was still in school and working part-time in a local chip shop. Mr Peterson was a very frequent customer! Now married for 7 years, they wed while Mrs Peterson was in college and Mr Peterson on the assembly line at BL. At present Mrs Peterson, aged 24, has been teaching for 4 years, while her husband, aged 32, has left BL for a position as an electrician in private industry. Mr Peterson left school at age 16 to undertake an electrical apprenticeship on the advice of his father, who told him: 'get a trade'. As yet the Petersons have no children and, as Mrs Peterson is actively seeking promotion within her school, intend to defer starting a family for some years.

The Thompsons: School Secretary and Train Driver

The Thompsons met as teenagers through Mr Thompson's friendship with his future brother-in-law. Married for more than 20 years, they have two children, one of whom still lives at home. Mrs Thompson left school with five 'O' levels and acquired certificates in shorthand and typing through 3 years at night school. The daughter of a factory worker, Mrs Thompson's first job was with the local education authority as personal secretary to a government officer. She held this position for 10 years, during which time she married. Mr Thompson left school at age 15 with no qualifications and is presently employed as a train driver after spending 18 years as a relief driver and fireman. In his trade, Mr Thompson, aged 44, has followed in the footsteps of his father. Mrs Thompson retired from active employment for 8 years to care for her children; aged 43, she resumed work on a part-time basis 5 years ago. Presently employed as school secretary, she would prefer full-time work should changes in the economy allow her school to hire her in such a capacity.

The Abbots: Head Teacher and Sawmill Foreman

The Abbots met as teenagers at an April Fool's party given by mutual friends. Mrs Abbot, aged 51, is the daughter of a postman and a cleaner, while her husband's father was a factory chargehand. Now married for almost 30 years, the Abbots have no children. Mrs Abbot attended grammar school, leaving at age 18 to enter college for teacher training. She then taught for 15 years prior to promotion to Deputy Head, and after 12 years in this capacity obtained the position of Head Teacher in 1981. Mr Abbot left school at age 14 with no certificates and 2 years later obtained a position with his present company. For the next 23 years, Mr Abbot was a worker in the sawmill until he was unexpectedly promoted to working-supervisor of a small section of the mill. Three years ago, he was once again sought out for promotion, much to his surprise, and made foreman of the mill. Aged 52, he still engages in physical work during the day, in addition to supervising the work of others.

The Ungers: Medical Laboratory Scientific Officer and Self-employed Roof Tiler

The Ungers met on the same school bus which took Mrs Unger to grammar school and Mr Unger to the secondary modern. The daughter of a bricklayer and a former school teacher, Mrs Unger left school at age 17 with seven 'O' and three 'A' levels. She began work in 1969 as a laboratory technician before studying for a Higher National Certificate (HNC) in 1974. She is now employed on a part-time basis as an MLSO. Mr Unger, who declined participation, left school at the minimum age and entered the roof-tiling business. While owning his own truck, Mr Unger, aged 33, does not employ others and usually works on a contract basis for the same general contractors. The Ungers have two small children; when they are older, Mrs Unger, aged 32, may decide to upgrade her qualifications and seek further promotion.

(b) QUALIFICATIONS OBTAINED AFTER MARRIAGE

The Merediths: Administrative Officer and Heating and Ventilating Fitter

Mrs Meredith left school at age 15 with no certificates, to realize 10 years later that if she was to advance in a career she must obtain some professional credentials. With the encouragement of her husband, she entered a College of Further Education and has now qualified for a Certificate in Management Studies and a Diploma in Management Practice. Further education awaits her as she feels the need for additional expertise. A City and Guilds training was the route chosen by Mr Meredith when he left school with three 'O' levels at age 16. He joined his present firm as an apprentice in the early 1960s. Mrs Meredith, the daughter of a plumber, met her future husband, the son of a factory worker, when he answered the wrong advertisement in the newspaper! Married for 16 years, the Merediths, aged 37 and 35, do not intend to have children.

The Fieldings: Teacher and Fireman

Both Mr and Mrs Fielding left school at age 15 without qualifications. Mr Fielding began a series of semi-skilled and unskilled jobs
before joining a London fire brigade in the late sixties, while Mrs
Fielding entered secretarial college and obtained various secretarial
certificates. After marriage and the birth of their only child, a
daughter now aged 16, Mrs Fielding held a series of junior grade
secretarial jobs. Dissatisfied with this, she entered college in the
mid-seventies and obtained a degree in education. Aged 33, Mrs
Fielding has taught full time for 6 years. She hopes, however, to
leave teaching for a career in educational research. Mr Fielding,
aged 36, is the son of a toolmaker; Mrs Fielding's father was a
printer. The couple met while teenagers at a youth club.

The Masons: Teacher and Self-employed Jointer

Like Mrs Fielding, Mrs Mason came late to her teaching career. She
left school at age 15 to begin a series of factory jobs. The daughter of
a construction labourer and a cook, Mrs Mason gave up work to
have and raise two daughters. In the mid-seventies, when her children were in school, Mrs Mason obtained a degree in education and
has taught full time since 1980. Aged 37, she hopes soon to fulfil a
second ambition, and is seeking a publisher for her recently written
children's novel. Mr Mason, aged 41, left school at 15 without qualifications. He works as a plasterboard jointer on a self-employed basis
although for the past 15 years he has worked on contract to the same
firm. Mr Mason, who declined participation in an interview, met his
future wife while working on a bus on which she was a passenger.

The Everetts: Senior Records Officer and Heating and Ventilating Fitter

After raising three children, now grown and away from the family
home, Mrs Everett returned to paid employment in the early seventies. For the past 10 years, she has worked as a local government
officer, in charge of a large records department and supervisor of
ten. The daughter of a factory maintenance man, Mrs Everett, aged
54, has no formal qualifications. Mr Everett, the son of a painter and
a part-time cook and cleaner, also left school without qualifications.
After an apprenticeship, he began work as a fitter. Aged 54, he is in a
precarious employment position although highly skilled. Seeking

advancement, he left a secure job to take employment with a new firm offering higher wages and more responsibility. Unfortunately, this firm quickly went bankrupt, forcing Mr Everett to seek re-employment with his previous company. Now although he has worked for more than 30 years for this firm, he is without seniority and liable to lay-offs at any time.

The Jasons: Medical Laboratory Scientific Officer and Turner Machinist

Like Mrs Unger, Mrs Jason also attended grammar school and went on to become an MLSO, although she has not obtained an HNC as such as is thus at a lower grade than Mrs Unger. Mrs Jason, the daughter of a clerk of works, left school at age 16 with eight school certificates including two distinctions. She met her future husband on a blind date arranged by friends. Married for 25 years, the Jasons have two grown children. Mr Jason, aged 63, left school at age 14 with no qualifications, and has worked in the same factory as a machinist for the past 43 years. Mrs Jason took several years out of paid employment to care for their children before returning to work as a senior secretary and accounts clerk for a food specialty firm. After 10 years in this position, she changed occupations, learning her new skills on the job. She has been employed as an MLSO for 2 years.

The Smiths: Teacher and Telecommunications Engineer

Mr and Mrs Smith have both been married before; they met, in fact, through Mrs Smith's attendance at the same college as Mr Smith's ex-wife: she introduced them! Now married for 12 years, the couple have two school-age sons. After marrying and completing her B.Ed. in History, Mrs Smith delayed her teaching career until after the birth of their sons and has now, at age 42, been teaching for 5 years. Unlike most of the husbands mentioned, Mr Smith, the son of a prison guard, continued his academic education after leaving school at age 16. As a mature student, he acquired two 'O' levels and an 'A' level in Biology, in addition to completing two years of City and Guilds training. After 9 years in the Army and 1 year driving sub-way trains, Mr Smith, aged 47, joined his present firm on their 'adult recruitment' programme. He has been employed as a tele-communications engineer for 20 years.

The Frenches: Teacher and Tanker Driver (HGV)

Prior to her marriage, Mrs French worked as a GPO telephonist. After meeting her future husband at a CND rally, Mrs French withdrew from paid employment to raise two sons. In 1968, when both boys were in school, she began studies leading to a teaching certificate. Mrs French, aged 48, has now been teaching for 12 years and is both department head and school librarian. Mr French, as with many men in his situation, left school at age 14 without taking any examinations. After a series of unskilled jobs and 6 years in the Army, Mr French began work as a tanker driver. Employed as such for more than 30 years, he took voluntary redundancy 2 years ago at age 57 in order that younger men would be able to retain their jobs. He now works part-time as a driver for a small industrial firm.

The Ashcrofts: Computer Programmer and Milk Roundsman

Both Ashcrofts come from troubled family backgrounds and each found themselves on their own at age 15. Mrs Ashcroft supported herself with various clerical and factory jobs; Mr Ashcroft with a series of unskilled positions in and out of factories. They met through friends just after Mrs Ashcroft had entered teacher's training college. Now after more than 10 years together, and a change of career direction for Mrs Ashcroft, the couple has decided to divorce. Mrs Ashcroft, the daughter of a storeman, was unable to find work as a teacher and entered training as a computer programmer, acquiring an HNC in computer studies. Now 29, she has been employed as a programmer for 4 years. Mr Ashcroft, aged 30, continued with his somewhat erratic job changes, spent 6 years on the shop floor at BL, and finally settled 3 years ago in his present job. He has had no education or formal training beyond age 15 and expects to continue as a milk roundsman for an indefinite period. The couple have no children.

In the sixteen families just introduced, husbands and wives come from very similar backgrounds; they have been brought into a cross-class marital situation through the educational or occupational experiences of the wives. However, occupational or educational mobility occurs downwards as well as upwards. In the following families, husbands and wives also share similar class origins but the occupational experiences of the husbands, rather than of the wives, have brought them into partnership in cross-class marriages.

Type Three: The Occupationally 'Downwardly Mobile' Husband

Five of the families located for research are cross-class families because the husbands have experienced downward occupational mobility. These men all come from middle-class families: their fathers, and mothers if employed, held middle-class occupations and most had the benefit of education beyond the minimum school-leaving age. Their wives too come from middle-class homes. They, however, continued their education beyond school, acquiring either a college certificate or a university degree.[1] Most of the husbands in this group of families attribute their present employment situations to poor educational performances: they achieved only a minimum academic education and no training which would qualify them for skilled manual work. Some of the husbands are still quite young, however, and it is possible that their downward mobility will one day be reversed and they will take their families out of a cross-class situation.[2] For a few this remains a possibility, however remote it may seem at present.

The Henleys: Teacher and Printer's Helper

Mr Henley, the son of an accountant, left private school at age 16 with two 'O' level passes. He now works as a printer's helper, cutting forms to their proper size before and after printing—a position he has held for the past 5 years and one he feels he will keep indefinitely, 'unless a miracle happens'. His wife, daughter of a company director, is a teacher, having continued her education beyond grammar school and obtained a certificate in education. Mr Henley, aged 27, and Mrs Henley, aged 34, are the parents of a 1-year-old daughter. They met in the church which both attend, and have endured one marital separation. Both now see their marriage as much more secure since the birth of their child.

The Robertses: Librarian and Unemployed Car Mechanic

Mr and Mrs Roberts met at age 15 while still in school: he left at 16 with four 'O' levels, while she stayed on until age 18, obtaining eight

'O' and four 'A' levels before entering university. Aged 25, Mrs Roberts has completed both a BA and a postgraduate Diploma in Librarianship. The daughter of a research technician and a secretary, she has been employed as a librarian for 4 years. Mr Roberts's father was a local government officer and his mother worked part-time as a secretary. At age 26, he has held more than ten jobs and entered, unsuccessfully, three different training programmes since the mid-seventies. His job history contains a variety of paid and unpaid, full-time and part-time, manual and non-manual occupations. At present, he is unemployed. Should the couple decide to have children, it is possible that Mr Roberts will stay home to care for them.

The Lights: Deputy Head Teacher and Self-employed Car-hire Driver

Like Mr Roberts, Mr Light has had numerous job changes since leaving school at age 15. The son of a restaurant owner, he now makes his living as a driver for a private hire-car firm. He uses his own car in this business and has been so occupied for slightly less than 2 years. His previous occupations include both manual and non-manual work as well as a period as a police constable. Aged 44, he has no formal qualifications and expects to continue in his present position indefinitely. Mrs Light, who left school at 18 to enter college, met her husband while dining in his father's restaurant. They married upon completion of her studies and now have two school-age children. Mrs Light, aged 41, took a few years away from teaching in order to raise her children. She resumed full-time teaching 11 years ago and has been Deputy Head of the school for the past 4 years.

The Astons: Teacher and Garage Driver

Mr Aston, at present employed to transfer new motor vehicles between the various outlets of a large automotive dealership, would like to open his own retail clothing store somewhere in a small town. This plan, however, is very tentative and exists as a possibility only because of the security and income provided by Mrs Aston's teaching position. The son of a costs estimator, Mr Aston left school at 18 with three 'A' levels. He entered college where he met Mrs Aston who was studying for her B.Sc. Failing his degree, Mr Aston, aged 28, took a job with a pub before entering his present firm with promises of early promotion. Now 5 years have passed and with their passing have gone any chances of advancement. Mrs Aston, the daughter of a farm owner, recently completed her Masters degree and is actively seeking promotion within the school where she has taught for the last 4 years. The couple have no plans to begin a family as Mrs Aston, aged 30, cannot envisage giving up the income and security which may some day allow her husband to leave his present, rather frustrating, occupation.

The Stones: Architect and Househusband (former Factory Worker)

Unlike many unemployed men, Mr Stone is voluntarily out of the labour force. Although the holder of a university degree, Mr Stone's work history is rather sporadic and involves only manual work, including 2 years on a factory assembly line. Aged 31 and 6 years younger than his wife, Mr Stone agreed to assume responsibility for the daily care of the couple's two pre-school children. He undertakes a small amount of carpentry work during the year and will begin this on a full-time basis once the children are older. The son of a teacher, Mr Stone met his wife through friends. Like her husband, Mrs Stone is a university graduate. Unlike her husband, however, Mrs Stone went on to professional employment and has been employed in her present capacity for 10 years. Mrs Stone was a fully qualified architect when she met and married her husband.

As mentioned, some of the above husbands may experience greater success in their future jobs and so move their families out of the cross-class pattern. Not all downward occupational mobility is potentially reversible, however. In the following families, illness and accident brought the careers of the husbands to abrupt ends, and so created cross-class families.

Type Four: The Disabled Husband

Two families coming into our cross-class category do so by virtue of illness and accident. At marriage, these families were not cross-class; husband and wife share the same family backgrounds and together enjoyed the benefits of high-level employment. Chance, however, intervened in their lives and the husbands now participate in the labour force as unskilled manual workers.

The Nortons: Training Officer and Kitchen Helper

In their early forties and married since the mid-sixties, the Nortons are both fully trained social workers. From the late seventies, however, illness has prevented Mr Norton from following his profession. He has held a series of progressively easier jobs as his health has deteriorated, and is now employed as a helper in the kitchen of a local school. After the birth of their first child, Mrs Norton worked part-time as a social worker and a teacher, resuming full-time employment when their second child entered school and Mr Norton found himself unable to cope with the demands of professional employment. Three years ago, Mrs Norton left social work to become a government officer responsible for the creation and implementation of internal training programmes—a position offering greater scope for advancement and higher financial rewards.

The Blacks: Home Help Organizer and Hospital Porter

Mrs Black was a full-time housewife and mother of five until an accident forced her husband to give up his own business. Unable to cope with intellectually demanding work, Mr Black has good physical health and finds some satisfaction in his work as a porter. Mrs Black entered employment soon after her husband's accident, beginning as a home help worker. Ten years later, she is now an organizer of home helps and spends her time on administration. She is continuing her education at night so that she may seek further promotion. The Blacks, who are in their early fifties, asked to be excused from further interviews because of family problems with one of their children.

These then, are the thirty families located for study. As seen, most of the individuals discussed come from the same sorts of family background as their partners in marriage. Class homogamy tends to be the rule even in those families which appear to contain husbands and wives with potentially very dissimilar social origins. Education and participation in paid employment have wrought changes in the circumstances of both husbands and wives leading to the creation of cross-class families. These changes, moreover, have occurred in different ways and at different stages in the life cycle of each family. Some of the families may perhaps move out of the cross-class pattern; indeed, one has already done so. For the majority, however, barring dissolution of the family itself, partnership in cross-class family life will be their future as well as their past.

A full analysis of cross-class families now begins. During this analysis, the typology just outlined is referred to whenever appropriate. Contrary to the author's expectations, however, the social origins of these families proved not to be an important discriminator of behaviour in regard to the various aspects of cross-class family life investigated. I suspect this proved to be the case largely because of the small number of families contained in each 'type', and that increasing the number of families would in fact reveal patterns of behaviour linked to the ways in which cross-class families come into being. In any event, the typology has a certain intrinsic value in itself, not least because it reveals the ways in which cross-class families are formed. Thus, in spite of the very few areas of family life in which social origins were found to discriminate between the families studied, the typology will remain in place as a convenient, and sociologically interesting, way of introducing the thirty families who are the focus of this work.

Notes

1. It is logically possible, of course, that a man experiencing downward occupational mobility might meet and marry a woman from a working-class background who had achieved upward occupational mobility, and thus form a cross-class family. I did not, however, locate any such families.

2. For a discussion of 'counter-mobility' see Goldthorpe (1980), especially pp. 53–4 and 124–31. Counter-mobility, or the returning of an individual to his or her class of origin after time spent at a different level in the occupational hierarchy, was found to be quite prevalent among males of Class I and II origin. However, as Goldthorpe points out also, counter-mobility is often dependent upon acquisition of professional qualifications or the securing of promotion within an occupational hierarchy. The chances of this occurring for most of the men in this study who have experienced downward mobility seem—at least at present—quite slim.

4

Husbands and Wives at Work

In this chapter the theoretical issues presented in Chapter 2 which underlie categorization of certain families as cross-class are made concrete through an examination of the differing work activities and conditions of employment experienced by the husbands and wives of such families. In this regard, the meaning of work for individuals, job autonomy and opportunities for innovation are explored. In addition, the relative positions of the husbands and wives with regard to job security, chances for promotion and plans for future occupational change are assessed. There are in fact considerable differences in the employment experiences of the men and women of this study. Moreover, these differences have consequences of some importance for their domestic lives and marital relationships. In examining and presenting such differences this chapter thus prepares the way for the analysis of the impact of work on family life which follows in the next two chapters.

The Meaning of Work

In a discussion of the meaning of work for individuals, Fox suggests that there are 'two great alternative meanings'—work may be an activity of 'central importance to his (*sic*) personality and life fulfillment', or it may be 'little more than a tiresome necessity in acquiring the resources for survival or for what he may define as the real living which he begins as work ends' (1976: 38–9). It is not surprising to find that husbands and wives in cross-class families attach such meanings to their work. Nor should it be surprising to discover that wives most often express the former meaning and husbands the latter.

The husbands:

Work for me is a means to earn a living. It's just a job.

Mr Everett, heating and ventilating fitter

I work because society says I must. I sell my body to the highest bidder. I am very bored with my job.

Mr Ashcroft, milk roundsman

It was always my ambition to be a lorry driver, so I was always looking for lorry jobs. Now, though, I just work for the money. I'm not trying to better myself. I just work as quickly as possible to get it done and forget it.

Mr Barnes, lorry driver

The wives:

At age 16 I felt called to do missionary work and so I went into nursing. My work is important to me as a person.

Mrs Henderson, health visitor

I didn't know what I wanted to do when I left school. By accident I dropped into a little village school and I always wanted to teach since then. So I worked towards it. Years and years of frustration—because I believed that that was what I was supposed to do. And I still believe. It's a vocation.

Mrs Mason, teacher

A careers interviewer suggested the idea of being a librarian and so I researched it. I thought it would be interesting and it is. I'm serving the public, making a contribution. It's not just commercial. And it's intellectually stimulating. You learn things, you develop.

Mrs Roberts, librarian

Moreover, these contrasting meanings which individuals attach to their work can be revealed by the same couple as the following examples illustrate. The first, the Patons, have been married for 4 years. Mr Paton has been employed as an agricultural fitter for 11 years following a 5-year apprenticeship. As such he services and repairs new and used farm equipment. Although he reports that 'if I won the pools, I'd still go out to work', his involvement with his work is minimal. He says 'It's just something I do to bring in money.' Mrs Paton, in contrast, sees her job as a district nurse as very much a part of her sense of self. In fact Mrs Paton became a nurse only over considerable opposition from her mother who wanted her daughter to be a shorthand typist. Her mother's attitude was that Mrs Paton 'wouldn't be able to take it' as a nurse. As a schoolgirl, however, Mrs Paton went on several outings to old people's nursing homes and found that not only could she indeed 'take it'—she enjoyed it. After 10 years as a hospital sister and 3 years as a district nurse, she reports: 'I've always wanted to be a district nurse and I've got what I wanted. I love my work . . . I see myself working as a nurse 25 years from now.' Similarly contradictory attitudes to work are revealed by Mr and Mrs Peterson who have been married for 7 years. Mr Peterson became an electrician on the advice of his father and following several years' factory employment now works for a small electrical contracting firm. Like Mr Paton, his work predominately involves the servicing of farm equipment and he is known to complain bitterly that he forever smells of pigs! Work for Mr Peterson is little more than a way of gratifying his passion for cars: 'Dad said "Get a trade," so I became an electrician but basically I work for money. I always have done. Money to buy cars. I love cars.' In almost complete contrast, Mrs Peterson reports her teaching career as the fulfilment of a long-standing ambition. After 1 year's employment as a systems analyst and 2 years teaching handicapped adults, Mrs Peterson entered college and obtained a teaching certificate. She has been teaching Home Economics and Needlecraft to boys and girls aged 11 to 16 for the past 4 years and derives great pleasure from her work. Moreover, she sees teaching as her way of making a contribution to society: 'I've always wanted to be a teacher. And I love working. I love my job rather than just working for money. I like the satisfaction of getting the kids through their exams. It's important.'

The contrasts in meaning which the husbands and wives of these two couples still in the early stages of married life attach to their work may well become more pronounced as time passes and husbands spend more years in jobs they simply tolerate as means to financial ends and wives develop their career interests more deeply. Mr and Mrs Light have been married for 20 years and have two teenaged children. Mrs Light completed her teacher's training in the same year that she married and, after nine years' sporadic employment while her children were young, returned to full-time teaching in 1972. She is presently Deputy Head of a junior school as well as responsible for her own class of 6- and 7-year-olds. Her job is vital to her sense of self; teaching is something she does because she has 'never wanted to do anything else'. Moreover, she is actively looking forward to promotion: 'Eventually I want a headship. I did very well in a questionnaire at a Deputy Head's conference. It seems that I am very good material for a headship. I've applied once already—just to get my name noticed.' How very different is her

husband's attitude to work. For Mr Light, all jobs are interchange-
able. Work is simply something he does. Once the dreamer of
dreams, he was unable to fulfil a youth's ambition to be a disc jockey
and since then has held a series of jobs in and out of manual work.
At present self-employed as a hire-car driver, he sees little change for
himself in the future:

> I'm not particularly ambitious. Life to me is just for the living. I've never
> had any particular plan other than one and that I've not been able to do.
> And if I cannot do that because I'm denied it, then I don't want to do
> anything else. That's been my attitude for so long. All the jobs I've had, I
> took them because they were available and because I could do them. My
> work stops when I leave the job. I'm resigned to what I'm doing now.

Perhaps not surprisingly the Lights suffer rather evident marital
conflict as Mrs Light resents her husband's unwillingness or inability to come up to her standards of work achievement and ambition.
For the present, however, examination of such conflict will await
further discussion of work-related differences between spouses.

This pattern of contrasting meanings between men and women is
the predominant one found among the couples interviewed. Generally, for the women work is a source of personal fulfilment. Only one
teacher, Mrs White, reports finding such fulfilment away from her
chosen occupation; only Mrs Thompson, a part-time school secretary, dismisses her work as 'just a little job'. For their husbands,
however, work is primarily a source of income; few would continue
in their present jobs if given the choice to do otherwise. Not all of the
men feel this way, of course, and as will become apparent, a purely
instrumental attitude towards work may be accompanied by feelings
of satisfaction and personal esteem. What then do such contrasts in
meaning signify? Does it follow that for the women work is all good
and for the men all bad? Are these contrasts in meaning associated
with clear contrasts in the degree of job security, autonomy and
satisfaction afforded by the two sets of occupations? In fact, they
often are not. In many ways such meanings are epiphenomenal to
other, more important differences. In order that the working lives of
these husbands and wives may be fully understood and the effects of
certain differences traced into their home lives, I will leave aside
momentarily the issue of the meaning of work and turn to the more
concrete reality of the day to day.

Autonomy and innovation

> Manual workers less often had before them a career with advancement depending upon their own efforts. They less often had a say in the day-to-day organization of their working lives. They were more often paced by machines they served. In all respects middle-class people generally had more autonomy.
>
> Young and Willmott, *The Symmetrical Family*, 1973: 154

Young and Willmott's characterization of the work of the manually employed is a familiar one. How far, though, does it represent the experiences of manual workers who are also partners in cross-class marriages? How far are these men restricted in their daily work activities to obeying the dictates of machines? To doing what others determine they should do? In what ways, if any, do their experiences of autonomy differ from those of their 'middle-class' wives?

Chapter 2 outlines the range of occupational skills held by the men and women interviewed. For the husbands such skills are highly diverse, ranging from virtually unskilled helpers, through those whose main skill is driving, to highly skilled telecommunications engineers. Not indicated by this list of job titles, however, is the overwhelming number of husbands who work almost entirely on their own, free from direct supervision during each workday. Setting aside the four men who are themselves supervisors of other manually employed men, we are left with only four others who work in close proximity to fellow workers or are subject to direct supervision during the day. The rest are either on their own entirely for most or all of the day or in relatively constant movement in the performance of their tasks so that they are thus indirectly free from supervision. A few examples will illustrate this point. Mr Allan, although he works within the confines of a factory, is constantly on the move during the day as a maintenance electrician responding to calls from foremen scattered throughout the plant. He reports that he is largely unsupervised in his work for this reason and because 'the machines are too complicated for close supervision; only the electrician really knows the machines'. Similarly, Mr Peterson, also an electrician, works from a radio-controlled van and is on his own for the entire work-day. Although his employer sets Mr Peterson's daily schedule, he is not himself an electrician and is therefore not able to monitor Mr Peterson's work closely. Freedom of movement and freedom from direct supervision, then, set these men apart from the manual workers cited by Young and Willmott. The experiences of the two men above are echoed by many others, whether it is Mr Barnes in his lorry, or Mr French in his 'You pick up your deliveries in the morning and then it's on the road—just you, no supervisors, on your own all day.' Or Mr Everett, a heating and ventilating fitter:

I've got several bosses but I hardly ever see them. Technically I'm supervised by a supervisor. But in reality there's only one person who knows the job and that's the person whose put in to do it. Someone else can't come along and say you're doing it wrong because they don't know how.

For most of the cross-class husbands studied here the situation is much the same: the level of personal autonomy during the working day is really quite high.

Unlike their husbands, however, the majority of wives work in the same place and in close proximity to others each day. Two of the three exceptions, Mrs Paton and Mrs Henderson, work in the community as nurses visiting their clients in homes and at clinics; the third, Mrs Young, travels from village to village in her capacity of mobile librarian. These women are subject to little supervision, as Mrs Henderson relates:

No, I'm not supervised at all. There is a nursing officer directly above and a senior nursing officer above her, but they don't interfere. We have meetings once a month and quarterly. You must fill in forms for each family, though, and you are monitored from these forms. But you are alone with the families.

For the other women, being stationary can mean they are more liable to control and scrutiny in their work activities than are their husbands. Teachers, for example, are dependent upon the will of the Head Teacher who is free to run the school almost entirely as he or she chooses. Occasionally this means loss of autonomy and close supervision:

Our Head is autocratic with many rules and regulations. He checks every child's book every year. I've never had this experience before. He comes into the classroom whenever he wishes and undermines the authority of the teacher. I've managed to get used to it—now I just smile, but it used to disturb me.

Mrs Henley, Junior school teacher

More often, however, the Head allows teachers considerable freedom, especially if they have many years of service:

I've been teaching for 18 years now, so the Head leaves me pretty much to myself.

Mrs Allan, Middle school teacher and department head

No, I'm not supervised, not now. I've been there 12 years; only the Deputy Head has been there longer than me.

Mrs French, Comprehensive school teacher and librarian

Outside of the teaching profession, the experience of autonomy is similar. If the immediate supervisor allows it, considerable freedom attends the job, while direct control from above can result in restrictions. Mrs Ashcroft, computer programmer, illustrates this dependence upon the goodwill of one's boss:

Under the previous programmer, it was impossible to work creatively. He was very rigid. I lost interest finally. He just wanted me to do what he wanted to do. But I'm in a new team now and it is much better. Most of my time is spent thinking about 'how to do it' problems. My senior programmer is there to consult but he doesn't directly supervise my work now.

Mrs Stone, architect, and Mrs Meredith, administrative officer, report similar experiences; now, however, both are free from direct control of their daily activities and look to their immediate supervisors only for advice and consultation.

Generally, then, the women report quite high levels of job autonomy, although their freedom of movement may be more restricted than their husband's. In reality, however, the experience of autonomy is quite different *in kind* for these husbands and wives. For the men, specific skills have been hired by their employers. The men are given considerable freedom to perform these skills, frequently being unfettered by direct supervision. If they fail to perform their skills adequately, the nature of their work ensures that this failure is readily observable: machines do not work, heating is not installed, milk remains undelivered. For the women, the situation clearly differs. As administrators and professionals, they are hired either to carry out delegated tasks and given the authority to do so, or to pass on the benefit of their expertise and specialized knowledge as teachers, nurses, librarians, and so on. They are thus hired to be autonomous. They must be trusted to carry out their work tasks, moreover, for failure to do so is much more difficult to detect, and may not become obvious for a considerable length of time. The restrictions on autonomy which do exist for these women come predominantly from the nature of the work they are hired to perform—from the fact that their work is done for and with other people. This fact sets them apart from their husbands whose main work activities centre on machines. Once the men have acquired the necessary skills, they may perform their work without need for constant or direct supervision. This gives them considerable freedom. The women, on the other hand, work in close and collaborative environments; often their work demands consultation, always it involves people. This in itself restricts freedom. This difference—of work with machines versus work with people—is, moreover, a fundamental job difference between these husbands and wives and, as such, more important than differences in meaning or freedom of movement. The experience of innovation, the opportunity to use one's own ideas in the performance of the job, illustrates the significance of this difference.

If autonomy is certain for most of the men interviewed, opportunities for innovation are not. Common to many of their jobs is a set of procedures, determined by the nature of the work to be done, and followed on a daily basis with little interruption in routine. Often the lack of scope for putting into play one's own ideas is a result of the minimal level of skill required for the job itself. Ferrying cars from one location to another (Mr Aston), delivering milk (Mr Ashcroft), cutting forms to their proper size (Mr Henley), or delivering goods (Mr Barnes) do not require nor allow much opportunity for innovation. However, even highly skilled jobs may require performance over and over again of the same tasks without demanding creativity from the worker. Mr Young, telecommunications engineer, reports being taught to do many different things as an apprentice. His training prepared him to solve problems, to be capable of seeing better ways of performing a variety of tasks. His actual daily work, however, contains virtually no variety at all, and little challenge:

My job at present is very boring, very mundane. It's a job that requires extreme concentration but no thinking. I'm wiring new telephone exchanges but all it means is the joining together of thousands and thousands of tiny wires. If I make a mistake, the system won't work. But it's very difficult to keep concentration. And you must because it's so easy to join the wrong wires. All day, just joining together thousands and thousands of tiny wires . . . the idea of changing my routine or how it's done just doesn't exist.

Only if Mr Young makes an error is the routine broken. In fact, it is only through errors or faults in systems or machinery that most of the workers here experience change in their daily routine. Occasionally this will mean that the worker in question is called upon to exercise his powers of ingenuity as he confronts a problem:

My job is fascinating at times. It's very intriguing and it can be extremely varied. There's set procedures for maintenance but problems can arise which mean you do things differently. A boiler blew up recently—worth £2,000—I discussed it with the on-site boss and then read up on the possible causes. And I figured it out. So now there's a new way of treating things. I saved them £2,000 in the future—I solved it.

Mr Meredith, heating and ventilating fitter

Even though Mr Meredith's experience is somewhat unusual in the degree to which it called upon his abilities for innovative thinking, it does illustrate the nature of work for many of the men of this research quite appropriately: breakdowns provide variety and the chance to use skills creatively; maintenance is routine. It follows from this that much of the day to day is the same, repetitive. Once the given skills are acquired, the machines understood, the job may be performed without much involvement of self in the work done. Mr Smith, a telecommunications engineer, underlines this detachment of self from the daily routine: 'As far as the actual work is concerned, I've been doing it for so long, I don't really have to think about a lot of it. Well, I do, but really not very much.' Sometimes, of course, performance of the job is accompanied by feelings of personal satisfaction, as evident in Mr Meredith's words and further illustrated by Mr Everett who installs heating and refrigeration into new buildings:

At the end of the day, there's quite a lot of job satisfaction. The jobs are prototype operations—one-off. Every job is different. And when it all works and everything works nice—you've done it all. It's something that you've done that will be there a long time: 50 or 100 years.

Despite this satisfaction, however, the lack of personal involvement in jobs with machines is such that Mr Everett also says 'It's just a job. I switch off after I finish.' The inability to bring individual expertise beyond the level of a specific skill into the normal working day tends, then, to result in the job itself being left behind at the end of the day. The following remarks are typical:

I shower my job away at the end of the day.

I hit the clock and it's all gone.

I leave it at work. Once I leave work, that's it—I forget it.

Of course, if the job is particularly trying or tedious, aggravation from boredom may follow these workers home, as may physical exhaustion. But generally, work with machines, work with only infrequent demands for individual creativity, is work which is left at the workplace. Carry-over into the home in the way of worry, planning, or preparations for the following day is, for these workers, virtually unknown.

In direct contrast, the majority of women interviewed report considerable opportunities to innovate, to involve much of themselves in their jobs by bringing their own ideas to their work, even if as Mrs Everett remarks 'They don't always admit that they are *your* ideas.' For the teachers, the freedom to work innovatively is somewhat restricted by the need to conform to a set syllabus. Even within this constraint, however, there is ample scope for creativity:

I teach to a syllabus but I cannot bear to teach the same thing in the same way. Every time I try to look at the subject and teach it from another angle. This means lots of preparation time.

Mrs French, English teacher

You must teach to the syllabus but you can add anything extra that you want. I always try to add something new.

Mrs Allan, Home Economics teacher

Moreover, the types of jobs that these women have are such that it is often for their ability to innovate, to think creatively that they are hired. Mrs Norton, a former social worker, is presently in charge of an internal training programme. In this capacity she is responsible for designing and implementing training courses, for arranging student placements through staff selection and interviews, and for acting as a liaison with outside educational bodies. Without the ability to bring ideas to her work, Mrs Norton would be inadequate for the job. In a similar vein, Mrs James has been responsible for the creation of an experimental educational programme for problem children; Mrs Miller for the innovation within her school of continual child study reports which follow each child from junior to middle school. Mrs Harvey is the supervisor of fourteen; Mrs Everett of ten; and Mrs Leonard of six: all are expected to use their own judgement in performing their duties. The only exceptions to this rule of freedom to innovate, to put something of one's self into the job are Mrs Jason and Mrs Unger, both employed as MLSOs. Routine is paramount for these two women. Entrusted with blood and tissue typing and testing, they must adhere strictly to the set procedures as deviations could lead to mistakes resulting in infection and death.

The differences between the work of husbands and wives are clear. Although on occasion the wives are subject to closer control of their work activities than are their husbands, they enjoy far greater opportunity to bring something of themselves into the performance of their jobs. In involvement with work they differ considerably from their husbands. This difference is, moreover, reflected in after-hours activities. Where husbands are content to leave 'work at work', wives carry the job home. Virtually every teacher brings work home in a physical sense—marking, reading, planning. Those teachers who do not carry work home with them frequently stay late at their schools, preparing for the following day. Those who are not teachers bring work home mentally (as, of course, do the teachers):

I'm emotionally drained, mentally exhausted at the end of the day. I must jolt myself to leave work at work. Sometimes, when I get home I forget to talk to the family.

Mrs Henderson, health visitor

I always bring work home in my mind. It's very stressful. I'm usually tense all week worrying about it, about whether I might have made a mistake. I usually manage to relax by Sunday.

Mrs Unger, MLSO

And, perhaps not unexpectedly, some husbands object to their wives' carry-over of work into the home. Mr Paton, an agricultural fitter married to a district nurse, is the most articulate but he speaks for certain others when he says:

I don't like my wife bringing work home. She works out of hours and doesn't get paid. Sometimes we have arguments about it—when she works after dinner. Sometimes she can be on the phone all night. I mean, she goes to bed at 9.30 p.m. and is up at 5 a.m. She just thinks about her job. I'd rather switch off and I wish she would too. She doesn't leave much time for me—not really much at all.

What may sound like a common complaint from the wives of

managers, in cross-class families comes from the husbands (cf. Pahl and Pahl, 1971, especially pp. 221–2). The differences in commitment, in involvement, and in after-work tiredness can and do cause conflict between husbands and wives. It will be seen in the following chapter, however, that the degree of such conflict is in large measure governed by the extent of normative agreement between spouses about the roles each play inside and outside the home.

Job Security

The security of one's job is often hard to judge. Despite employment contracts, union support and years of long service, changes in Governments and the economy are liable to make the most secure job seem uncertain. In addition, the type and size of the employing firm affects the quality of security. The men of this research represent a wide variety of employment situations with commensurate degrees of security. The women are all employees in the public sector and so experience very nearly identical security of tenure. This section examines the consequences of these differing employment situations, in large measure to set the scene for future analysis. For perhaps the most important aspect of security for these men and women is the fact that, with only a few exceptions, all of the men have wives with incomes sufficient to support the family should the husbands become unemployed—a fact of some importance for the marital relations of many of these couples. I will begin this examination by exploring the range of situations in which the husbands are found and then proceed to a brief look at the wives.

In general, those men employed by local governments as industrial civil servants and those working in public corporations are in the most secure positions. The former include Mr Abbot, a sawmill foreman employed by the county; Mr Fielding, also employed by the county, a fireman; and Mr Henley, employed in local government as a printer's helper. Although their years of tenure vary from 6 to 37, all three report themselves in highly secure situations. For the men employed in public corporations, such as transportation, the car industry and telecommunications, job security is seen to be dependent upon the attitudes of the present Conservative Government. For these men, feelings of security are marred by doubts about the trend towards privatization and the demand for cut-backs. Among workers at BL and British Rail (BR), such doubts are minimal and provide only a backdrop of insecurity:

It's very secure but contracts don't mean a thing any more—not with this government.

Mr Jason, employed 43 years at BL

It's very difficult to judge, very difficult. It's not too likely I would be made redundant though. But the contracts are no longer recognized.

Mr Allan, 15 years at BL

It's really quite secure but, then, I don't know—the government wants cuts.

Mr Thompson, 30 years at BR

A background of doubt has become a positive threat, however, for the workers at British Telecom (BT). During the course of the interviews the Thatcher Government moved from suggestions of privatization to concrete actions towards this aim. This change is reflected in the responses of the men involved, from Mr Young who was interviewed in the early stages through Mr Meredith and Mr Smith interviewed at subsequent six-month intervals:

Right now, my job security is excellent but it could change if the government decides to sell BT.

Mr Young, 4 years' employment

It's been very secure up till now but BT may be sold and the union says we will be less secure. The Government says there will be no difference at all. I feel just a little worried because mine is the type of job they could do away with, could contract out. I'm not particularly threatened at the moment and if you believe management, I'll be okay—if you believe them.

Mr Meredith, 22 years' employment

If you had asked me a year ago, I'd have said absolutely secure. But now with this privatization thing—I don't think my job is as secure as it was. They want to knock 40,000 off the employment list and I think I'd be a front runner.

Mr Smith, 20 years' employment

It is difficult to predict the consequences of cut-backs and privatization for these men. Those with long-service records would, of course, be financially compensated through substantial redundancy payments should their jobs disappear. In addition, they are all protected by strong union organizations. Compared with

many others in the labour market, then, it could be said that these
men enjoy relatively secure existences.

Much less secure are those without union support and those with
comparatively short records of employment with their present firms.
Among the former are men employed by small, privately owned
companies. Continued employment for these men is often dependent
upon maintaining good relations with the employer. Mr Paton
manages to achieve such good relations, as does Mr Parker although
to a more doubtful degree. But both Mr Peterson and Mr Aston
report having failed to establish good terms with the men
responsible for their security of employment. As a result, they both
feel it quite probable that they may lose their jobs in the immediate
future. All four of these men are in non-union firms and subject to
only 1 week's notice of dismissal. Of course, the existence of a union
does not in itself guarantee against unwanted dismissal. If a worker
has little seniority, or breaks tenure with his firm, then he may well
find himself out of work. Mr Everett had been employed with the
same heating firm for more than 25 years. But when offered an
opportunity to better his working conditions and income by joining
a newly opened firm, he left his long-term employer. After only 8
months in operation, the new business went bankrupt, sending Mr
Everett back to his previous employer—but now without seniority.
Six months later, on the 'last in, first out' principle, Mr Everett was
made redundant. Securing employment with yet another firm, he
once again suffered the consequences of bankruptcy. At the time of
our interview, Mr Everett had been re-employed with his old
company for 5 months:

Usually once you start at this company, you stay your whole life. But I
broke my service with them and now I'm back again, trying to build up
seniority. I'm the first one to go now and I don't need to be paid
redundancy. It's quite likely I will be out of work again . . . if you worried
too much, you'd get sick. Right now, it's not too bad, we've got three
workers.

In addition to losing seniority when he left his company, Mr Everett,
aged 54, also lost his pension. He now has virtually no job benefits
beyond paid holidays.

The reality of job insecurity for manual workers becomes even
more plain, however, when neither union support nor seniority
protects the worker against unwanted redundancy. Mr Creighton

began work as a welder as a boy of 15. For 40 years, he continued with the same firm experiencing both promotion and several changes of management. Promotion for Mr Creighton meant moving from welder to foreman-welder to supervisor of four departments, responsible for the work of more than fifty others. The final change of management meant redundancy. Four years prior to the loss of his job, new managers at Mr Creighton's company introduced 'efficiency experts' into the firm. These young, American, college graduates reorganized the factory, bringing in two new departments of 'Inspection' and 'Progress'. Very quickly, Mr Creighton's years of experience were to count for little as new rules and regulations for the management and control of the work flow were introduced. Eventually needing to leave the factory for a short time in order to undergo an operation on his foot, Mr Creighton returned to work to discover he had been demoted from supervisor back to working-foreman. Three months later, he was asked to be on the night shift; 3 months after this, the night shift was closed down and Mr Creighton was asked to take 'early retirement'. The union could not help him, and so feeling that worse might occur if he refused, Mr Creighton agreed. Now unemployed, and at age 55 virtually unemployable, Mr Creighton feels considerable resentment that his 40 years of good service and loyalty could not prevent his being 'eased out'.

The job security of these men is, then, quite variable. Most feel no immediate threat to their positions although the workers at BT are clearly worried. For the others, their sense of job security may well be ephemeral should they find themselves in similar circumstances to those of Mr Everett or Mr Creighton. In contrast, it is highly unlikely—with only two exceptions—that any of the women interviewed for this research will be made redundant or find themselves unemployed other than as a result of their own desires. As employees in the public sector, their jobs are very secure, protected by contract. The two exceptions are Mrs Thompson and Mrs White, both employed on a part-time basis and thus subject to notice at any time. Although Mrs Unger and Mrs Henderson also work part-time, their employment has been agreed as a continuation of previous full-time work and they are therefore entitled to the normal benefits and rights of full-time employees. The position of these women in the labour market, Mrs White and Mrs Thompson apart, is thus markedly different from that of their husbands. Only

husbands themselves employed by the county share the same degree
of job security. For the rest, despite varying degrees of confidence
about job security, the possibility remains that changes in the
economy will force them into unemployment. Their wives face no
such threat.

The situation of county employees has changed somewhat in
recent years, however. While actual job security remains untouched,
employment contracts have been modified such that, while
unemployment may not be an issue, redeployment may be. Until the
1970s teachers, nurses, librarians, etc. were hired to a specific job in
a specific location. This is now altered so that the hiring authorities
can cope with demands for cuts in staff, and all new employees are
contracted to the county rather than to a specific school, library, and
so on. With respect to teachers, Head Teachers and Deputy Heads
are exempt from this new contract. For some of the women in this
research, redeployment is an issue which causes worry. This
concern, however, extends only to where they might have to work,
not to whether they will be able to continue working. Mrs Mason
discussed this point in our interview: 'At the moment, you are
redeployed if your school doesn't want you. But it's very hard to
actually get rid of a teacher, so one could say that I'm there as long
as I want to be.' Redeployment is, however, a far different matter
from unemployment and the majority of women interviewed share
Mrs Mason's confident: 'I'm there as long as I want to be.' In doing
so, moreover, they differ from their husbands.

Promotions and the Future

If job security is very certain for the wives, and of varying degrees of
certainty for the husbands, what then of advancement possibilities?
Given that all are able to avoid unemployment, will they seek or
achieve change in the future? Four husbands have already been
promoted to differing levels of authority. Mr Creighton's success in
progressing beyond the rank of welder did not protect him from
unemployment, as we have just seen. Similarly, promotion from
worker to supervisor has not changed the material conditions of
work for Mr Henderson or Mr White. Both men remain hourly paid
workers, are docked pay if more than 5 minutes late, continue to be
paid for any amounts of overtime worked, and are expected to
perform manual work in addition to their supervisory duties. For

Mr White, though, his promotion—which came as a surprise— awakened unknown feelings of ambition. He now looks higher and thinks that within six years or so he might be able to enter management: 'I never expected it at all, but since getting promoted I've certainly set my sights higher. I'd like to be my own boss.' The same sense of surprise is expressed by Mr Abbot, promoted twice in his 37 years with a sawmill. On both occasions, the previous incumbents left unexpectedly and Mr Abbot was sought out to take their places, first as charge-hand and finally as foreman. That promotion found him rather than the reverse is clear from his words: 'I was really quite happy doing the job I was doing before.' And his wife confirms his sentiments: 'He's very bright really, but he has no ambition. They had to force on him the foremanship of the mill really.' Like the others, Mr Abbot remains an hourly paid worker, is fully recompensed for any overtime work, and continues to perform physical labour. We see with these four husbands, then, that promotion for manual workers can sometimes mean little change, that future conditions of employment remain quite similar to past conditions.

If promotion can come without conscious efforts towards such an end by the worker, as it did for Mr White and Mr Abbot, then it is possible that more of the men of this study will gain advancement at work. In practice, however, only one husband is actively seeking such advancement. The rest either do not want promotion, or work in situations where opportunities do not exist. For some, the worker's own lack of ambition itself denies the availability of promotional prospects (cf. Goldthorpe, *et al.*, 1969: 72):

I'm not ambitious. I've no desire to give orders so I've never explored the possibilities.

Mr Fielding, fireman

I suppose it is theoretically possible, but I'm not interested at all.

Mr Henley, printer's helper

It's not that kind of job really. There's no prospects ... but then I'm not very ambitious.

Mr James, forklift driver at BL

Only Mr Young, at present a telecommunications engineer with BT, is preparing himself for future promotion by taking the courses necessary to pass upwards in the BT hierarchy in fulfilment of his aim to become a 'non-worker'. If lack of ambition is an important reason why many of the husbands do not seek promotion, it is not the only reason. For Mr Allan, for example, the conditions of work itself make him unwilling to move beyond manual work:

I'd be loath to take promotion with the situation as it is now in BL. There's too much pressure, the place is run by hatchet men. Outsiders don't really understand—it's a completely different world at BL.

Similarly, moving out of the ranks of the manually employed was perceived by Mr French as an avenue to job insecurity. Actively involved in the creation of a union within his industry, Mr French reports on the dangers of promotion:

Oh yes, possibilities certainly existed. But being a suspicious character, I could see and did see what happens to someone like me who takes a promotion. We were giving the company a hard time, you see, standing up and fighting—quite a few got the opportunity for upward promotion and they took it and they lived to regret it. There was no union for white collar workers, no protection. I wasn't interested in following that route after seeing what had happened to a couple of them. No way. But the offer was there and I turned them down *flat*! I was a troublemaker you see. And the company, well, their attitude was: if you can't beat 'em, get them to join you. And once they've joined you, if you don't like them, then you can just get rid of them. And they did. And the men didn't have any redress at all.

If both Mr Allan and Mr French are somewhat unusual in their reasons for not wanting advancement, they are not alone in assigning specific work-related reasons to their lack of ambition. More common, however, is a reluctance to give up the relatively autonomous existence these men enjoy in pursuing their occupations. As described earlier, the majority of these men work alone, often away from the plant or office during most of the working day. Mr Meredith speaks for others when he says:

I'm very much my own boss, I can decide pretty much on a day-to-day basis where I'm going to go. I can organize my life most of the time very much to suit myself. And at 4.30 p.m. I lock up my van, come home and the job is finished. The next step up would be lower management. It would mean being in an office, in one place, looking at the same walls every day and shuffling bits of paper. Bits of paper come in, you sign them and push them on. And you take the job home with you, the worries home with you. You're liable to be phoned up at home. The increase in salary, the rewards, I think, just don't match the demands.

Again and again, echoes of this feeling were expressed by the men of this research, from Mr James: 'Right now, I hit the clock and it's all gone . . . there's no worries, no responsibilities . . . no worries—it's definitely an advantage.'—to Mr Paton: 'I wouldn't want office work—it's too boring. Right now, for 60% of the time, I'm my own boss.'—and to Mr Jason, a turner machinist with BL:

Work never comes into my mind. It might be different if you had problems you have to solve. I think it's a bonus—all them directors and that, they've got ulcers and that. They worry. It's always on their minds— Business—they must have everything right—Guilt—it's not good for you.

And so we return, finally, to the beginning—to the meaning of work for these men. Work is simply something they do during the hours set aside for earning a living. It is not something they carry with them into the hours away from this necessity. It is not something in which they invest much of themselves. They are free from direct control, free from anxiety about what the next working day might bring. In general, they want neither promotion nor responsibility beyond that which accompanies the performance of their own tasks. For those who have achieved advancement at work, most are content to remain more or less within the ranks of the manually employed and all are content to leave 'work at work'. Their work, as such, is not without certain intrinsic satisfactions, although from time to time it can be both tiring and tedious. For most, what they have is a 'job' and what they have is enough (cf. Goldthorpe *et al.*, 1969: 67). It follows from this that the future is likely to resemble closely the past and present for the majority of those interviewed. This was often reflected in their responses to my queries about what they are looking forward to with respect to work. Mr James's 'Nothing at all. It's that kind of job.' speaks for many of the others. He does not, of course, speak for all. Mr Young is seeking promotion; Mr White has discovered latent feelings of ambition. Likewise, both Mr Aston and Mr Peterson hope some day to become self-employed. These four apart, however, the future holds little likelihood of change in the working lives of these cross-class husbands.

If little change in the future is likely for the husbands, what is ahead for the wives? In Chapter 2, Gidden's comments are noted regarding 'career blocks'—impediments to further advancement once the given occupation has been achieved. Giddens specifically cites teachers as vulnerable to this problem. However, as noted also, teachers are frequently able to progress within their profession, although often only within certain limits. Of the fifteen teachers studied here, nine have already been promoted to varying levels of authority as department heads, pastoral heads, Deputy and Head Teachers. Three teachers are seeking promotion; one wishes to leave teaching for educational research and two others work on a part-time basis. The majority, then, have achieved advancement at work. The nature of their occupation is such, moreover, that most do not want added promotion beyond the level already gained for they would then lose contact with the ultimate objects of their work—the children:

I really enjoy the kids. I wouldn't want administration.

Mrs Henley

I'd like to be department head but not much higher. I like the kids, higher would mean too much administration.

Mrs Peterson

The remarks of these two stand for many of the others. The satisfaction of teaching comes from the children taught, not from paperwork—a feeling made plain by Mrs Abbot, a Head Teacher who retains her teaching duties:

If I get the opportunity, I may retire early. I love the children but there's so much red tape now. I spend so much time filling in forms and so on. The pressures are becoming so much more now. I think I shall be quite happy to retire when the occasion arises.

Teaching is, in fact, like many other professions—satisfaction comes from achieving and performing the chosen occupation. Promotion takes the individual away from the work they want to do. Outside of teaching this is expressed by Mrs Paton and Mrs Henderson both of whom have gone beyond hospital nursing to the positions of health visitor and district nurse. Further advancement now would take them away from the people they try to help.

For those in administrative-type occupations, feelings are mixed about future plans. Mrs Everett and Mrs Leonard do not want promotion: Mrs Everett for reasons of age—she is now 54 years old and content with the present demands of her work—and Mrs Leonard because she intends to give up work for family responsibilities. For the others, promotion is something they definitely want, if only to escape the possibility of performing the same work until retirement:

It's a career. I have to think of it as a career. When I moved to this job, I thought of it as a step on the ladder up . . . but I'm still looking upwards. I don't want to do the same job until retirement. Right now, the chances of promotion are slim because of cut-backs, but perhaps in another county.

Mrs Harvey, head librarian

It certainly is a career. I'm fully qualified now and can only add to experience. As for ambition, well, I'd be horrified to stay there for the rest of my life. I would like to think I could change my life if I wanted. But I want financial independence and the only way to have that is as a professional person.

Mrs Stone, architect

Hopefully I'll be promoted . . . you see, there's a pattern. I'm very ambitious. Every job I've undertaken, I've learned something new and carried that learning with me and gradually progressed. I think I'd like to move into higher management. All my work career, I've gone into messy situations, set them straight, and then lost interest. There's no more challenge.

Mrs Meredith, administrative officer

These two general attitudes towards advancement at work—career satisfaction and the seeking of new challenges—represent the future working lives of the majority of women interviewed. Unlike their husbands who, for the most part, would choose alternative work if given the opportunity to do so, these women are happy with their chosen fields. They invest much time and energy in their work, carry home their worries and thoughts about the next day and look forward to continued professional development. Unlike their husbands, they attach meaning to their work which links job and self most closely. In the next two chapters, these husbands and wives will be brought together in an analysis of the impact of their differing work experiences on family life. In this analysis, it will become clear that for many cross-class families such differences in work involvement and commitment can be disruptive of family harmony. For both husbands and wives, however, the preceding comments on the overall nature of work represent only the predominant pattern. For a very few, work holds quite different meanings, is of different conditions. In the analysis which follows, these few will stand apart.

5

Linking Work and Home in Cross-class Families, Part One

If purely moral rules are at stake, the public conscience restricts any act which infringes them by the surveillance it exercises over the conduct of citizens and by the special punishments it has at its disposal. In other cases the constraint is less violent; nevertheless, it does not cease to exist. If I do not conform to ordinary conventions, if in my mode of dress I pay no heed to what is customary in my country and in my social class, the laughter I provoke, the social distance at which I am kept, produce, although in a more mitigated form, the same results as any real penalty. In other cases, although it may be indirect, constraint is no less effective . . . Even when in fact I can struggle free from these rules and successfully break them, it is never without being forced to fight against them. Even if in the end they are overcome, they make their constraining power sufficiently felt in the resistance that they afford. There is no innovator, even a fortunate one, whose ventures do not encounter opposition of this kind . . . Here, then, is a category of facts which present very special characteristics: they consist of manners of acting, thinking and feeling external to the individual, which are invested with a coercive power by virtue of which they exercise control over him.

Emile Durkheim

This chapter begins with Durkheim's formulation of the force of social facts over the individual because cross-class families—by their very existence—contravene one of society's most pervasive social norms: the occupational supremacy of husbands. It is the norm in Britain as elsewhere for husbands to form the most enduring and economically rewarding attachment to the labour force. It is the norm for husbands to determine their families' standing in the community through their occupational attainments. It is the norm for wives to shape their labour force participation to the demands of husbands' employment and family commitments. Sandra Burman captures the essence of these 'social facts', this pattern of family and work organization, in her introduction to *Fit Work for Women*:

One set of assumptions that became all pervasive in British society in the recent past, and which is likely to persist for many years to come, embraces the ideas that a woman's primary duties are as wife and mother and that her proper place is therefore in the home. Any work she does outside it must be subordinated to her domestic obligations and should not inferfere with men's rightful priority in paid work. (1979: 9)

In cross-class families, however, it is the wives, and not the husbands, who have occupations which provide higher status in the community. The wives have higher educational qualifications. They frequently earn more and are often much more committed to their jobs than are their husbands. And while there is no intrinsic reason why such differences between spouses which favour the wife as these do should be problematic for family life, the social fact of male supremacy makes them so.

Male occupational supremacy is more than a norm in most societies, in the sense that it is the typical pattern of family and work organization. It is also an ideology, a belief system which is extremely influential in forming images of how work and family life ought to be organized. In contravening this norm cross-class families thus have an additional burden to carry—a burden which is only rarely experienced by other two-earner families. In addition to the expected problems of balancing two jobs within one family, the men and women of cross-class families must come to terms with deviation from both norm *and ideology*. They must, moreover, accommodate whatever penalties arise from such deviance. For, as Durkheim reminds us, social norms may indeed be broken but not, however, with impunity.

The relationship between home and work is discussed in two parts. Part One, the present chapter, examines the way in which home life may affect participation in paid work by showing how an individual's attachment to the labour force may be conditioned by or alter as a result of family circumstances. The labour force attachment of both husbands and wives is considered in this section. In Part Two, Chapter 6, the carry-over of work into domestic life is discussed by examining the degree of separation of work and family worlds. The extent to which husbands and wives share the work-day's activities in conversation and the degree of understanding between spouses which exists regarding differences in post-work tiredness and commitment to extra-work activities are assessed. An overriding concern in both parts one and two is the relationship between income, long-term financial security, and the normative agreements between spouses which provide the foundation of family life. In all, the words of the participants themselves will be relied upon to illustrate the issues at hand. Throughout a balance will be struck between narrating the personal experiences of the husbands and wives—for little is known of this—and analysing the ways in which such experiences are a reflection of and a response to deviation from the norm of male occupational dominance. In this way it will be possible to gain both an understanding of cross-class family life itself and an awareness of the efficacy of social norms in defining and controlling the lives of individuals.

From Home to Work: Decision-making and Attachment to the Labour Force

For an individual worker, making decisions about future employment possibilities can often be a difficult process. When, however, there are two earners in one family, this decision-making process may become much more complicated.[1] Such decisions as might be made include taking on added responsibilities through promotion, or moving home and family to a new location in order to obtain promotion. Conversely, decisions may entail reducing the amount of work undertaken, or extend to the giving up of the job itself in order to conform to the demands of one's spouse. Like other two-earner families cross-class families must often cope with employment decisions, and in looking at how they do so we may begin to develop some sense of how these families may differ from others.

Geographical Relocation

In the previous chapter it became clear that a predominant feature of cross-class family life is the greater career involvement and desire for promotion on the part of the wives. With regard to geographical relocation for enhanced occupational opportunities, then, one could expect that the wives' careers would govern the families' responses to such occurrences. In fact, several other factors intervene and reduce mobility. For both husband and wife, attachment to specific homes and cities, either for reasons of sentiment or of proximity to other family members, overrides the desire to advance occupationally through relocation. In addition, the presence of dependent children in the home restricts mobility as parents are reluctant to disrupt their children's school lives. Perhaps more important, however, is the recognition by both husbands and wives of the difficulties presented by a very uncertain economy. The kinds of jobs held by these men and women are not ones which are, in times of recession and Government cut-backs, easily regained once given up. As manual workers, the husbands are often under greater threat occupationally than are their wives, and for them relocation could well mean an avenue to unemployment. For the women, as employees of county and local governments, promotion is available to a certain extent without having to change employer or location. Moreover, leaving the county in which they presently work would be likely to result in unemployment as social services in most areas are being reduced. Nearly half the men and women interviewed report unwillingness to move for these reasons.

In spite of such reluctance, however, a distinct pattern emerges. If familial and economic restrictions on mobility are set aside from consideration, the predominant employment decisions taken by the majority of families would be to move for the enhancement of the wife's career—should she so wish—and to acknowledge the improbability of doing so for the husband's work. In this cross-class families are quite distinct from other families. Moreover, they contradict Talcott Parsons's expectations concerning restrictions on labour mobility arising as a result of joint occupational participation of husbands and wives.[2] For in fact these families would, by and large, be willing to relocate; they would do so, however, not to further the husband's chances as assumed by Parsons, but to further the wife's. Of course, not all of the families interviewed reported this willingness for husbands to relocate in response to the demands of their wives' employment. In particular, those families in which the wives are employed on a part-time basis would not move for reasons concerning the wives' work, but would move for the husbands' work. Of the rest, however, only two families indicated that the wives would give up their jobs in order to accompany their husbands elsewhere. Only one of these husbands would actually ask his wife to do so. The first of these families, the Merediths, will be discussed more fully in the next chapter. Mrs Meredith reports herself willing to move in acknowledgement of her husband's greater earning capacity. The other family, the Astons, illustrate most clearly the difficulties inherent in dual commitments to the labour force within one family and in doing so give substance to Parsons' suggestions concerning restrictions on mobility.

Mr and Mrs Aston have been married for 4 years, throughout which time Mrs Aston has worked as a teacher. Mrs Aston became a teacher in part because she saw teaching as a secure occupation and in part because she enjoys working with children. She loves her work and is eager for promotion. Her husband, however, is very unhappy with his job as a garage driver and wishes to relocate geographically with the hope of opening his own retail clothing store. The Astons are thus confronted with a dilemma, for not only is Mrs Aston due for promotion very soon, but the added income from such advancement will aid in the realization of her husband's ambitions. Acceptance of promotion would mean, however, a greater commitment from Mrs Aston to her present school and increased reluctance to leave the area in which it is located. On the other hand, obtaining a transfer to a school in another area is extremely unlikely, and quitting her job to accompany her husband elsewhere could entail the loss of work as a teacher altogether. Moreover, the loss of her teaching position would mean that they were without the financial security necessary for Mr Aston's venture into retail trade. At the time of our interviews the Astons had not resolved this dilemma. Mrs Aston reports willingness to accompany her husband to a new location if and when he is ready to move; she is, however, unable to decide for or against any promotion offered to her. Mr Aston, while wanting to move as soon as possible, readily acknowledges that his plans depend upon his wife's continued employment as a teacher and refuses to consider her relinquishing her job: 'If she couldn't get a transfer, she'd stay behind and continue to teach here, and commute weekends. We need her guaranteed income.' For the time being, both Mr and Mrs Aston are delaying taking any decisions about their future and are thus delaying any changes in their working lives. Eventually, however, decisions will have to be made—or will be made in default—and it is quite likely that the importance of financial security to this couple will mean that such decisions will reinforce the already apparent primacy of Mrs Aston's occupational position within their marriage. If this indeed becomes the case, then this family as well will join the many others in which it is the wife's and not the husband's occupation which guides the family's future.

Attachment to the Labour Force

The dilemma confronting the Astons illustrates the difficulties of

coping with two jobs in one family in the face of geographical relocation. Moreover, they illustrate problems not often found in most
two-earner families. Mrs Aston's secure job and guaranteed salary
(which exceeds her husband's income by £2,000 annually) both allows
her husband to consider changing his job and prevents him from
doing so easily. Should Mrs Aston be less committed to her work, or
in the position of secondary earner within her family—as are most
wives in two-earner families—then the decisions confronting this
couple would be of quite a different order and it is plausible that Mrs
Aston would simply give up her job in acquiescence to the demands
of her husband's employment future. This would in fact be the
normal pattern of decision-making. As discussed in Chapter 1, wives
usually match their employment to the demands of family responsibilities. Most often, married women give up paid work for a period
to care for children, and frequently return to work on a part-time
basis after doing so. In addition to childcare responsibilities, the
employment choices facing husbands also precipitate modifications
in the labour force attachments of wives with women either not
taking up or giving up paid work in order to accommodate their
husband's labour force participation.[3] Although the Astons have not
yet chosen—and may not choose—to follow this normal pattern of
decision-making, others in this research have.

Thirteen of the wives interviewed took time away from the labour
market to have children, some bringing their families into the cross-
class family pattern only after returning to work. These women are
now at various stages of career development, with many having
already achieved promotion and others just beginning to think in
such terms. They will continue their attachment to the labour force
until retirement. Of the six women who intend to but have not yet
had children, most report an intention to withdraw from paid work
for only a short time before resuming their careers. Only one of these
women, Mrs Leonard, has decided to quit work more or less perma-
nently to raise a family. Mrs Leonard is presently employed as a
senior secretary and supervisor of six others. As such, she has been
encouraged by her superiors on several occasions to seek promotion. She, however, declines to do so and views her attachment to the
labour force as a prelude to assuming the role of full-time
homemaker. Her decision not to pursue career advancement is tied
closely to her home situation as she perceives little support from her
husband for any other course of action:

I think my husband would be supportive if I wanted more of a career but I'm not really sure. He's a man's man, if you know what I mean. I could never contemplate him staying at home and me going out to work. He'd never be one of those people who said: all right, dear, I'll give up my work. You go out to work. He identifies himself with working.

In concordance with her husband's identification of himself as a worker, Mrs Leonard sees herself primarily as a wife and future mother. Consequently, she has not prepared for a long working career:

I think I've always thought I'd give up my job for a number of years. I also think you are brought up to think that you grow up, you get married, you have children. You only work up to a certain stage. If I thought I would be working for the next 30 years, I would have tried to do something different [from her present job].

In her explicit adherence to the traditional role of women, Mrs Leonard is quite unusual among the wives of this research but she is not entirely alone. It is possible to find similarity in the part-time employment of Mrs Thompson and Mrs Unger. For these wives, part-time work is a way of balancing traditional roles within the family with their desire to work outside the home. They have each curtailed their participation in the labour force in response to the demands of family life. For Mrs Unger, who reports working part-time 'mainly because of the children', full-time employment or promotion at work exists only as a vague possibility some 10 or 15 years in the future. Mrs Thompson refers to her work as 'just a little job'; any change in her labour force attachment would conflict with the demands of marriage to a worker on alternating shifts. Furthermore, all three of these wives report willingness to relinquish their jobs should their husbands choose to relocate elsewhere. None, moreover, expect their husbands to oblige them in a reciprocal manner. In fact, no such necessity on the part of their husbands is likely to arise as a result of employment decisions taken by these women. In their assent to tradition, then, these families avoid the need to negotiate work-related decisions. Maximum potential for occupational mobility is maintained for the husbands through the relegation of the wives' employment to a position of secondary importance within the family. Although cross-class in occupational positions, these families in fact closely resemble the more traditional families cited by Parsons as necessary for the optimal functioning of a modern society. The wives in these families have minimized their involvement in paid work as part of a family strategy which allows a more or less traditional division of roles inside and outside the family; they have shaped their attachments to the labour force in agreement with their husbands so that only one member, the male, retains full commitment to paid employment. In doing so, moreover, they have attenuated the extent to which their families can be considered 'cross-class'. In these families, the husbands are the primary earners. Both husband and wife look to his income for long-term financial security. The differences in occupational attainment are mitigated by the contingent nature of the wives' labour force participation. Certain aspects of these families' contacts with others in their social worlds (which will be discussed in subsequent chapters) continue to allow their acceptance as cross-class families, but in economic terms alone they have ordered their lives so that few of the characteristic features of the other cross-class families are found.

Mrs Henderson, a health visitor, also works on a part-time basis. Unlike the other wives in this position, however, Mrs Henderson's form of labour force participation appears to be a direct result of the problems which may exist in marriages between men and women in markedly different occupations. It is, in fact, the *cross-class* aspect of occupational participation in this family which has been largely responsible for a reduction in the amount of work undertaken by Mrs Henderson. Aged 50, Mrs Henderson has been a nurse since age 18. During much of her working career, she combined full-time and part-time employment with periods away from the labour market in order to raise three children. Five years ago, when her youngest child was 12, Mrs Henderson resumed full-time nursing as a health visitor. Recently however, in response to pressure from her husband, Mrs Henderson reduced her working hours to three-quarter time, as she explains:

It is not essential financially for me to work full-time and I was still expected by my family to be a wife and mother full-time even though I was working full-time. So I said: OK, if they want me home, I'll be home when they get home. Of course, it doesn't always work out that way. The hardest part has been to adjust my work mind. My colleagues have found it difficult as well to accept me as part-time. As a result, I'm trying to squeeze a full-time job into part-time hours. I hope it will eventually settle into part-time work.

Giving up even some part of her attachment to nursing has not come particularly easy to Mrs Henderson as her work has considerable significance in her life: 'Work is important to me as a person. I couldn't be happy as a full-time mother within the family—it's just not essential, not of primary importance any more.' She has undertaken to reduce her commitment to work though, and has done so primarily as a way of minimizing the differences in occupational involvement and professional attainment which exist between her and her husband, a printer. These differences reveal themselves initially in contrasting post-work behaviour:

I'm involved with machines, my wife with people. You don't just turn off when you're involved with people. I turn off the machine, and turn me off as well. Work, I leave at work.

I'm emotionally drained, mentally exhausted but not physically at the end of the day. I must jolt myself to leave work at work. Sometimes when I get home, I forget to talk to the family.

They are, however, made worse by Mr Henderson's traditional views about the role of women within the family, and by his perceptions of the occupational differences which exist between husband and wife:

My husband is very traditional. He's been brought up to believe that a wife stays home. It's been very difficult for him to accept my going out to work. He feels that I'm in a profession—that he's in a trade—and that my job is higher than his. He feels some resentment towards me because I've become more extroverted than he as a result of my job and he attributes this to the fact that I am a professional.

Within this family, then, many of the problems which potentially exist in cross-class marriages—differences in work involvement, in after-work behaviour, in perceptions of status between the spouses' occupations—have come to the fore. They have, moreover, combined with a husband's traditional views to change the labour force attachment of a wife. Mrs Henderson has, like many other wives, modified her work to suit the demands of her family. She has done so, however, for reasons not normally found in other two-earner families. For Mrs Henderson, cross-class marriage, and the difficulties which can accompany such a union, has meant the loss of at least part of a career of some importance.

It is not unusual, however, for a wife to change the nature of her labour force participation to meet family obligations as Mrs Henderson did, although her reasons for doing so are, I suggest, quite unusual. It is in fact the expected pattern. More unexpected within two-earner families in general is for a husband to find his labour force attachment in many ways dependent upon the occupational participation of his wife. But within this group of cross-class families such a situation is not unusual. Five husbands here have modified their work relationships in greater or lesser degree as a direct result of their wives' employment. Mr Stone has withdrawn from work to care for his two children while his wife continues her career as an architect; Mr Roberts, unemployed at the time of interviews, has curtailed his job search in order to find work in the area of his wife's job; Mr Barnes has reduced his work-load so as to minimize the carry-over of work-related stress into an already stressful home; Mr Abbot and Mr French have been able to pursue poorly paid but agreeable occupations as a result of the high incomes earned by their wives. As all of these cases reveal important aspects of cross-class family life, they are explored in some detail.

THE STONES: ARCHITECT AND HOUSEHUSBAND

Staying at home and caring for two pre-school children on a voluntary basis is an unusual occupation for a man. 25 years ago it was virtually unheard of, as is nicely illustrated by the 'normal' families investigated by Elizabeth Bott in 1957:

All couples took it for granted that there would be a basic division of labour between husband and wife in which the husband was primarily responsible for supporting the family financially and the wife was primarily responsible for looking after the children and seeing the housework and cooking was done. The world would be upside down if the woman went out to work and the husband stayed home to care for the house and children. (1957: 197)

Times have changed considerably since Bott's work but in spite of such change, being a househusband means living if not in an 'upside down world' then at least in a slightly tilted one. Mrs Stone comments on her husband's occupation:

My husband is a man in a woman's world. Mostly he does very well at it, but sometimes he feels that people think he's odd. Although he's quite enlightened, he feels his masculinity sometimes threatened—his sense of male self somewhat undermined. The neighbours, for example, sometimes say: 'He's not really doing a man's job, is he?'

Given, then, that such difficulties arise, that—as Durkheim noted—penalties exist when norms are broken, what convinces a couple to take employment decisions which set them apart from the majority of those around them? What sustains such decisions and what, if any, are the consequences?

Jane and David Stone have been married for seven years. Jane is six years older than her husband and was well established in her career when she met and married David. Following a university education, David Stone turned away from professional or white-collar work and became instead a self-employed window cleaner. This lasted only four months, however, and David then entered a factory undertaking work on an assembly line. Two years later, when their first child was born, David gave up his job in order to assume responsibility for her care. Behind this decision was the strong conviction of Jane Stone that women have an obligation to participate in society to the utmost of their abilities. Jane is, in fact, the only woman in the study with explicitly stated feminist views:

It's important for a woman to make a stand, to make a contribution to improving the women's movement. I could go off and grow mushrooms, but because I'm a woman, I can't. It confirms too much the 'woman's role' in society . . . we married with a clear understanding that I wouldn't give up my job. Male careers can be interrupted without too much danger, female careers cannot.

David Stone acknowledges his understanding of his wife's views and, through willingness to stay at home with the children, his agreement with them: 'My wife refuses to be dependent upon anyone. It was clear when we married that, if I wanted children, I'd have to be prepared to stay at home and care for them. And I was—I am.' What motivates this couple, then, is ideology—a belief in the rights and obligations of women to assume equal roles to men in public life—and an understanding that the strength of traditional thinking is such that, should Jane interrupt her career for childcare, achievement of her goals would be threatened.

The Stones, of course, are fortunate in that their chosen stance coincides with the reality of their differing abilities in the labour market. Opportunities for advancement and financial gain are much greater for Jane as an architect than for her husband. David does not wish to return to factory employment and hopes instead some day to undertake carpentry on a full-time basis. At present, he attempts to supplement the family income through occasional work as a carpenter, but his primary responsibility is for the children, as it will remain for the next 10 to 15 years. If the Stones are fortunate in having a belief system which is not only in line with reality but is also shared between them, does it follow that they are free from conflict arising from adherence to norms contrary to convention? As the initial remarks of Mrs Stone indicate, no, not entirely. As a househusband David is, like most housewives, dependent upon his spouse for income and financial security. This can, in a society which often equates money with manhood, cause stress for a man without his own source of funds. The Stones try to ameliorate the level of this stress by seeing their financial security as a joint venture, but Jane's more realistic appraisal contains hints of the difficulties inherent in her husband's role in the family. When asked who provided economic security for the family, David Stone responded:

Both of us—that's our strength. If Jane was made redundant, I'd find work. Whether it's true or not, it's what we believe. I have a wide range of skills, while she is more limited in her skills. Her income does provide security but not only her income—I exist. My skills can be fallen back on.

Jane Stone, while acknowledging her husband's ability to provide income if necessary, assumes much greater responsibility for the provision of financial security:

Mine is it basically. Mine is the professional job, the guaranteed income. He can learn his trade (carpentry) without worrying about bills. He hasn't got the anxiety of worrying. If I lost my job, though, he would provide some income. I believe him to be capable of that.

The intimation of difficulties manifest in these slightly varied responses became a reality of problems when David Stone one day went on a spree and managed to spend the couple's entire savings of more than £1,000. Since this occurrence, Jane has assumed complete control of the bank accounts. Moreover, the attitudes of others towards the Stones' attempts to live according to their beliefs became clear at this time when David's parents responded with 'We knew something would go wrong eventually.'

Generally, however, David and Jane manage to cope successfully with their chosen life-style. In times of stress, they have strong egalitarian ideals to fall back upon even though such beliefs occasionally fail to sustain David in his attempt to contravene the normal, expected pattern of men's behaviour. Both their successes and their failures illustrate, moreover, two issues of central importance within this study—the force of ideology and the power of money. As we proceed through the lives of more cross-class families, these two issues will arise again and again. The following couple, for example, share the Stones' views on the role of women.

THE ROBERTSES: LIBRARIAN AND UNEMPLOYED CAR MECHANIC

At the time of our interview, Tom Roberts was indeed an unemployed car mechanic. Ten months previously, however, he had been an under-employed painter and decorator; and before that, a voluntary worker, a typewriter repairman, a clerk, unemployed, at training school, and so on. In fact, in the 10 years since leaving school, Tom entered and left the labour force six or seven times. Sara Roberts meanwhile was obtaining her credentials as a librarian before beginning work as such in 1979. Throughout these varying work histories, the couple maintained a close relationship which culminated in marriage 3 years ago. Both Mr and Mrs Roberts are very open about their different successes occupationally, as Tom says:

Ours is the inverse of the normal pattern. Sara is far better qualified than I am. She has a far better job than I have—it has an ongoing future. I'm the one who has had a pretty patchy employment record, and at present don't have much going. I tend to spend most of my time here, at home, re-decorating, mucking about . . .

And Tom is quite right—his behaviour in the labour force more closely resembles that of a wife than a husband. It is the reverse of the norm. It is, however, sustained in this couple's lives together by a strong belief on Sara's part of the obligation of women to be financially independent:

I have always thought of myself going out to work and earning money. I don't see myself as 'providing'. It's just something I'm having to do at the moment. I'd prefer it greatly if he got a job and it was more equal but I've never imagined not working. I've always assumed I would be going out to work and earning my own living. Just being self-supporting. It seems a very basic fact of life: you work to live.

Sara's view that both men and women must work to live allows, then, for either partner to assume the breadwinner role when necessary, while always striving towards some sense of financial equality.

At the moment she is earning and her husband is not; should the couple have children, they may reverse these roles, they may not. What is important to them is the understanding that either spouse *can* provide income and that both spouses have an *obligation* to do so:

It would be fairer if he had a nice job, but he doesn't and I knew that when I married him. I hope he does get a job soon, but he's really trying hard. If he wasn't I'd be upset, but he is.

The money she's put into the partnership over the past 6 months has been much greater than what I've put in. Ideally, there would be a balance. Recently this has broken down, hopefully it will be restored soon.

At the moment, then, financial contributions to the family are out of balance; Tom, however, hopes to restore some semblance of equity through acquisition of training as a repairer of computers. In his discussion of this aim, Tom's awareness of the lack of equality between him and his wife is apparent, as is his understanding of the importance of her job in his life and his subsequent reluctance to look for work in areas away from their present city:

At the moment my idea is trying to get a job with microprocessors—the new technology. It's an idea to get a job with a future. But also there's a status thing in it. To say that you're a mechanic mending cars and to say you repair computers, people's attitudes are different; the money you get for the job is different. There's definitely, on my part, an element of catching up—to a social level—to my wife. The odd thing is, the actual skills are much the same but the world view is worlds apart, really. But finding work like this might mean applying for openings in different parts of England. The reason I don't do that is my wife's job is here. The house is here. Her job exists—don't underestimate the importance of her job: it is *the* job at present. Hopefully, it will be her and my job in the future, but right now, her job is the job.

Tom Roberts is only 26 years old; he may thus be able still to achieve parity with his wife occupationally and financially. At the moment, the couple's beliefs sustain the obvious lack of parity. Whether they will do so in the future should Tom fail to realize his ambitions is unknown. Mrs Roberts's words, however, suggest that they might:

Our outlook on life is very similar. And I don't see him as any less intelligent. He should have worked harder at school. But I don't see any difference between us—that's a sort of external thing that other people put on us. People at university asked: what do you have in common? I used to think how stupid they were. They were imposing such narrow views.

THE BARNESES: POLYTECHNIC LECTURER AND LORRY DRIVER

Unlike the previous two husbands, John Barnes is in full-time employment. He interests us here because of his actions to reduce the amount of stress in his work in order to accommodate the high level of tension associated with his wife's work. As a lecturer, Pat Barnes has the greatest involvement of all the wives in after-hours work, if the idea of non-working hours may be applied to one, like her, who reports: 'My job is with me 24 hours a day—always. It affects our sex life—everything. It's slightly worse when I'm writing.' In addition, Pat is away from home two or three evenings each week, either talking with colleagues or visiting former university friends in London. Spouses of people like Pat must themselves be so involved in their own work as not to mind the other's lack of attention, or must invest so little in their work that they are able to shrug it off and find something else to do at the end of the day. For the first few years of their marriage, John Barnes was neither of these. Fulfilling an ambition to drive lorries, he worked with large vehicles, often travelling to overnight destinations. Physical exhaustion and tension were the most immediate results of this work. After considerable conflict with his wife, however, he gave up these large vehicles and now drives smaller trucks with only rare long-distance loads. His 'something else' is—as it was before—his home village and the friends he has known there all his life, only now he spends much more of his time with these friends. Mrs Barnes, for her part, would not consider any career moves which would take her husband away from this village. She sees their continued residence in close proximity to her husband's friends and family as essential to their marital stability.

In giving up responsibility for the larger lorries, Mr Barnes also gave up part of his income. He was able to do this because of his wife's income which now nearly doubles his own. In an attempt to minimize conflict over money, Pat gives her husband a weekly £50 supplement to his earnings. She is, however, only partially successful in this attempt and reports resentment on her husband's part which manifests itself in bullying and argumentative behaviour—especially when he's 'had a few'. Although this couple indicated no explicit beliefs about who should or should not be the main earner in a family, this difficulty over money suggests the existence of implicit and contradictory views. Financial reality, moreover, supports contradiction. Pat Barnes is completely in charge of the household finances; she makes all financial decisions and pays all bills. The couple also live in the home she bought for herself prior to marriage. John's income is largely devoted to supporting his former wife and their two children. He is, then, the major earner of a family—his former family—while in his present marriage his income is superfluous. Accepting the role of breadwinner in one family and denied it in another: there should be little surprise that John Barnes sometimes finds it hard to come to terms with marriage in a cross-class family.

The Barneses illustrate the difficulties in coping with unequal incomes in the absence of an agreed system of beliefs between spouses which allow and explain such differences. Moreover, they demonstrate the problems which can arise when contradictions exist. While Mrs Barnes is content with her role of primary breadwinner, Mr Barnes is not. The result is occasional 'bullying' and considerable conflict. In the lives of the following couple, no such conflict is evident although the income disparity between husband and wife is very nearly identical with that in the Barnes family. Instead, there is an understanding that the high wages of one spouse can often allow the other ample freedom to pursue the occupation most wanted.

THE ABBOTS: HEAD TEACHER AND SAWMILL FOREMAN

Like Mr Barnes, David Abbot has modified his attachment to the labour force as a direct result of the employment of his wife. But for David this has meant keeping a job he loves in spite of the relatively low income it affords. As a young man, David worked in a factory for 2 years. He disliked this job very much and so, when offered an opportunity to work outdoors in the local sawmill, he responded with alacrity. He has continued working in this mill for 37 years and has been, in spite of himself, promoted twice. As foreman he earns just less than £5,000 per annum with a perquisite tied house at £10 per week rent. The size of his income is quite unimportant to him, as he relates:

I've always had the principle that I'm not worried about the money so long as I'm happy doing the job I'm doing. I wouldn't do a job like Cowley or a factory. I wouldn't work there; I'd leave. My wife's income allows me to do this; it allows me to stay in a job I like.

Diana Abbot's income is £9,000 per annum. As Head Teacher of a small junior school, her work-day begins before 9 a.m. and lasts, on most days, until 6.45 or 7 p.m. She normally works through the lunch hour, trying to cope with the administrative demands of running the school during the short time she has free from teaching duties. In addition, she drops into work at least once every Saturday and Sunday to ensure that the school, which is in a remote location, remains free from vandals. If this was not a sufficient work load, she is also faced with meetings each month outside normal school hours, courses to keep herself up to date as a teacher, and during term approximately 2 hours of 'homework' each evening. Diana Abbot fully earns her salary. She is, moreover, conscious that income disparities in marriage which favour the wife may be problematic:

We've never had any arguments about money, I've made sure of that. I've always felt that many men would feel hurt by the fact that their wife earns more, but I don't think David has ever felt like that. But I've always been a bit worried about it. I've never looked at my income as being more important; it just gives us lots of room to breathe and be ourselves.

In pursuing her career to its utmost, and in allowing her husband and herself to be 'ourselves', Diana Abbot is rejecting an ideology which says that men must be breadwinners, women only secondary earners, homemakers. In its place is an understanding that people must be accepted for what they are, not for what they do or what they earn. She speaks about the educational differences between herself and her husband:

What is education? I have paper qualifications, he doesn't. But as I said before, as far as being knowledgeable, he beats me completely. He's much more interesting to talk to than I am. His interests are much more varied than mine are. The profession of teaching can be a very narrowing thing; you can end up talking about nothing but teaching if you are not careful. He's really very bright. I suppose I used to look at him critically sometimes and think: what a waste. But he's so complete. He's so complete that the fault was in me, not in him. In me for not completely accepting him as he is—he's really a most extraordinary person.

Diana Abbot did not, however, enter married life with this understanding. Rather, she assumed she would be much like any other wife—work for a while, until children came, and then retire into the home and financial dependence upon her husband. When it proved impossible to have children, she began to put her energies into her work, with the result that she is now in charge of her own school. During the development of her career, in response to both reality and her husband, Diana gradually evolved a new belief system, one which dispenses with rigid adherence to conventional roles in the family (as will become clearer in the chapter following on the division of labour in the household). I suggest that this woman's beliefs changed in part as a response to her husband. This is perhaps not surprising in a marriage, even less so in one which has lasted more than 29 years as in the Abbots' case. I make this suggestion mostly as my response to David Abbot himself. A gentle, cheerful man, his work history and general demeanour is such that one doubts he has ever rigidly adhered to any notion of expected behaviour (see p. 67 for a discussion of his promotions at work). When I asked him if he was the major breadwinner in his family, he laughed quietly to himself and said:

Me? Oh no, I wouldn't think so, no. I would think that my wife is the main breadwinner. She earns more money and always has—ever since we were married. It's never worried me. It worries some people, but not me, oh no.

And, as said before, this 'more money' has allowed David to remain working in the out of doors he so enjoys, as well as to pursue his many hobbies.

The Abbots thus introduce something new into the analysis of cross-class family life. Rather than such life being built on a foundation of mutually agreed beliefs about the roles of men and women, or enduring in spite of the lack of such agreement, David and Diana show how cross-class life can result in the changing of beliefs. Diana Abbot has, through years of marriage in which she has been the main source of income and financial security, come to accept a system of beliefs which dispenses with rigid adherence to norms which would be in contradiction to the reality of her own life. She has changed her views. In the following family the husband, like David Abbot, has also escaped unpleasant and unwanted employment as a direct result of his wife's occupational position. Moreover, as it did for Diana Abbot, the relationship of employment status between husband and wife inspired a change in both actions and beliefs, this time, however, of the husband.

THE FRENCHES: TEACHER AND FORMER TANKER DRIVER, NOW REDUNDANT

For the first 12 years of married life, the Frenches followed the conventional pattern: wife at home with the children and occasionally undertaking part-time work; husband in full-time employment, frequently working overtime to support his family. Ann French then decided it was time to think about her future and so entered college and became a teacher. She has been teaching now for 14 years. Her change in employment status had a considerable effect on the family's housing situation in that after many years of council house tenancy, the Frenches are now owner-occupiers of their second home. The second major change of their lives came, however, as a result of employment decisions taken by Martin French. Very active in his union, Martin was on the committee which negotiated agreement with the company concerning redundancies and productivity. When it came time to implement this agreement, he chose to be one of four required to give up their jobs. He recounts this decision:

I could've stayed if I'd wanted but, having been directly responsible in reaching these agreements, well, the company said if they didn't get voluntary redundancies, then—although they didn't say it in so many words—then there'd be compulsory redundancies. I was then coming up to an age, I suppose 80% were reasonably young people, in their thirties with small children—you know, what do you do? It would have been last in, first out. They'd get rid of them and you'd hang in there for a few more years and see them on the dole. So, I thought, right, I'll go. But not realizing at the time it was going to be so difficult. There was certainly no work. I thought I'd find work easily—*easily*—not highly paid work perhaps, but *full-time* work. But it just isn't there, full stop.

In fact all Martin, at age 57, was able to find was a part-time job as a driver, working perhaps 2 or 3 days per week, with no pension, no sick pay, no paid holidays. He retains some anger at his previous company and feels that management ought to counsel the workers, advise them of the difficulties they will most likely face in finding alternative employment, especially when of advanced age.

Martin French was able to give up his search for full-time work and accept a poorly paid part-time job instead because of his wife's occupation as a teacher and her salary of nearly £11,000 per annum. Without this income, his present situation and participation in the labour force would be entirely different:

If my wife wasn't what she is, if she didn't earn what she does, then I'd have had to get something—anything. I'd have had to gone labouring, back to haulage—to the crummiest haulage firm, anything.

And, perhaps not surprisingly, Martin's changed work role has had a significant effect on his perceptions of financial security and the role of breadwinner within the family:

Being a male chauvinist, I suppose I always thought of myself as the main breadwinner. I always tended to think—yes—I thought: well, your job, if you pack it in, I'm here. But never the other way round. But I do now. When she gets upset with work, I say: steady on, steady on, you've got 12 more years to work. It's a standing joke with us now.

This change, and Martin French's easy acceptance of financial dependence on his wife did not, of course, simply arrive all of a sudden with his change in employment status. Rather, it had been slowly developing over the years of his wife's employment as a professional. Acceptance of this change—from husband of a housewife to husband of a teacher—came with much more difficulty. Martin's hesitancy in recounting his feelings about the occupational differences between him and his wife reveal this difficulty, as well as illustrating once again the importance of money:

I've never been the sort of person who felt, you know, inferior, because of the professional person. Well, I don't think I have—I might—sometimes—but I don't know. I might have used it inadvertently in an argument or a row . . . but you don't know . . . I'd always been in a position to equal her salary. I suppose had I—yes—there could have been conflict; there could have been jealousy . . . I would have been jealous—unfairly so—if she had earned more. But I've changed on that score [*laughs*] I must have done.

He changed because he began to realize that a weight had been lifted from his shoulders with his wife's employment and high earnings:

You have no idea what a relief it came to be to me that she has her own income and has a pension in her own right. That she's not dependent on me. Before I used to worry: what if I died, would she be all right? would she be able to keep the house? have I got a big enough pension for her? Now I don't need to worry. She's got her own income, her own pension.

Mr French's awareness of the psychological load which attends the conventional male role in the family and his willingness to shed that load show a remarkable flexibility of mind as well as a change

directly attributable to his wife's choice of employment. For had
Ann French continued in her traditional role, perhaps even worked
full time in her pre-marriage job of telephonist, none of these
changes could have occurred for her husband. As he says himself,
he would have had to take any job possible in order to continue
his role as provider. Cross-class family life has changed this man
dramatically.

In the preceding discussions, the importance of both family norms
and money has been brought out. I have tried to show that the
existence of agreed norms within the family can be the basis of
cross-class life but that, in spite of such agreement allowing the
superiority of the wife in both occupational and monetary terms,
conflict can occasionally arise; that husbands in this situation do
indeed have something they must cope with. I have tried, further, to
indicate that the lack of agreed norms between spouses can precipitate substantial conflict centring on money and unequal work
involvement. And, in the last two families, an attempt has been
made to relate the level of the wife's income and degree of work
participation to normative change. In the following chapter, I will
continue to focus on the beliefs held by these couples, on the relationship between beliefs and occupational participation, and on the
problems which result from contradictions between felt convictions
and reality. It is important to note that it is most often the contradictions between reality and belief that cause problems for many of
these cross-class couples. Each man and woman came to marriage
with values inculcated from early childhood. For most, in the past,
this meant acceptance of the primacy of husbands in the occupational world. Only one man and four women in these cross-class
families were raised in intact homes where the mothers undertook
full-time employment during the years when their children were
young. Many others, of course, had mothers who were employed on
a part-time basis but, in general, their fathers assumed the dominant
role occupationally, their mothers domestically. Thus their child-
hoods were, in important respects, radically different from their
adult lives and marriages. In coming to terms with the present
reality of cross-class family lives, then, these men and women must
also come to terms with left-over beliefs and expectations from their
pasts. Moreover, they must, as husband and wife, do so jointly. I do
not think it is too much to suggest that one important condition of

stability in a marriage is the existence of a common value system which defines the expected behaviour of each spouse. Failure to negotiate the content of this value system together so that husband and wife are in basic agreement over the norms of their marriage can result in considerable discord. And while this is true of any marriage, for the husbands and wives of cross-class families, it is perhaps even more imperative. For these families stand in contrast not only with their own past lives but also with the majority of marriages which surround them. They cannot simply accept, without thought or without conflict, the pervasive norm of male dominance. To do so would be to bring contradiction between belief and reality into their lives—and with this contradiction, marital discord. Moreover, while such discord may manifest itself in a variety of ways, disputes over money and a lack of understanding about the nature of work for one's spouse are among the most important. In the following it will become clear that for some families, the almost complete separation of work and family life is a direct result of this type of marital conflict.

Notes

1. See Gowler and Legge, 1982 for a literature review and discussion of the ways in which decision-making is modified by the nature of the (predominately) wives' labour force participation. Only in dual-career families is there any attempt at joint decision-making between spouses regarding employment.
2. Parsons argues that sex role segregation allows 'for equality of opportunity, for mobility (of labour) in response to technical requirements, for devotion to occupational goals and interests unhampered by "personal" considerations . . .' (1942: 191). Although Parsons sees such sex-role segregation as a functional imperative in modern industrial society, it is possible to disagree with the functional aspects of his theories and to continue to examine the substance of those theories. Thus, I am not concerned to show that joint labour force participation of husbands and wives is either functional or dysfunctional, but rather wish to assess the consequences for the men and women involved in personal terms.
3. Cf. Goldthorpe, 1983: 475, who reports that between 15% and 25% of wives married to men stable in Social Class I withdrew from paid work in order to accompany their husbands to new locations as a result of husbands' job changes. Also Pahl and Pahl, 1971: 221.

6

Linking Work and Home in Cross-class Families
Part Two

From Work to Home: the Carry-over of Work into Cross-class Family Life

More than money follows a worker home: mental strain, physical exhaustion, paperwork and the telephone can all mean that the job enters into domestic life. In Chapter 4 it was seen that one characteristic of cross-class family life is the far greater involvement of the wives in their daily work activities, in addition to their greater propensity to bring the job home. In this chapter I investigate how this differential work involvement carries over into home life, in part by examining the extent of work-related discussions between spouses and the degree to which husbands and wives recognize each other's post-work exhaustion, and in part by considering long-term financial security and the importance of money in the family. By pure chance, half of the wives earn higher incomes than their husbands, half do not. This simple distribution does not, however, serve as a useful distinction between families. Rather, as suggested earlier, the type and extent of normative agreement between spouses acts on the realities of their circumstances and, in some families, allows for unequal incomes and financial contributions to the household. In other families, however, the lack of such agreement causes stress between spouses. None the less, money is important[1] and so in the following it is in the juxtaposition of norms and money, of family ideology and family income that the ways in which work comes home are investigated.

Normative Agreement: Equality

Certain of the families in this study may be characterized by normative agreement between spouses that it is the obligation of both husband and wife to make an economic contribution to the household. As is the case with the Roberts family, this agreement is captured in declarations of financial independence on the part of the wives, and supported by the husbands' freedom from adherence to conventional norms about their roles within family life:

I feel it's my part to work. To contribute. It was one of the things that used to worry me when I was at home. It used to worry me. I would hate it—being supported by somebody else. I don't like it. I'd never done it before. I know women whose children are older and they just stay at home and let their husbands support them. I don't know how they do it, it's quite wrong.

Mrs Smith, teacher and mother of two

Mrs Smith is married for the second time and worked throughout her first, childless marriage. Choosing to have children in her second marriage, she stayed at home with them for 4 years. Her desire to contribute her share of the family income led her to undertake a second part-time job as a secretary in the Department of Education when the only teaching work available was also on a part-time basis. In both jobs she has 'permanent' status and thus the benefits and security of a full-time teacher, although a smaller salary. If the present freeze on hiring changes, Mrs Smith hopes to obtain full-time teaching. Her husband, a telecommunications engineer with BT and therefore in a somewhat uncertain position of job security, views their economic future as a joint responsibility. When asked how he would feel if his wife's income exceeded his earnings, he responded:

Indifferent really. If she earns more, she earns more. It really wouldn't matter, not in the least. At the moment, mine is the larger income. But if she went full-time teaching, she'd be on a par, and eventually she'd earn more than me. I've never considered her income as an 'extra'—it's just an income, and someday it could be the main income.

The views of the Smiths are echoed by the Merediths and the Fieldings:

It would delight me if she earned more. I don't have the average male need to dominate and to be the breadwinner.

Mr Meredith, heating and ventilating fitter

I couldn't live an aimless, parasitic life. I must contribute.

Mrs Fielding, teacher

In these families, then, there is an agreed system of beliefs which for the wife says that she has equal obligations with her husband to

provide for the family financially, and for the husband dispenses
with any sense of 'male ego' standing in the way of her pursuing this
obligation to the extent of surpassing his income. This lack of male
ego with respect to earning power is apparent in Mr Meredith's
response when asked if he would move location to further his wife's
career. He replied:

Oh yes, pride doesn't enter in. I'd have to drop a rank to transfer, but I'd
certainly go. Provided, of course, we would be living somewhere I liked.

It is, moreover, this lack of male pride, lack of male identification
with the size of one's pay cheque, which leads me to argue that
although at present these three husbands are in the position that
they have no real need to test their beliefs against reality—that is,
they all at present have higher incomes than their wives—should the
future career advancement of their wives change reality so that the
women exceed their husbands in earning capacity, the system of
beliefs which holds between spouses will ensure that the evident lack
of conflict in these couples' lives remains. It has already been seen
that Mr Smith is well aware that a definite possibility exists that his
wife will overtake his earnings should she obtain a full-time teaching
position. Similarly, Mrs Fielding is a late entrant to teaching and
therefore still low on her salary scale. It is thus possible that she will
exceed her husband's income in the future. Only for Mrs Meredith
does some doubt exist about her future earning capabilities. This
doubt is expressed in her willingness to leave her present job as
administrative officer to relocate for her husband's work should any
such opportunity arise:

Yes, I think I would, I'd follow Alan. Even though we've got this very
shared outlook, I've got to be realistic. He's the large wage-earner, whether
I like it or not. He's the one who's got the capacity to earn more money . . .
my view is that it's not my fault. I work as hard if not harder than Alan,
because as a woman you've got to prove it over and over again. But you still
never get the high paid job unless you have professional qualifications.

Given, however, that Mrs Meredith considers it possible that she
may at some stage enter university to obtain these professional qualifications, it is likely that she too may one day exceed her husband's
earnings.

These husbands and wives, like Sara and Tom Roberts, do not
experience conflict over occupational or financial dominance in the
household. Instead, they see themselves as equal partners with

equal financial obligations. They have an agreed family ideology of equality which allows for family income from both spouses, permits occupational primacy for either spouse, and dispenses with competition between spouses. This agreement is, moreover, a reflection of solidarity between husband and wife which Parsons suggests would be directly threatened by joint occupational participation:

If both were equally competitive for occupational status, there might be a very serious strain on the solidarity of the family unit, for there is no general reason why they would be likely to come out very nearly equal, while in their capacity of husband and wife, it is very important that they should be treated as equals. (1940: 80)

These families, however, demonstrate that rather than competition between spouses straining solidarity, solidarity itself dispenses with competition. The agreed system of beliefs held by these couples—their solidarity—demands joint labour force participation and allows for unequal rewards from unequal occupational attainments. In dispensing with competition between husband and wife, moreover, these agreed family norms allow mutual interest in each other's working lives. There is recognition that tiredness from physical work is no worse than mental strain: 'exhaustion is the same, no matter what'. There is opportunity to discuss the day's events with each other. Although the technical aspects of the men's work are often kept out of such discussions, the anecdotes, personalities, and conflicts of work are not. The women as well are able to bring work home with them:

Oh yes, I discuss both work and situations which arise at work with my husband. And sometimes my ideas about teaching. He advises or commiserates with me.

Mrs Fielding

I discuss my work with him to a certain extent because it's part of me and because he's very astute. If I'm having problems with some of the people who work under me, he can make some very succinct remarks which help me to a certain extent.

Mrs Meredith

Moreover, the extra work which attends these women's occupations is accommodated into their home lives without causing conflict between husband and wife. Mrs Smith reports bringing home at least 1 hour's work each night; Mrs Fielding slightly less. Neither

Mr Smith nor Mr Fielding report any distress over their wives' post-work involvement. For Mrs Meredith, extra work and the extra commitment to her career which such work symbolizes are part of a bargain struck with her husband in negotiating the future of their marriage. Mr Meredith prefers to remain childless; in accepting her husband's choice Mrs Meredith turned her energies to her working life. Accommodating the consequences of his wife's commitment to a career is Mr Meredith's part of the bargain, as his wife relates:

> When I realized that he didn't want kids, I said to him: well, if I can't have children, I have to have something and if I'm going to commit myself to a job, you know what I'm like—it will be a total commitment. And you'll have to accept it. And he's been very good. He reminds me to come home, to pack up work. He's very supportive. Occasionally there's slight conflict over this. He thinks I'm putting too much into it. You see, his attitude to work is different than mine. He tends to feel that you work from time 'a' to time 'b' and the rest of your time is play time. But he recognizes that it's different for me. I tend to work most of the time. I'm a workaholic! And generally it works out well between us.

Work and family worlds merge, then, in these families. There is no strict line drawn at the end of each working day. Although the husbands are somewhat less likely to talk about their jobs in the hours after work, there is no similar demand placed by them on their wives. Slight friction may result from time to time, as noted by Mrs Meredith and echoed by Mr Fielding: 'if she doesn't turn off after work, she can get somewhat boring—not annoying, just boring'. Generally though there is little conflict evident. Instead, there is in these families willingness to share and to listen to the day's events.

The family norms which allow such mutual interest in each other's working lives and which dispense with competition between spouses over occupational or financial dominance are, in these three families as in the Roberts family, quite explicit. There exists between husband and wife, in effect, a spoken agreement of equality. It is possible, however, for agreement between spouses to be found in other ways. In the following families relatively explicit agreement between husband and wife also exists. In these families, though, the agreement is not of equality between spouses but rather of acknowledgement of the dominance in both occupational and financial terms by the wife. There is, in these families, a coming together of normative agreement with economic reality which results in the wife assuming financial responsibility and control with the willing acquiescence of the husband.

Normative Agreement: Female Superiority

Mr and Mrs James provide an illustration of female-dominant family organization as a result of agreement between husband and wife. A second marriage for both, the Jameses live in the house Mrs James purchased from her former husband. Mrs James is the family accountant and makes most financial decisions for the family although usually with some consultation of her husband. Mrs James earns approximately £1,500 per annum more than her husband. She is, moreover, the acknowledged family 'boss', as Mr James reports:

I like things to be nice and smooth. I don't want to be boss. I've got no worries at all—not money worries, I mean. My last wife used to lean on me, depend on me. Jane's great—she's so much in control of her own life. It gives me so much more freedom. She's the boss—whatever she says is fine with me.

Jane James confirms her husband's acquiescence in her control of the household:

I'm the boss but only because Mike defers to me. I'm bossy by nature and he seems to choose to agree.

The roles this husband and wife assume at home are in large measure a reflection of their occupational roles. Mr James drives a forklift in a factory. He has been in this job for 29 years and has no desire to advance beyond the level of worker. When asked what he was looking forward to with respect to work, he replied:

Nothing at all. It's that kind of job, really. There's no prospects. I guess you could try for a foreman's job, my brother did. But that would mean being shifted around, even to another factory and I really am not interested.

His lack of interest is, moreover, directly related to the ease with which he slips in and out of his work role each day:

Right now, I hit the clock and it's all gone. There's no worries, no responsibilities. I feel safe there. The job's the sort of job where it's finished at the end of the day. I really have nothing to think about at the end of the shift. If you were a high-powered fellow, you'd worry all night. I've got nothing to bring home—no worries. I see it as a definite advantage.

Mrs James, however, has a very different orientation to her work. A teacher for 12 years, she was recently responsible for the creation and implementation of an experimental educational programme designed to respond more effectively to the needs of problem children. She works on a one-to-one basis with children who are maladjusted, disruptive or have specific learning disabilities. This programme has now been implemented on a permanent basis with Mrs James responsible for the supervision of two other teachers. She speaks about her work:

> I take my job very seriously. I think it's important, a useful job to be doing. I think I contribute. To me, that's important as a person. I couldn't do a job that in my mind wasn't useful and fulfilling. I couldn't do it, not even for the money . . . I say I switch off at home but really, there's usually something going around in my head which is to do with something that's happened at school.

The differences, then, between the working lives of Mr and Mrs James are very great indeed and, as such, reflect the nature of their roles within the family. But because there is no contradiction between reality and belief, and because husband and wife agree on their family organization, there is little conflict evident. Mrs James is in charge at work; she remains in charge at home. Mr James is content with his work without responsibilities in the factory; he is content with his role at home. For Mr James cross-class marriage has relieved him of the necessity of fulfilling conventional definitions of the husband's familial role, relieved him of the obligation to be primary breadwinner and decision-maker. He is able to leave this to someone far better qualified to do the job—his wife.

Mrs James's dominance at work and at home is revealed in the degree of work–family separation in this household. Mr James leaves work at work, rarely discussing the day's events at home:

> Well no, not really. I guess I only talk about the odd thing, amusing things. Mostly though my wife doesn't have time for car workers and generally I agree with her. Anyway, my work doesn't interest them [his wife and stepdaughters] one little bit—I'd bore them to tears.

Mrs James, on the other hand, does not separate work from family life so completely and will frequently discuss the day's happenings and problems with her husband, although often only in a restricted manner:

Yes, I do, but not in great detail. He's not a teacher and therefore not involved in all the ins and outs of teaching—it's too mystifying to an out-sider . . . with Mike I can only talk about problems superficially because I know that a lot of what I'm saying doesn't mean to him what it does to me. But I do talk about it. And I don't find it a problem. In addition to Mike I've got plenty of people at school I can talk to about problems.

A line, then, is drawn between Mr James's work and family worlds, while for Mrs James the separation is less complete. The same general agreement which characterizes their roles within the family governs the separation of work from home with, moreover, little evidence of conflict or disappointment over either the inability to talk at all or to talk in great depth about the problems faced on the job.

Considerable similarity to the James family is found in the Allan and Creighton households. Mrs Allan, a teacher, earns nearly £4,000 more each year than her husband, an electrician. Both husband and wife see the long-term security of their family as resting on the shoulders of Mrs Allan, for not only is her job perceived by both to be more secure in the long run, but as Mr Allan notes: 'inflation has put everything past my wages'. His wife's economic dominance in the family is evident in her words: 'my income is there to enable the family to *live*', and in her remarks when discussing financial decision-making: '*I* cleared the mortgage when it went to 13%'. For Mr Creighton, a foreman welder earning £6,000 p.a. prior to redundancy, his wife's high earnings and assumption of financial responsibility afforded him considerable feelings of personal security:

I never worried. If I'd spent all the money I had, I could fall back on my wife's income. I never felt I had to watch or save. I became very dependent on her income being there.

Mrs Creighton was, at retirement, Deputy Head of a large comprehensive school. In this capacity she earned £13,000 per annum—more than double her husband's income. During our interview she was quick to acknowledge the importance of her income to family security and ready to depict herself as the family 'boss':

Oh yes, certainly. Financial security rested with me. Because over the last 10 years I became the major earner. I earned more than my husband. I 'overtook' him. And I suppose the job made me more bossy—in charge at work, in charge at home—once a teacher, always a teacher. I tend to boss everyone around. But then, my husband hates any organizational things so I have always done them.

Like Mrs James, moreover, both of these wives discuss their work with their husbands, bringing home both anecdotes and problems about colleagues and students alike. The separation of work from family life occurs only with regard to the daily activities of the husbands. Mr Creighton reports: 'I didn't discuss work with my wife, partly because of the technical nature of my work.' But, in addition to job content which might not be understood by his wife, this man's silence at home reflected a desire to escape from work itself. Unlike his wife who derived immense personal satisfaction from teaching and administration, Mr Creighton wished only, at the end of each working day, to forget his job (cf. Sennett and Cobb, 1973):

I'd never come home and just sit down and talk. I'd go out gardening or do some carpentry—to keep my mind occupied outside work. It would take the edge off work definitely. I'd never take my problems out on my wife or family. I'd keep myself busy, not allow my mind to think, to get to the bottom line.

For Mr Allan, the separation of his work from family life is a response to the demands of his wife's teaching responsibilities. Although he reports working in very strained and stressful conditions, he does not discuss these difficulties at home:

No, I don't talk about it. I have trained myself to leave work at work. My wife has a difficult job. It would make it [family life] too tense if I also got uptight.

Mr Allan's words suggest not only his understanding of the greater responsibilities faced by his wife in her work, but also his acquiescence in the rank-ordering of jobs which gives highest priority to hers, second place to his.

These families are, then, characterized by agreement between husband and wife that the wife is generally responsible for long-term financial security; she is the family 'boss' and decision-maker; her work and family worlds may overlap, while his do not. Competition between spouses is eliminated not by norms of equality but by acceptance of the primacy of the wife's occupational position and earnings. Husband and wife agree on the norms which govern family life and, more importantly, their agreement reflects reality. If I have perhaps seemed to belabour the issue of agreement between husbands and wives, in these and the preceding families, or to have brought to the fore seemingly obvious points, it is only so that these families may serve as comparisons for those which follow. For, as will be seen, within the next group of families agreement between spouses is often missing, contradictions between beliefs and reality exist, work is more clearly separated from home for both husband and wife, and a considerable lack of understanding about the nature of the wife's work is evident.

Normative Disagreement: Disappointed Wives

In the following families, the wives see themselves as responsible for long-term financial security of the family as well as for present management of the household. Unlike the wives in the families immediately preceding, however, these women wish that their lives were otherwise. Unfortunately two of the husbands to be discussed here refused participation in interviews and so I am unable to include their views. It is possible, though, to infer a certain amount from the responses of their wives. Generally, these families are characterized either by high levels of marital conflict (resulting, in one family, in divorce) or by mechanisms on the part of the wives to subvert reality and thus prevent such conflict. There is some agreement between husband and wife about the primacy of her occupational position and income, although this agreement may be accompanied by considerable resentment. It is, in fact, in these families that money once again assumes great importance. Mrs Light speaks about the place her income and secure job takes within the family:

I certainly don't see my husband as the main breadwinner. I never have done. Even when I wasn't working—we lived too close to the breadline. Since I've been working, my job has been very much more secure. I'll have to work until retirement, my job is our security. When he's been made redundant, or left a job, we still have to pay the mortgage, and live, and if it hadn't been for my wage—in fact, because of my wage he didn't get unemployment benefits. I feel the security rests on my shoulders. I feel I've got to work full-time.

Mrs Light's husband has held a succession of jobs over the 25 years he has been employed. Once denied an ambition to perform on radio, he now takes whatever work is available within his capacity to perform. More importantly, he is totally devoid of ambition or of the desire to come up to his wife's standards of achievement. Presently self-employed as a hire-car driver, Mr Light is at last earning an income comparable with his wife's salary as Deputy Head teacher. His past inability to equal or surpass his wife's income has been a source of resentment for both husband and wife:

I think he used to resent the fact that I've always earned more; I don't think he liked that at all. And I've always resented it. I mean, comparing his jobs with the jobs my colleagues' husbands have, and the way their standard of living is much higher than mine, I feel a lot of resentment that I work extremely hard and get a good wage and yet my standard of living isn't as high. It's definitely caused problems; oh yes, we've had lots of rows about money.

Mr Light, however, was unwilling to talk about the past when asked to discuss his role as breadwinner in the family, although he was willing to admit the greater security afforded by his wife's occupation:

For the first time in a long time I'm now on a par—earning more or less the same as my wife. Her basic income compared to mine is £300 less—it's pleasing to me. The first time. My expenses bring it down to about the same level. Is her job more secure? I would hope so. One would expect it to be secure. And it's important. I can't deny that it's nice to know there's a cushion there.

Although Mr Light's estimation of his wife's job as a 'cushion' jars somewhat with her reports of its importance, there is in his evident relief at finally equalling her income at least implicit acknowledgement of the place that secure income has taken in family life, as well as of the resentment which has accompanied it.

The Lights suffer considerable marital conflict in their acceptance of an ideology—the male should be the major earner in a family—which contradicts reality. Mrs Light's disappointment in her husband's work career and inability to fulfil her expectations of accomplishment is evident. In the Ashcroft family, this conflict has come to its ultimate conclusion and the couple have separated, pending a divorce. Like Mr Light, Mr Ashcroft has held a series of jobs since meeting his wife 11 years ago. He is now employed as a milk roundsman and earns an equivalent income to his wife, a computer programmer. Mrs Ashcroft's sense of disappointment in her husband's work history is plain:

I suggested that he should get himself trained in something that would set him up for life. Make him fulfil himself more. Get away from dead-end jobs. He'd have to take a drop in wages to do this, but I'm quite prepared to go without. It's more important to have fulfilling work—something more worth while, more skilled. Something to give him more self-respect. He lacks self-respect. I don't know how much of this I have caused—with the differences in our jobs—but then, there is a social stigma about being a milkman which comes out. I'm sure he's fully aware of the gap between our occupations.

During the course of our interview, Mrs Ashcroft made it clear that she would like a husband she could look up to, depend upon; someone who could, in her words, 'teach me'. She, however, has been the one who is depended upon, who is responsible for economic security and financial good sense. No longer willing to assume the primary role within the family, she has chosen instead to divorce. Sometimes, perhaps, it is easier to change reality than to change disappointed expectations.[2]

Both Mrs Light and Mrs Ashcroft came to marriage with definite expectations about the behaviour of husbands and wives. Their husbands have not fulfilled these expectations and so the women experience feelings of disappointment in their marriages: they have been 'let down'. The Lights suffer considerable marital conflict while the Ashcrofts have chosen not to come to terms with this disappointment—not to persist with cross-class family life by finding some way around their obvious occupational differences. Unlike the Ashcrofts, however, other families have so chosen, although not without difficulty. The Harvey family is such a family. Like Mrs Light, Mrs Harvey is the primary earner in her family. She assumes, as does Mrs Light, long-term responsibility and makes most financial decisions. But unlike either Mrs Light or Mrs Ashcroft, Mrs Harvey affects specific behaviour in her relations with her husband designed to avoid the conflict evident in the other two homes. She shares, however, the same sense of disappointment:

I feel I am the breadwinner, but I wouldn't let him know I feel like that. I play the helpless female because I think that's how he wants it. I think I'd like to be more stereotyped. I'd like him to take more responsibility. Perhaps because I think that's the way it *ought* to be. But then, I'd worry about whether the bills were paid . . . In some ways, on the financial side, I'm more mature in my approach. I wish it were different.

Mrs Harvey's income exceeds her husband's by almost £5,000 per year. And, like Mr Barnes mentioned earlier, Mr Harvey devotes much of his income to the support of his former wife and their son. Mrs Harvey's income is, moreover, not only greater than her husband's, it is also much more likely to increase over the years as she progresses up a set salary scale. The importance of this income is reflected in her readiness to report her husband willing to relocate to further her career: 'We'd say: do we want more money? My job's the one that's going to get it. And then we'd have to move.' As Mr Harvey declined a personal interview it is not possible to know if he would agree with his wife or to assess his views regarding her financial dominance in the family.

Mrs Harvey plays the 'helpless female' at home in order to negate the obvious superiority of her job security and income. In doing so she is, in effect, pretending to a system of beliefs about the abilities of men and women which is in contradiction with the reality of her own situation. She does so, moreover, in order to avoid conflict with her husband over the extent of financial inequality between them. Mrs Mason undertakes similar behaviour towards her husband for corresponding reasons and with the same sense of disappointment:

With me paying all the bills, writing all the letters and all that—I completely run the house. All he has to do is bring money home. The rest is up to me. I plan the holidays, everything. I'd love someone to plan a holiday for me . . . He needs lots of bolstering up. He knows I'm useless at fixing anything, so I ask him to do lots of things—it usually works. He does think he's boss of the household, but I keep it going. I try to let him think he's boss.

Unlike the other wives in these particular families, Mrs Mason does not earn more than her husband. A late entrant to teaching, she has been contributing to the family income for only 4 years. Her income and the security of her job, however, qualified the couple for a mortgage of sufficient size that the family was able to move from a small, cramped cottage on the outskirts of an industrial housing estate into a detached, three-bedroom home in a quiet cul-de-sac. Her income is also much more secure than that of her husband, a self-employed jointer. In recent years the building trade has slowed considerably and Mr Mason has endured relatively long periods without work. Continuity of income thus has come more to rest with Mrs Mason:

Yes, I do see my income as providing security. Yes, I think so. With my husband's bad back, with the building industry the way it is, yes. At least I know that the bills can be paid. If I lost my job, it would have an enormous effect—we'd have to sell the house.

Mr Mason's higher income and his wife's actions to reinforce his view of himself as household boss work together to prevent— usually—the development of conflict over the growing importance of Mrs Mason's professional employment:

He earns more and I think it's very important to him that he does. I don't think I'll ever earn more, unless he has a very bad year. I make sure I never rub it in his face the fact that I have my own cheque book—unless, of course, I'm provoked.

In these families, then, we begin to see the results of contradictions between reality and belief; we begin to see the difficulties which can accompany cross-class family life. Mrs Light has been the main earner in her family for some time now; hers is the more secure job. She wishes, however, that her husband assumed the primary occupational role, does not act to change the appearance of reality and, as a result, experiences conflict in her marital relations. Mrs Ashcroft, wanting a husband whom she can look up to, chooses to divorce. Mrs Mason and Mrs Harvey, both responsible in varying degrees for the security of their families, would also like their husbands to assume more dominant roles. Both act, however, to subvert the appearance of reality and thus avoid most conflict. None of these women have negotiated, with themselves or with their husbands, a system of beliefs which would allow for and explain their occupational or financial dominance in the household. Instead, these wives accept the convention of male dominance. They do so, moreover, in spite of obvious contradictions between convention and reality. In not negotiating a new system of beliefs within themselves they experience, at best, disappointment, at worst, divorce. In not agreeing a new set of beliefs with their husbands, and in acting to sustain beliefs which are out of step with reality, they shut away a major part of their lives—their work—from their marriages. None of these wives discuss work with their husbands. For each, a line is drawn between work and home, clearly separating the two:

No, I don't talk about it. He knows nothing, for example, about the dispute with my Head I was telling you about. I don't think he's very interested, so I don't talk about it, really.

Mrs Light

He's really not interested, so I do occasionally but not much . . . sometimes I find it frustrating. Frustrating that he doesn't understand the sorts of things I'm on about.

Mrs Mason

No, I don't, not really. Gossip sometimes, but not anything about the work content.

Mrs Harvey

For Mrs Ashcroft, this separation between work and home was one of the factors influencing her decision to divorce:

No, we don't talk about work. He hasn't any office or computer experience at all. He wouldn't really be able to grasp it. I'd like to be able to discuss work with him. When I was studying for this job, I'd go up the street to one of my colleagues and ask him if I got stuck on anything. I can't talk to my husband at all about these things and I'd like to.

Generally, then, by not developing family norms which allow for the greater career involvement of a wife—and for the consequences of such involvement—either because of their own reluctance to do so, or because of their husbands' unwillingness, these women find themselves in the position of emulating their husbands' after-work behaviour. Married to men who leave work at work, who do not wish to discuss work at home, who see their jobs in monetary terms rather than as sources of personal fulfilment, these women act the part of conventional wives and once at home, in conversation with their husbands, assume domestic interests only. Moreover, their inability to negotiate new understandings with themselves and with their husbands means not only the denial of career commitment while at home but also, in very tangible terms, the denial of after-work tiredness:

I do get very very tired, especially mentally. I'm on the go all the time from 7 in the morning till 10 or 11 at night—it's bound to wear one out. My husband gets physically tired, but he doesn't see my tiredness as tiredness at all—no, not at all. He's more obviously tired. I mean, it's easier to see. I tend to be an optimist, I tend to go on and on. So perhaps it doesn't show with me. I am sure, though, that he doesn't recognize that I am mentally tired. I suppose because I tend not to show it because if I did show it, there'd be an argument. He goes and watches TV, drops off to sleep, and then I can get on with it [extra work].

Mrs Mason

Mrs Mason speaks for the other wives with these words.

A further consequence of the lack of agreement between husband and wife allowing superior career involvement on the wife's part is that the extra work of these women's jobs (Mrs Ashcroft apart) must be done without disrupting domestic routine. For Mrs Mason, this means waiting until her husband falls asleep in front of the television before she can 'get on with it'—preparations for the following day and her work writing a book on children's education. For Mrs Harvey, it entails squeezing extra work editing a book into the early morning hours, or planning her life very carefully: 'I try very hard to be here, without work to do, on the evenings when I know my husband will be home.' In practice, however, she is not always successful. Mr Harvey refused an interview with me; he intervened in my interview with his wife, however, just as she was discussing the ways in which she attempts to fit after-hours work into her home life. He interrupted her to express considerable discontentment with her work involvement and about her working in the evenings. He referred specifically to her work editing a colleague's book, an undertaking for which Mrs Harvey was to receive a large fee. Mrs Harvey was very surprised at his outburst and, after he had left us, reported that this was the first she had heard of his dissatisfaction. She went on to say: 'That was very unfair of him. I did it in a way that did not upset his life at all—by getting up at 6 a.m. That really was unfair. I planned it all not to bother him.' Mrs Light also plans her working life so that it does not disrupt her role as a 'conventional' wife. She manages to do all the extra work of teaching before her husband returns home at the end of the day. The result of this, however, is that Mr Light does not quite understand—or at least acknowledge—the full extent of a teacher's job: 'I suppose my wife's job is more demanding than mine. I do feel, however, that 9 o'clock in the morning to 3.30 in the afternoon is hardly a working day.'

The underlying cause of these misunderstandings is, of course, that these wives attempt to be what they are not. They are not conventional wives in conventional families with husbands who assume the dominant role occupationally—although they would like to be. They attempt to balance the reality of their lives with this belief in—or wish for—conventionality by subverting reality. The true extent of their work commitment and the exhaustion and extra work which accompanies this commitment remain hidden. For these women, cross-class family life means a confusion of belief and reality. Unable to fit the reality of their marriages to their beliefs, and unable to match their beliefs to reality, they may—like Mrs Ash-croft—experience conflict marked enough to warrant divorce. Or they may persist with cross-class life, all the while experiencing a certain sense of disappointment. Solidarity between spouses may indeed be threatened by the occupational superiority of a wife, but not simply because of the fact of superiority itself. These families show rather that it is the lack of agreement—the lack of solidarity of agreed family norms—allowing and explaining occupational attainments of wives surpassing those of husbands which acts on and weakens family stability.

Normative Disagreement: Troubled Husbands

In the preceding two groups of families, contrasting ways in which husbands and wives cope with female occupational dominance have been illustrated. In the first group, characterized by agreement bet-ween husband and wife, the wives' willingness to assume the prim-ary role is supported by their husbands' acquiescence in their doing so. In the latter group no such agreement is found, and the wives are unwilling participants in their own dominance. There is as well a third response to female occupational dominance. In certain of the families, the wives are content to accept the reality of their superior occupational attainments and to carry the benefits of this attainment into their homes by providing both higher incomes and long-term financial security. The husbands of these women, however, find their secondary roles difficult to accept. Such families are character-ized by lack of agreement between husband and wife and consider-able marital conflict. One of these families, the Barneses, was discus-sed in Chapter 5. Mr Barnes, a lorry driver, attempts to acquiesce to his wife's dominance, and readily acknowledges the much greater importance of her income to the couple's economic well-being. When asked if he would relocate to further his wife's career, Mr Barnes responded: 'I'd leave it up to her; she has the better job. If she wanted to go, I'd go.' In addition he leaves to his wife all financial decision-making and management. Mrs Barnes tries to ameliorate the monetary imbalance between her and her husband by giving him a generous weekly supplement to his income. Mr Barnes's apparent concurrence with the dominance of his wife and Mrs Barnes's actions to lessen the effects of her higher income are not wholly successful, however. Lacking in this family is a system of beliefs which would allow Mr Barnes a satisfactory explanation of his position in the family; as a result, this couple's marital harmony is broken by discord. And, as noted earlier, this discord most often focuses on money and differential work involvement.

A second family, in which husband and wife seem to pull in opposing directions, are the Parkers, a teacher and farm worker married for 10 years and parents of a 3-year-old daughter. Like Mrs Barnes, Mrs Parker commands a higher income than her husband and is in a much more secure occupational position. Both Mr and Mrs Parker agree that long-term financial security rests with Mrs Parker:

Oh definitely. My job is more secure than my husband's. He has a tenuous relationship with his boss; it's a small farm and could fold tomorrow. I can't really see the future any different than it is now.

It's not particularly on my shoulders. Her income is much better than mine.

Mr Parker, however, is not content with the income disparities between him and his wife and attempts to supplement the £6,000 per annum he earns as a farm-hand through ownership of a small herd of cattle. Each morning before work and each evening after work Mr Parker attends to his cattle, with the result that an already long working day is greatly extended. Through these endeavours, he manages to earn an extra £1,000 yearly, added income which brings his contribution closer to his wife's £8,600 annual salary. Perhaps not surprisingly, Mrs Parker resents her husband's involvement with his cattle, not the least because of the extra time they demand, taking her husband away from the family and causing a disproportionate share of childcare and housekeeping duties to rest with her. She sees these cattle as wholly unnecessary and has taken steps to put aside part of her income for the purchase of anything other than cattle:

I've opened an 'anti-cattle' building society account in my name only with £500 in it. I don't know what I'm going to use it for, but whatever it is, it will be something I want, not for animals I hate. They take so much of his time. I have a secure, well-paying job; it should be enough, but it's not—at least not for my husband.

Mr Parker's reluctance to accept the income disparity which favours his wife leads to frequent quarrels between husband and wife over his actions to increase his financial contributions. In fact I arrived to interview Mr Parker in the middle of one of their many arguments about his cattle and so witnessed their conflict first hand. Mr Parker's reluctance is, moreover, a reflection of his inability to accept the role of secondary earner in the family. While his wife is content to assume the 'breadwinner' role, he is not happy for her to do so. If Mr Parker was able to negotiate with himself a new system of beliefs which allowed for the superiority of wives both occupationally and financially, his cattle could be sold (as both Parkers agree, they do not really need the extra income they provide) and a major source of conflict between husband and wife resolved. His failure to do so means that the solidarity of his marriage—like that of the Barneses—is indeed threatened by competition between spouses.

With regard to work–family carry-over, these two families are somewhat unique in this research. Mrs Barnes is a lecturer in economics; her work is always with her and intrudes into family life to a much greater extent than that of the other wives. And as noted this intrusion causes considerable difficulty between husband and wife. In the Parker family, it is Mr Parker's work which most directly carries over into the home. The couple resides in a tied cottage on the isolated farm where Mr Parker is employed. The degree of social isolation experienced through residence in this remote rural area compelled Mrs Parker to continue her teaching career after the birth of her daughter although she had originally planned on giving up paid employment. The long hours which Mr Parker puts in as a farm worker interfere with family life by taking him away from both domestic responsibilities and social activities. The times in which Mr Parker is in greatest demand for farm work are the same times that Mrs Parker has available for relaxation and holidays. The difficulties which reside in these differing work schedules are sufficient in themselves to cause conflict between husband and wife. They are, however, further exacerbated by Mr Parker's attempts to equalize the income disparities which exist between this couple. As a result, Mrs Parker maintains an almost studied indifference to her husband's work activities. They really do not discuss his work at all, as Mr Parker notes: 'I talk a bit, but not much; she's not interested.' In return, Mrs Parker shares a little of the gossip of her school but none of the problems associated with her job. For this couple, then, the separation of work and family worlds is virtually complete. Mrs Parker's resentment at the inability of her husband to accept the benefits of her secure, well-paying job, and thus to dispense with his cattle and to minimize the extent to which his work intrudes into family life, leads to a shutting away of a major part of their lives—work—for both husband and wife.

A similar clear separation of work and family worlds is found in a third family in which the wife assumes the dominant, breadwinner role while her husband finds some difficulty in accepting her doing so. The Henleys have been married for 8 years and are parents of an infant daughter. Like the Parkers, both Mr and Mrs Henley look to her income as the source of their security:

I feel it is the source of our security. I'm the major wage earner. It's difficult being older and earning more.

Mrs Henley, teacher

My income's not very good for security; it's not enough money. It costs more to run the house than what I get.

Mr Henley, printer's helper.

Mrs Henley assumes control of the family's finances and acts as bookkeeper. The couple profess to share expenses equally but, like Mrs Barnes, Mrs Henley attempts to soften the income differences between herself and her husband. She does so, however, in a manner unlike Mrs Barnes by under-estimating, unbeknown to her husband, his share of the costs of running their home. Thus conflict between this couple seldom arises over money. Differences in work involvement and in professional status have, though, caused discord.

After some years of marital discord, including one period of separation, Mr Henley has now come to terms with the differences in status between his wife's occupation and his own. The couple lives in a small village where Mrs Henley teaches at the local junior school. She is very well known to parents and children alike in this village and for some time Mr Henley found it difficult to adjust to the differential public treatment accorded them. He has now accepted this difference and reports: 'It used to get to me, bother me. I'd feel inferior. I got over it by getting involved in the village, by getting to know the people she works with. I've got used to being Mrs Henley's husband.' One source of cross-class conflict has thus been resolved. Differences in work involvement and after-work tiredness, however, continue to be problematic for this couple as Mr Henley finds it difficult to accommodate the extra degree of commitment which his wife's professional employment demands. Employed in a position which asks little of him either physically or mentally, he leaves work 'raring to go', while his wife is 'exhausted because of her job'. Mr Henley reports preferring to 'leave work at work' and seldom discusses the day's activities with his wife. He resents his wife's inability to do the same. In contrast, Mrs Henley invests a great deal into her teaching and comes home to rest for the next day:

Work has come first most of the time. I put all my energy into my job and am exhausted when I get home. My relationship with my husband improves when holidays come. My husband isn't home when I get home and that's good. I'm really wound up from teaching and clubs and talking. He just wants to switch off. And no, I don't talk about it to him. I leave it there. He doesn't want to hear about it and I've learned not to talk about teaching.

Mrs Henley acts in two ways, then, to lessen the effects of her superior occupational attainments in the face of her husband's difficulties in accepting the obvious lack of parity between them. She keeps to herself the daily occurrences of her working life and she quietly minimizes income disparities between husband and wife by assuming a greater share of expenses. In these ways she is able to help her husband come to terms with his deviance from the norm of male dominance.

In a fourth family, the wife adopts a markedly different approach in helping her husband accept a similar position in family and community life to that experienced by Mr Henley. Like Mrs Henley, Mrs Paton is the higher earner in her family and is in a more secure occupational position than her husband. Moreover, as a district nurse she is, like Mrs Henley, very well known in her community, more well known than her husband who is employed as an agricultural fitter. Mrs Paton reports that the local townspeople are very friendly towards her, greet her by name, and so on. Her husband resents this differential public treatment and sees it as a direct result of her participation in professional employment. In suffering such resentment Mr Paton is in fact acting out Talcott Parsons's suggestion that dual occupational linkages by husbands and wives are likely to result in confusion of status in the community with concomitant psychological insecurity for those involved.[3] Mrs Paton attempts to mitigate this resentment and to gain her husband's acquiescence to her continued professional employment by conceding to him the role of 'head of household'. Mr Paton is the only husband in this study who undertakes entire responsibility for financial decision-making and management. He pays all household bills, plans all holidays, carries any cash needed for socializing. In addition, when asked about long-term financial security Mrs Paton underlined the role her husband takes in family life by saying: 'I don't worry about the future, my husband does.' In reality, however, Mrs Paton's income and secure job provide the foundation of this family's future. Mrs Paton acknowledges the importance of her income: 'we couldn't live without my income, I earn more'. Moreover, her income will remain above her husband's as time passes and she progresses each year up a set salary scale, while increases to Mr Paton's income depend entirely on the goodwill of his employer. Employed in a small, non-union firm, Mr Paton is also dependent upon goodwill for the continuation of his employment: subject to only one week's notice of dismissal, his job security is well below that of this wife's.

In giving to her husband complete financial responsibility, in allowing him the role of 'household head', Mrs Paton is in effect denying the supremacy of her occupation within the family, denying the commitment to work which leads her to state: 'I love my job. I see myself working as a nurse 25 years from now.' A contradiction between belief—male occupational dominance—and reality—female superiority—results in mutual connivance by husband and wife in the appearance of conventionality. Such collusion between spouses is not, however, sufficient to offset the consequences of cross-class occupational attainment, and, like others who lack the beliefs necessary to sustain deviance from the norm, the Patons experience discord over differential work involvement:

I don't like my wife bringing work home. She works out of hours and doesn't get paid. Sometimes we have arguments about it—when she works after dinner. Sometimes she can be on the phone all night. I mean, she goes to bed at 9.30 p.m. and is up at 5 a.m. She just thinks about her job. I'd rather switch off and I wish she would too.

My husband likes me to work, for the money. But he would be much happier if I was in a different job. He doesn't like me to be so involved. I have to bring work home, you see; there are just not enough hours in the day. He does go on to me: you should do it in the daytime.

The Patons and the three preceding families demonstrate once again that deviance from male occupational dominance is something quite difficult to accommodate into family life. These four families lack the beliefs necessary to sustain such deviance, lack agreement between husband and wife allowing for or explaining female occupational superiority and, as a result, experience discord in their marital relations. Moreover, they show that it is most often at the point of deviance itself that such discord occurs. Thus conflict frequently centres on money in those families in which the wife is the higher earner or in the more secure job—unless the wife takes steps to lessen the effects of her greater earnings. In a like manner, stress between spouses arises from differential work involvement and commitment as wives pursue their career interests well beyond the hours which their husbands set aside for work. At the point at which they differ—from each other and from the families which surround them—lies the centre of conflict and distress.

In the preceding families, various responses to cross-class occupational attainments have been observed. We have seen cross-class family life built upon norms of equality between spouses, and upon acceptance by both husband and wife of female occupational superiority. Further, we have seen that considerable conflict between spouses can arise when either husband or wife (or both) lacks the beliefs necessary to sustain and explain the deviation from conventionality which such female superiority brings. At the beginning of Chapter 5, however, certain families were introduced for whom the extent to which they may be considered cross-class is attenuated by the contingent or part-time nature of the wives' employment. In these families the husband maintains the role of household head; his position in the family is supported by the economic realities of the labour force participation of both husband and wife. As a way of providing some contrast to the preceding discussions, and to reinforce the importance for marital harmony of normative agreement between spouses, this chapter will end with a brief illustration of the carry-over effects of work for these families. Into this group—which may be thought of as neo-traditional in family organization—fall the Ungers and the Thompsons, families in which the wives are employed part-time, together with the Jasons and the Leonards. The husbands in these families are the higher earners. Both husband and wife look to his income for long-term economic security. With the exception of the Jasons, who do not wish to leave their present home, all of these families would relocate to help the husbands' occupational prospects; would not move to help the wives'. Although some misunderstanding occurs between spouses about the nature of the wife's employment, these families may generally be thought of as free from overt work-related conflict. They are in fact characterized by normative agreement between husband and wife which both creates and sustains male occupational dominance.

Normative Agreement: Male Dominance

The Ungers provide an example of neo-traditional family organization. Mrs Unger, an MLSO, worked full time for 9 years before taking 4 years out of the labour force for childcare. For the past 18 months she has been back at her previous job working 20 hours per week as a permanent part-time employee with full benefits and security of tenure. The Ungers live entirely on Mr Unger's earnings as a self-employed roof tiler. Mrs Unger is the family bookkeeper, paying all bills and writing all cheques. She does so, however, with the money given to her by her husband; in fact, while she may write all of the cheques, she does so only for her husband's signature as the bank accounts are all in his name. Mrs Unger prizes her job very highly, but she has no real intention of returning to full-time employment unless the costs of educating her children necessitate extra income:

I'm working part-time mainly because of the children, but to be honest, I wouldn't really go back full-time. I have the best of both worlds really. Unless work pressurizes me to take it full-time, or we need the money for the kids' schools, I'll stay part-time. But I also think I could never go back to being full-time at home either. That would be like going backwards somehow.

Mrs Unger's sentiments are echoed by Mrs Thompson: 'I don't know how anyone who is married works full-time'.

Mr Unger declined participation in a personal interview and so it is difficult to know if he would prefer his wife to undertake more or less employment. His wife, however, reports that he is quite content with the present situation. His satisfaction may, moreover, be inferred from the minimal level of separation between Mrs Unger's work and family worlds:

Oh yes, I talk to him about work a lot. And although he hasn't a clue what I'm on about half the time—the technical details—he's smashing about listening, letting me tell him all about it. He rarely discusses his work, mind.

He comes home quite exhausted—likes a hot bath—he's happy just to sit and listen.

In spite of Mrs Unger's remarks that her husband rarely discusses his work, there is little enough separation between work and home for Mr Unger that his wife can speak both informatively and at length about the content of his work as she was pleased to do during our interview (and which, I might add, Mrs Harvey was quite unable to do). This lack of separation between work and family worlds, moreover, means that Mr Unger shares his wife's understanding of post-work tiredness regardless of which job is producing the exhaustion. In the above, Mrs Unger notes that her husband comes home very tired. She went on to say that he fully recognizes her tiredness but with a slight twist in understanding which reinforces a view of this couple as male-dominated, or neo-traditional, as well as bringing to the fore one of the problems of cross-class life:

Yes, he realizes I get very tired—he's sympathetic—but I think he also thinks that it's a trait in women [*laughs*] because he's never done my type of job. I mean, although his is very tiring, it's also relaxing. It doesn't have a lot of worries with it. When he's finished, he's finished. He doesn't have to worry about mistakes.

This apparent lack of understanding about the nature of the wife's occupation is found again in Mrs Leonard's words:

We talk about the odd thing but our worlds are so different. Office life is so different than a building site. I sometimes think that we don't exactly understand what goes on in the other person's work life. What they actually do at work. General office life, he can't understand. You need to talk about it. He listens, but . . .

As noted earlier, however, Mrs Leonard's job is only something she will do until having children and so this vague misunderstanding does not translate itself into marital conflict. The agreement between spouses that the husband's work has primacy, that he is responsible for long-term support and security of the family, that her job is either temporary or secondary to his, allows for misinterpretation of her work and post-work tiredness. By agreement, the wife's job is without vital importance in the family and so some misunderstanding about it does not provide a source of conflict. It is in fact only Mrs Jason, about to take over responsibility for the family's welfare upon the retirement of her husband, who expresses aggravation with her husband's unwillingness to discuss either his or her work:

> He says that once he leaves the factory gates, he doesn't want to think about it and he doesn't want other people to talk about their work. I don't agree with him. I think it's part of your life and you've got to talk about it.

A part-time secretary for the majority of the working years of her marriage, and now employed full time as an MLSO, Mrs Jason faces 10 years of continued employment beyond the retirement of her husband. Without her income the family's financial situation would worsen considerably upon Mr Jason's withdrawal from the labour force. Mrs Jason might well be anticipating her transition to primary earner in her discontentment with her husband's taciturnity. For the others, no such discontentment exists.

In all of the families discussed in this and the previous chapter I have tried to show the importance of the relationship between the reality of family life and the system of beliefs held by husband and wife. I have tried to demonstrate that this relationship is neither static nor given, that it is something which must be negotiated over time between spouses. As noted earlier few of the men and women reported here were raised in other than traditional homes in which the mother's primary role was as homemaker, the father's as breadwinner. Their own marriages have, however, brought them into very different circumstances and so, for most, a negotiation of new understandings has become necessary. I have tried to show that these new understandings do not simply occur as a result of cross-class marriage but must be achieved, and that failure to do so jointly such that husband and wife are in general agreement over the norms which govern their lives often results in conflict or disappointment for one or both.

It is hoped that some understanding of the relationship between work and home for these cross-class families has been gained. However, perhaps the most important aspect of this and the previous chapter is that they have brought to the fore the realization that unequal attachments to the labour force favouring a wife can exist without destructive competition between spouses. Talcott Parsons argued otherwise and suggested that solidarity between husband and wife would be endangered by joint occupational participation. And although his theories have been tested in a variety of ways, they have perhaps not been put to the test quite so clearly as with cross-

class families. Moreover, many of the families have shown Parsons
at least in some instances to have been mistaken: rather than solidarity being weakened by competition between husband and wife,
competition is eliminated by solidarity. In those families in which
there is an agreement of norms—solidarity—conflict and competition are absent. In addition, however, cross-class families characterized by conflict and competition do exist. In these families, solidarity
is indeed threatened by the superior occupational attainments of the
wives. Moreover, such families experience greatest difficulty at the
point of their deviance from the norm of male occupational dominance. Thus, conflict and competition centres on differential work
involvement and income disparities between spouses. Such couples
lack normative agreement allowing and explaining the realities of
cross-class family life, and in lacking such agreement—such solidarity—face threats to the stability of that family life. What seems,
then, to be of paramount importance is not the outward attachment
to the labour force itself, but rather the extent and nature of agreement, or lack of agreement, between spouses. As suggested at the
outset of Chapter 5, there are no intrinsic reasons why the occupational differences experienced by cross-class husbands and wives
should cause difficulties beyond those normally associated with
balancing two jobs in one family. In a world without specific beliefs
about the correct, or expected, behaviour of husbands and wives,
which family member makes the most money or is the most committed to a career would not matter; decisions about work involvement,
promotions, or moving home and family would be made without
reference to the sex of the person facing such decisions. Other
criteria would enter in, of course, but such things would not necessarily carry the same overtones of conflict and disagreement. In this
world, however, specific beliefs most certainly do exist. And for
cross-class couples who stand in opposition to the most pervasive of
these beliefs—male occupational supremacy—it seems clear that
some degree of agreement between spouses allowing and explaining
their normative deviance must be achieved if marital conflict is to be
avoided. Or to put it slightly differently, in a world of male occupational dominance, cross-class couples must reject or modify prevailing beliefs about family life in general in order to accommodate
the realities of cross-class life in particular. Failure to do so is to
bring contradiction between belief and reality into their lives, and
with contradiction, marital discord.

The question of changing one's beliefs to match the realities of one's life is, however, much more complex than has been suggested so far. Few individuals make explicit the underlying norms which guide their behaviour. This seems especially so with regard to 'taken for granted' behaviour such as that associated with being a husband or wife (Bott, 1957: 195). For many, such behaviour is based upon unexamined beliefs; it is simply accepted as 'natural' or 'proper'. But in order for change to occur individual awareness of the assumptions which underlie internalized standards and expectations must be achieved. Gaining such an awareness is difficult, however, because individual beliefs about the appropriate behaviour of husbands and wives are in large measure a reflection of individual gender identity. As Hiller and Philliber note, gender identity 'is the degree to which a man or a woman incorporates traditional masculine or feminine role definitions, including dominant and subordinate statuses, into his or her own self-concept.' (1982: 55). And, of course, among the most important masculine and feminine roles are those of husband and wife. Moreover, as Burke and Tully point out, gender identity is one of the 'most central, pervasive, encompassing, influential, and salient role/identities' (1977: 883), and as such strongly resistant to change.[4] In this way, then, threats to individual beliefs about the right and proper behaviour of husbands and wives are threats also to individual beliefs about what it means to be 'masculine' or 'feminine'. By challenging traditional role behaviour of husbands and wives, cross-class marriages may also challenge individual perceptions of gender. In fact, for some cross-class husbands and wives, gender identity may be an insurmountable barrier to a realistic approach to the realities of cross-class marriage, with the result that changing beliefs is impossible and marital discord or dissolution the only possible response.

Certain writers have in fact presented gender identity as an important element of stability in marriages of wife occupational superiority. Safilios-Rothschild (1975), for example, argues that a wife's occupational superiority to her husband presents a threat to the gender identities of both: his economic dependence on her threatens his masculinity; her apparent dominance lessens her femininity. Hiller and Philliber (1982) also regard gender identity as a 'critical variable' in determining the success of marriages in which the wife's occupational achievements exceed those of her husband. Similarly, occupying the primary breadwinner role has been shown to be an avenue for men of validating their masculinity (Gronsëth, 1972; Yankelovich, 1974; Pleck, 1977). While for women, fulfilling the role of homemaker has been shown to be inextricably bound to perceptions and definitions of femininity (Oakley, 1974). Gender identity is, however, a culturally learned attribute of men and women. As such it varies considerably from individual to individual.[5] The degree to which such identity presents barriers to change within cross-class families, and thus barriers to marital harmony, can therefore be expected to vary, and is largely a matter for further empirical investigation. When individuals have strongly traditional gender identities, such as has been suggested about Mr Henderson, Mrs Light, or the Leonards (for example), cross-class marriage can be problematic, resulting in conflict or disruption to the wife's occupational career. In contrast, the ease with which Mr Meredith, Mrs Stone, or the Smiths (for example) accommodate differential occupational achievements between spouses suggests the internalization of gender identities less closely tied to traditional stereotypes. In the next chapter, one of the most enduring symbols of gender identity for both men and women will be examined: the performance (or not) of household chores. Hiller and Philliber suggest that for individuals to whom traditional masculine or feminine role identities are important, the 'trappings of traditional sex stratification *per se*' are also important (1982: 55). There is little more indicative, more a 'trapping' of traditional gender identity, one would suggest, than the assumption (or avoidance) of responsibility for housework. Ann Oakley confirms this tie between gender identity and household chores:

Women locate their orientations to the housewife role within the context of a general view of feminine and masculine roles, according to which the place of each sex is clearly defined. This definition of appropriate gender role behaviour thus covers not only the equation of femaleness with housewifery but also the patterning of the division of labour between the housewife and her husband. (1974: 185–6)

Although Oakley was primarily concerned with wives without paid employment, the following chapter shows that for cross-class wives the same link between gender identity and the housewife role exists. The strength of this link varies considerably, however. For those women to whom traditional 'feminine' behaviour is important, housework is important. In fact, for some of the wives studied, *control* of housework is explicitly retained, and seems to be a way of asserting traditional feminine behaviour in the face of occupational achievement which could suggest otherwise.

Notes

1. The importance of money is stressed by Safilios-Rothschild (1976) when she suggests that the wife's higher occupational status can be tolerated within a family as long as her income is lower than her husband's. Also Paloma and Garland, 1971, who write: 'When the wife's income is greater than her husband's (unlike differences in education or status alone) the husband's role in the family is clearly threatened. It is significant that no wife *wanted* to earn more than her husband, but some in fact did in order to meet the family's needs' (p. 756).

2. Hiller and Philliber (1982), in constructing a typology of marriages in which wives are occupationally superior to husbands, refer to 'wife reluctant' marriages. In such marriages, incongruity between role expectations and performances exist for the wife but not for the husband. They suggest that if the wife places responsibility for this incongruity upon herself, she is likely to change jobs and thus eliminate her occupational superiority. If, however, she places responsibility on her husband, she is likely to withdraw from the marriage. In the Ashcrofts' case, Mrs Ashcroft sees her husband as responsible for her marital unhappiness. And, in accordance with Hiller and Philliber's expectations, has chosen to divorce.

3. Talcott Parsons goes on from his discussion of sex role segregation: '. . . secondly, it aids in clarity of definition of the situation by making the status of the family in the community relatively definite and unequivocal. There is much evidence that this relative definiteness of status is an important factor in psychological security' (1943: 191).

4. It is often thought that, once established, gender identity is difficult or impossible to alter. Symbolic Interaction theory, in suggesting that role identities are the 'meanings a person attributes to the self as an object in a social situation' (Burke and Tully, 1977: 883), allows, however, for the possibility of change. Such meanings come to be known and understood by the individual through interaction with others; others react to the individual as if he or she has the identity appropriate to a specific role performance. Thus, role identities come to be learned through a *process* of social interaction. In this way, gender identity could change in response to the social roles in which individuals find themselves. However, such change does not come easily. Just as gender identity is learned through social interaction, it is also supported and defined in specific ways by others and by society in general. As Hiller and Philliber note: 'If gender identities are tenacious, it is because they are supported in childhood and adulthood through a variety of cultural norms' (1982: 56). If, however, an individual cannot change the social expectations of

others and/or the norms of his or her society, an individual can change his or her acceptance of such norms as legitimately defining appropriate gender behaviour (cf. Eichler, 1980: 61). This individual attempt to change behaviour may mean, of course, changing the social settings in which one lives.

5. Gender (and sex) is frequently presented in the literature as an either/or attribute of individuals. This dichotomous relationship is found in both folkloric knowledge and social scientific investigations (for example, masculinity–femininity scales). In fact, such differences between men and women are best represented by a continuum, with a large 'grey' area in the middle where gender attributes overlap considerably, and differences thus disappear. For a discussion of this, see Eichler, 1980; and Tresemer, 1975: 319).

7

Domestic Life: Housework and Children

It is almost an axiom of research into family life that there is an unequal division of domestic labour between husbands and wives. Wives do housework. Husbands help wives with 'their' housework. If wives are employed outside the home they frequently do less housework than wives not so employed, but they always do more housework than employed husbands. Moreover, when husbands do participate in housework, they are more likely to undertake tasks which are seasonal or occasional in nature, such as gardening, household repairs and decorating, than to perform daily, repetitive tasks such as cooking and cleaning. Domestic chores which are qualitatively more constant and time-consuming are quantitatively more likely to be performed by wives than by husbands. Studies throughout the seventies confirm this gender-specific division of labour (Bahr, 1974; Boulding, 1976; Clark and Harvey, 1976; Hunt, 1980; Edgell, 1980). This chapter examines the domestic division of household chores between cross-class husbands and wives. A plausible assumption held prior to undertaking such an examination might be that cross-class husbands and wives would differ from other families, most particularly from families in which the husband assumes the dominant role occupationally. After all, wives in cross-class families contribute, if not more than their husbands to the family financially, then almost as much. Their jobs provide a considerable degree of economic security for their families. They are most often much more involved with their jobs than are their husbands. All this has been seen in previous chapters. Might not one assume, then, that cross-class wives would carry less of the domestic burden, cross-class husbands carry more?

In fact, such an assumption would be largely mistaken. Cross-class husbands and wives do not, for the most part, differ greatly from other husbands and wives. In general, the majority of wives in this study assume personal responsibility for domestic chores, for seeing that the house is clean, food is prepared, clothes washed and ironed. This is itself an interesting finding for it suggests that neither career commitment, nor financial power, nor occupational superiority, either alone or in combination, are sufficient to overcome traditional beliefs about what is the responsibility within the home of women, what is the responsibility of men. Of greater interest, however, are the reasons and explanations behind this perhaps unexpected conventional division of labour between cross-class husbands and wives. Although the wives generally do assume personal responsibility for all or nearly all the household work, *why* they do so varies considerably. Therefore, an examination of their reasons and explanations forms the focal point of part one of this chapter. Such an examination will lead to an enhanced understanding of the force of conventional or traditional thinking on the actions and beliefs of married couples, for if wives in cross-class families persist in assuming control of, or accepting responsibility for, housework in spite of all the resources at their command which could be brought to bear in creating more egalitarian relationships, what hope is there for change among more traditional families?

With respect to childcare, previous research has demonstrated that husbands frequently undertake a certain amount of responsibility for their children's needs. This often extends, however, only to the pleasant side of children—reading to children, bathing them perhaps, playing with them before bedtime, and taking them on outings so that mothers can get on with other household chores (Young and Willmott, 1973; Oakley, 1974; Clark and Harvey, 1976; Edgell, 1980; Martin and Roberts, 1984). Feeding children and providing them with clean clothes remains the work of mothers. In addition to these tasks which confront all parents are those which apply only to two-earner parents. Providing adequate care for children while both mother and father are at work; transporting them to and from the minder or school; attending to them during times of illness—all this must be done as well. These chores also fall with considerable regularity upon the mothers of cross-class families. Of course, children eventually grow up and the amount of work involved in their care diminishes and finally disappears. Of interest regarding the children of cross-class couples are the occupations that these children follow once grown. Such children have two very different models to choose from: mothers in white-collar, professional employment; fathers in blue-collar, manual work. This chapter ends, therefore, with a discussion of the occupational achievements of the children of the families studied.

Part One: Responsibility for Housework

Wives are constrained by their own idea of ideal feminine roles.
They are very concerned about their possible infringement on
their husband's provider role and they are unwilling or unable to
relinquish their traditional feminine role.

Paloma and Garland, 1971: 757

The sense of self as a housewife (or not) is a deeply rooted facet of
self-identity as feminine; the equation of femininity with housewifery is basic to the institution of family life and to the gender
divisions which obtain in the paid work world . . .

Oakley, 1974: 185

The link between femininity and housewifery is sufficiently
ingrained in women to overcome any advantage which might
accrue to wives through occupational participation. This follows
decisively from the authors' statements quoted above. Paloma and
Garland investigated the domestic division of labour among American dual-career husbands and wives and found, like Rapoport and
Rapoport (1976) in Britain, that primary responsibility for housework and childcare tends to remain with wives. Oakley studied
wives who, for the most part, did not engage in paid employment.
Oakley's findings parallel those of Paloma and Garland. The sense
of personal responsibility for housework is so closely aligned to the
sense of self as a woman that few wives escape this responsibility,
even in families where husbands contribute actual labour to the
housework needing to be done.

There is little in previous research findings to suggest that wives
in cross-class families will differ substantially from wives in other
family configurations.[1] It has been shown, however, that equality of
income is an important precondition of male participation in household chores (Scanzoni, 1978; Model, 1981), and as many cross-
class wives equal or exceed their husbands in earning capacity, it
might be that this factor would lead to greater participation by
cross-class husbands in housework. In fact, as has been suggested in
previous chapters, money—while important—is not a sufficient
motivating force to overcome beliefs about the correct and proper
behaviour of husbands and wives. Moreoever, one study of dual-
career families indicates that once wives' incomes exceed their husbands', male participation in housework decreases rather than
increases:

While in the neo-traditional family (where income was supplemental to the male breadwinner) we saw some 'helping' with female domestic roles, the cases in which the wife's income exceeded her husband's revealed little such assistance. While the husband was not able to assert himself as the sole breadwinner and main economic provider, nor was he willing to assume any extensive or sharing role with domestic tasks. (Paloma and Garland, 1971: 756)

This study will largely confirm Paloma and Garland's findings; it .will, in addition, shed light on an issue these authors were unable to address fully: the reasons why equality (or, near equality) of income does not lead to equality of performance of domestic labour—and indeed seems sometimes to lead to quite the opposite. In a footnote, Paloma and Garland write:

It is not clear whether the wife wants her husband to assume a sharing role as far as domestic work is concerned and he is not willing or whether the husband is willing . . . but the wife is reluctant to share the feminine role with her husband . . . One or two husbands claimed that they were willing to assume more of a responsibility for domestic tasks, but that their wives would not let them. Whatever the reason, the domestic work remains the wife's *responsibility* even when the wife is the prime breadwinner. (1971: 760 n. 14)

In fact, both possibilities suggested by Paloma and Garland exist as explanations: in some families wives do refuse to relinquish control of household chores; in other families, husbands refuse to assume any responsibility for their performance. The decisive factor behind these explanations seems not to be, however, whether the wife is the primary breadwinner or whether she enjoys occupational but not financial superiority relative to her husband. Rather, the distinguishing characteristic between husbands and wives who do not share domestic responsibilities and those who do appears to be the degree to which husband and wife have incorporated traditional gender roles into their identities. For those to whom traditional 'masculine' or 'feminine' behaviour is important, the performance (or not) of housechores is important. Doing housework (or not) is an important confirmation of traditional gender identities.

It would be surprising, however, to find no husbands and wives at all in cross-class families who share equally both housework and responsibility for housework.[2] More surprising would be to discover that those couples characterized by normative agreement between

husband and wife obliging each spouse to make an economic contribution to family life do not extend this agreement to include participation in housework. And in fact, for the most part, they do.[3]

Couples who Share

The Fieldings, Merediths, and Robertses all share both the amount of
time spent on household chores and the decision-making and organization of those chores. The Fieldings make joint decisions about
what needs doing and when; whoever is able to execute these decisions most easily does so. There are no tasks in this household which
are exclusively 'woman's work' in the sense that Mrs Fielding alone
undertakes to do them. Only two chores are assumed by Mr Fielding as predominately his responsibility: laundry and car maintenance. The egalitarian ideals which demand joint participation in
paid employment extend into all areas of this couple's marriage and
result in joint responsibility for housework.

In a similar manner, the Merediths share most household tasks
between them, with Mrs Meredith taking sole responsibility for only
laundry and ironing, Mr Meredith for gardening and household
repairs. The extent of joint responsibility for the remainder of the
household chores is such that in interviews each spouse informed me
that the other spouse actually did more work than they:

> The housework isn't organized. We both tend to leave it until we can't stand
> it any more. We do so much else we don't have time to fuss about it. I always
> feel I ought to do more. My wife tends to do more cooking than I do.
>
> Mr Meredith

> We do it as and when we can. It's shared out and it tends to be a blitz. We
> get fits of cleaning and luckily usually at the same time, although he tends to
> do more cleaning than I do. I don't feel it's *my* responsibility to keep the
> house clean, or to get food on the table.
>
> Mrs Meredith

Implicit in Mrs Meredith's words, and plainly stated by her husband, is a generally low level of household cleanliness. This is not
entirely uncommon among two-earner families and is one way of
easing the demands made on husbands and wives by joint occupational participation. The Robertses share attitudes towards housework
similar to those of the Merediths: a relatively small amount of time is

spent on such work; work that is done is shared equally between husband and wife:

Neither one of us much likes housework, so it gets done maybe once a week on Saturdays. The pair of us will get something done.

Mr Roberts

We do it at weekends really. Not much gets done during the week except Tom usually tidies up. We tend to see it as putting in a certain amount of work rather than who does what. Sort of trading jobs. Like: I'll spend the morning doing this, if you spend the morning doing that. I think so long as you're both putting the same amount of effort in, one of you isn't sitting there with their feet up while the other works, it's okay. It works out in the end.

Mrs Roberts

One result of seeing housework as the responsibility of both husband and wife rather than as something wives do is that behaviour often associated with housewifery, and thus with being female, such as nagging or fussing over cooking and cleaning, is revealed as a consequence of the job done. It is the housework itself, and not the sex of the houseworker, which produces such behaviour. This is very clearly seen in Mr Roberts's description of the times when he and his wife are most prone to argument:

The time we tend to argue the most is in the first 10 minutes when one of us steps through the door. Particularly if I've been working all day and have cooked a meal. For example: you know, cooking the meal and I'm all steamed up and then she's had a hard day, she's driven all the way from Slough or something—it's the first few minutes—maybe I'll have done cabbage or something with the dinner and she'll say: you know, you really ought to have done potatoes with that meal. Which would be true of course because potatoes give you padding and all that sort of stuff. But I'll go: ya, ya, Hell! I've just cooked you this fantastic stew and I've got sweetcorn and cabbage and you come in here and you wind me up about the fact there's no potatoes. You want potatoes—do your own damn potatoes!

Mr Roberts's words not only paint a colourful picture of a typical family feud, they would serve well as dialogue in almost any television situation comedy—provided, of course, they were spoken by a harassed *housewife*. The important point is that this husband's reaction to the perils of cooking for others is simply a logical response to the situation in which he found himself. Responsible that day for providing a meal, and unappreciated for his efforts, he gets angry. Not an unusual nor unexpected response, but one most often associated with wives, not husbands—at least with respect to housework. When, however, men do the same work as women, when they assume the same roles, the same behaviour develops. Such behaviour is most clearly not biological in origin as is often assumed, but part and parcel of the role performed.

These three families, then, share responsibility for housework between husband and wife. They refrain from labelling some chores as 'women's work' and other chores as 'men's work' and share equally the labour necessary to get the work done. For all three families there is an interchangeability of housework and houseworker—whoever is the most able or most inclined undertakes the necessary chore. It is possible, however, to achieve equality between spouses with regard to domestic labour in other ways. The Everetts, for example, share chores between them by each assuming responsibility for a certain number of specific tasks and by pooling their labour to do the remainder of the housework. Mrs Everett retains responsibility for cooking, planning meals, washing, and ironing, while her husband undertakes much of the cleaning, the hoovering, and general picking up and putting away. The rest of the domestic work is done together or by either husband or wife. In the past, Mrs Everett was responsible for all aspects of domestic labour. Her entry into paid employment after 15 years at home raising three children led to a redistribution of both responsibility for and performance of the household chores:

When I was at home with the kids, I did it but now it's shared between us. My husband does a lot of cleaning—on his own—he doesn't wait to be asked. I do most things in the kitchen plus the beds. He hoovers, dusts, puts things away.

Mrs Everett

We pull together. We're both at work. None of us is in charge—we pull together: that's how you make a marriage work. I do my share. I like to see things tidy, polished up [he laughs] I wouldn't do it if I was *told to*!

Mr Everett

Mr Everett's assumption of responsibility for his share of the housework once he was no longer the husband of a housewife is paralleled in Mrs Everett's willingness to share responsibility for her family's

financial security now that she is employed. The reader will recall
that Mr Everett is in a very insecure position in the labour market,
having left his long-term employer for a new opportunity, only to
find himself forced back into employment with his previous firm but
now without the protection of seniority. In addition, he suffers from
back trouble—a serious problem for a man dependent upon his
physical strength for work. His wife's employment thus has considerable importance for their economic security, as she explains:

I don't know if I will work to retirement. I'd like to be able to finish earlier
but my husband has spinal trouble and he may not be able to work forever
and so my job is very important. Even if my husband was healthy, my job is
more secure than his. With his health as it is, mine is much more secure.
Originally I went back to work just to help out but now it's different. He did
everything for us [her and the children] when I wasn't working. Soon it may
be my turn, and that's only fair.

And so, like the Merediths and the Fieldings, the Everetts also trade
joint responsibility for financial security and economic contributions
to the family for joint responsibility for housework. There is no sense
in these families that 'women's work' is in the home, while 'men's
work' is providing and supporting that home—although this traditional division of activities did typify the Everetts' marriage at an
earlier stage.

   In addition to the egalitarian notion of 'fairness' alluded to by
Mrs Everett which underlies the trade-off these couples make with
respect to domestic and paid labour, differential work involvement
itself can lead to husbands and wives sharing responsibility for
housework. In this way, the domestic division of labour may be related directly to the *nature* of paid work undertaken rather than just to
the fact that paid work is undertaken. Cross-class husbands and wives
differ considerably in the amount of involvement in daily work and
post-work activities. The husbands most often leave 'work at work',
spending a well-defined amount of time at their jobs. Their wives, in
contrast, frequently work late hours or bring work home with them
physically at the end of the day and thus spend more hours 'at work'
than do their spouses. In the Abbot family, this differential occupational participation has had considerable economic consequences in
that Mrs Abbot's earnings as Head Teacher nearly double those of
her husband, a sawmill foreman. In addition, a very non-traditional,
but equal, division of domestic labour between spouses has resulted.

Mr Abbot assumes responsibility for all marketing, meal planning and food preparation, as well as doing all of the ironing. These are time-consuming, ever-present chores. They are chores most often done by wives. In contrast, Mrs Abbot assumes responsibility for tasks which do not need doing every day: laundry, hoovering, window-washing, and general cleaning. Behind this unconventional division of tasks are work schedules which permit Mr Abbot's return home by 4.30 p.m. each day; prevent Mrs Abbot's return until 7 o'clock, laden with 1 or 2 additional hours' work. The Abbots have thus altered tradition to suit the realities of their differing work involvement, as Mr Abbot acknowledged in our interview:

I learned very early on in my marriage that if I wanted a hot meal cooked at a reasonable hour, I'd better learn to do it myself. Anyway I'm home first.

Not only have the Abbots chosen to alter the normal division of labour between husband and wife with regard to cooking, they have done so with shopping also. Mr Abbot is paid in cash. He uses this cash to purchase the food he subsequently prepares, in addition to other minor household necessities. Mrs Abbot is responsible for major purchases such as furniture, appliances, and utilities. The Abbots have thus ordered their lives domestically in response to the positions husband and wife hold occupationally. Few of the other husbands and wives studied are quite so willing to alter tradition. In regard to shopping, although—like Mr Abbot—it is the husband's pay packet which is most often used to buy food, unlike the Abbots, it is most often the wife who does the actual shopping.

With these families, then, we see that egalitarian divisions of domestic labour do occur among cross-class families, although these families are the minority pattern. Moreover, we see that freqeuntly behind such sharing of roles is a relinquishment of traditional gender roles. The families just discussed include the same families met earlier who enjoy freedom from traditional ideas about which family member should be the primary earner; enjoy freedom from ideas of male supremacy financially and occupationally. They are the families without conflict and competition over occupational dominance. Their normative solidarity dispenses with such competition and, as just observed, prevents an unequal division of domestic labour. In these families performance of household work is frequently a matter arranged with a high degree of flexibility between husband and wife: whoever is best able or most willing undertakes the work needing to be done. In families where chores are apportioned to specific persons, traditional ideas of who ought to do what do not dominate. In the families to be discussed subsequently, we will see that this type of freedom from conventional role behaviour is quite rare. Instead, there are husbands and wives who feel that certain work in the home ought to be done by wives, ought not to be done by husbands. However, unlike the families above who share norms common to participation in both the domestic and occupational spheres, in the following families no similar congruence between norms governing these activities holds. That is, although those families who have egalitarian ideals governing joint participation in paid work also have egalitarian ideals about the performance of domestic labour, for the rest of the families there is no simple, or single, connection between the husbands' and wives' responses to cross-class occupational participation, as documented in Chapters 5 and 6, and the household division of labour. Instead, there are three main variations which cut across the respondents' responses to female occupational superiority: husband refusal to participate in domestic work; husband willingness to help out with such chores; wife unwilling to allow husband participation. Of these variations, the first and third are the most interesting from a perspective of gender, for although in all three the wives assume personal responsibility for housework, it is in 'husband refusal' and 'wife in control' that the clearest links between household work and gender identity are seen.

Husband Refusal

There are certain wives for whom assumption of full responsibility for housework is not a matter of personal choice: their husbands refuse to participate in domestic labour beyond an occasional 'helping hand' given at the husband's discretion. Most of these wives. earn considerably higher incomes than their husbands and include Mrs Paton, Mrs Creighton and Mrs Harvey. The exceptions to higher earnings are Mrs Henderson and Mrs Mason. Mrs Henderson, it will be remembered, recently gave up full-time employment in acquiescence to her husband's demands; as a part-time health visitor, her income is now just slightly less than her husband's. Mrs Mason also earns less than her husband, but since she is only a recent entrant to teaching, it is possible that their relative earnings will alter in the future. These families challenge the idea that equality of income between spouses leads to greater male participation in housework, and indeed confirm Paloma and Garland's finding that husbands who earn less than their wives often contribute no labour at all to running the home. Behind these husbands' refusals to undertake household chores are their traditional ideas about the role of men in family life:

My husband has a traditional family background—the husband goes out to work and doesn't expect to do housework when he gets home. He doesn't do much in the house other than washing up.

Mrs Henderson

I do the housework mainly. My husband will do things as the mood takes him such as Sunday lunch or washing up but he never does any cooking or cleaning. He's fairly traditional and thinks it's my job. But usually he just doesn't think of it, doesn't think of how houses get clean.

Mrs Harvey

My son is capable of cooking and cleaning for himself; my husband is not. I'm totally responsible for the housework. He will do the odd bit if asked, but he doesn't volunteer. He sees it as my job.

Mrs Creighton

The husbands of these women confine their participation in domestic work to traditional 'masculine' activities such as gardening, decorating, house repairs and car maintenance. Their responses to my queries about housework confirm their wives' reports. Mr Creighton found these questions tremendously amusing, replying: I do not do any housework, never have, and have no intention of starting. He added, quite proudly, 'I don't do any housework *at all*—not even Christmas shopping'. Mr Henderson, however, at first implied that he participated fully in household work, but then amplified his answer to indicate quite the opposite:

It's a shared responsibility. My wife's always been very active. She doesn't let the housework pile up. I will hoover sometimes.

Mr Henderson will also wash up the dishes and, occasionally, lay the table for meals.

Often this lack of participation by husbands in domestic work produces resentment in the women who must thus carry two full burdens:

I tend to get snappy. Especially on weekends if I've got all the housework to do and I've had a really hard week. Then I get resentful. I think: why is he down at the pub and here I am pushing the hoover around. I hardly ever see him at weekends . . . so sometimes I get resentful. I feel very much that I have to do two jobs.

Mrs Harvey

I'm not in charge of the house—my husband is—but I am in charge of the chores. He fusses at me about getting things done. He's more tidy than I am, neat and precise. He expects me to come up to his standards but won't do it himself. He nags at me to get up and do things. He sees it as my job.

Mrs Paton

The housework is my job, my responsibility. My husband does none. I frequently feel I have two jobs, especially at end of term. I work so hard and then come home and have to start again. I begin to resent the demands put on me. I toyed with the idea of working part-time but I knew that I wouldn't be satisfied with that. My husband helping is not an option. There are times when he's sitting watching the telly and I'm out there in the kitchen and I feel a bit frustrated about it all, but I don't do much about it.

Mrs Mason

Such resentment does not, of course, exist in isolation. The Creightons apart, these families also experience difficulties in coming to terms with the very different occupational achievements of husband and wife. Mrs Henderson, as noted, has given up part of a career of some personal significance in order to comply with her husband's traditional attitude towards the roles of men and women. Mrs Paton, in spite of a higher income, greater job security, and a lifetime commitment to employment, has given to her husband all financial control and responsibility for now and in the future. Mr Paton experiences jealousy and resentment over his wife's greater public recognition. The traditional attitudes held by these husbands (and acquiesced to by their wives) which argue against female occupational superiority argue also against male participation in domestic work. For Mrs Harvey and Mrs Mason, however, agreement with the convention of male occupational dominance, seen earlier in their mechanisms to subvert the reality of their work-life accomplishments, rebounds back upon them in the domestic sphere. These women attempt to bolster their husband's views of themselves as 'heads of household' either by playing the 'helpless female', or by encouraging him to be the family 'boss'. They accept the convention of male dominance and in doing so minimize the extent of their own career commitment and involvement. By failing to negotiate new understandings with themselves, and with their husbands, they are left not only with a sense of disappointment in their marriages, but all of the housework as well. While their husbands do in fact refuse to undertake any household work, these women are, in a sense, accomplices in their refusal.

Wife in Control

If Mrs Mason and Mrs Harvey end up with all housework as their responsibility through a somewhat passive compliance with tradition, there are other wives who are active participants in the defining of housework as 'woman's work'. For these women, performance of household chores is felt to be their personal responsibility. They define it as such and, for the most part, refuse any assistance from their husbands. Unlike wives met earlier who are willing to let standards of cleanliness slide in order to accommodate all of the demands on their time, these wives set very high standards. Moreover, they attempt to live up to these self-imposed standards, and are often exhausted by the effort:

It is too much, I get very tired. But a lot of it is my own fault. I'll be honest, I keep the work to myself. I've spoiled them [husband and children]. I find it quicker and easier, without a lot of arguments, to do it myself. And that's how it's gone. And it's wrong—I pay. I'm tired. But then, no one could do it the way I wanted it done. I'm very houseproud. It's my own fault. And if they do do it, I have to sort of bite my tongue and leave it for a day or two and then do it all over again.

Mrs Jason

I do every bit of it. I think it's because I'm a perfectionist: if a job's worth doing, it's worth doing well and I do not suffer fools gladly. If they [husband and daughter] don't do a job well, I'll do it over again myself. It's been my undoing really, because it's ended up with my doing everything. I get very tired really.

Mrs Light

The standards these two women set, which lead them to exhaustion, lead them to redo the occasional work done by husbands and children, are strong indications of high personal identification with housework. Oakley argues that the assumption of personal respon-

sibility for housework is not only associated with personal identification with that housework, but also that 'those women with a high
identification were likely to have a high specification of standards
and routines' (1974: 185). Being 'houseproud' or a 'perfectionist' are
clear signs of high standards and strong personal identification with
housewifery. Mrs Leonard echoes the words of Mrs Jason and Mrs
Light:

I do it, my husband does virtually nothing. But I feel it is my fault, really.
He wouldn't do the chores the way I wanted them done. I prefer to do them
myself, in my way. Sometimes he'll do it if I ask him, but he doesn't think of
it himself. But then, I'd rather do it. I think it's my responsibility, and if I
left it to him, I'd still worry about whether he'd do it right.

One source of this identification with the performance of domestic
chores may be seen in the words of Mrs Unger or Mrs James:

It's my upbringing, really. Do everything for your man. I must admit it's
how I want it. I'd rather, for instance, be out in the kitchen washing up
while he kept the children amused. Then I get them ready for bed, and he
reads them their story.

                                                              Mrs Unger

I'm a bit old-fashioned, I think. Going back to the old days when my mum
did everything and I think: well, if I can't wash the clothes myself, there
must be something wrong. My husband doesn't know how to use the
washing machine . . . I think he'd do more if I weren't so bossy. The thing
is, I don't think he would clean the house as conscientiously as I do. I think
he'd think that he did, but I would know that he didn't. I suppose if I asked
him to. He sometimes suggests changes—suggests helping—but I guess I'm
a bit old-fashioned.

                                                              Mrs James

Participation in paid employment has changed little in these
women's views of what is the personal responsibility of women; for
them, housework is woman's work. The same themes run through
all of their responses: he wouldn't do it as well; it's my fault, but it's
my responsibility; I prefer to do it myself. In spite of tiredness, in
spite of paid employment, in spite of occupational achievements
which exceed their husbands', these women remain, in a large part
of themselves, housewives. They undertake employment as teachers,
secretaries, medical workers because they *want* to, their work is
important to their senses of self. They undertake housework because

they feel they *ought* to, such work is *part of them* as women. The feelings expressed by the wives above are found in other wives:

I've been in charge of the housework. I make the decisions about everything. I don't mind doing it all, as long as I don't get complaints.

Mrs Ashcroft

The housework is my responsibility. I make sure that it is done. But then, that's what I've been trained to do.

Mrs Allen

I do it all until I flake.

Mrs Henley

I run the household, Perhaps we decide jointly 'who does what', but I decide what needs to be done. The responsibility is mine. I tell him what to do.

Mrs Barnes

I do it, I'm in charge: he's quite hopeless, really.

Mrs Parker

This is by far the predominant pattern among the wives studied: ten wives retain personal responsibility for and undertake to do virtually all domestic work as a matter of personal choice. They retain control of the housework willingly, and occasionally in spite of suggestions from their husbands that domestic chores ought to be organized otherwise. The question is, why? Why, with all the resources at hand that these women could bring to bear in creating more equal divisions of chores between themselves and their husbands, do they not even make an attempt, and in fact, seem to do quite the opposite? It seems an inadequate answer at best to say, simply, it is their socialization. And yet, in many respects, that is all that we are left with. These women have little else in common beyond the fact that they are all women and have thus all been brought up to be women. Asking direct questions of these wives about why they do all, or nearly all, of the housework provoked the responses just seen. In essence they do it because they think they should, or have come to want to, which is tantamount to saying the same thing twice. For one or two, help from their husbands is not an option. Mr Light, for example, comes from a traditional family and agrees with his wife that housework is her responsibility:

Absolutely yes, it's my wife's responsibility. I suppose that's the case. It's how it's always been. I've allowed it to continue. I can't see myself doing the ironing—I wouldn't *consider* doing the ironing.

Similarly, Mr Jason sees himself as outside any responsibility for household chores, especially shopping:

Oh no, I'd be terrible at food shopping. I'd spend too much money, buying it the first place I went to. No, that's all my wife's responsibility. I wash up though.

For others, very high standards of cleanliness preclude husband participation, as has been indicated by Mrs Jason and Mrs Light who redo work done by their husbands. Regardless of why the husbands of these women do not participate in housework, however, the question still remains of why such male participation is not wanted, not accepted. These women do not do the housework because their husbands will not, as with the wives just discussed. These women do the housework by choice. And, as suggested, little else distinguishes them from the other wives studied beyond their strong sense of personal identification with housework, beyond their relatively traditional gender identities which, for them, equate femininity with housewifery. With respect to age, stage in the family life-cycle, ages and number of children, there is no commonality. Mrs Leonard is 28 years of age, married for 8 years and childless. Married for the second time, Mrs James is 45 years old and mother of two teenagers. Mrs Henley is in her early thirties, has been married for 7 years and is the mother of a 1-year-old. And so it continues. Mrs Jason is 49, married for 25 years and mother of two grown children; Mrs Barnes is in her forties, childless and married for the second time. Similarly, their patterns of participation in paid employment do not distinguish these women from the others. Mrs Allan, Mrs Henley and Mrs Parker have worked continuously since marriage in addition to having children; Mrs Light and Mrs Jason both withdrew from paid employment for childrearing. Mrs Unger works on a part-time basis only. Mrs Barnes, Mrs Leonard and Mrs Ashcroft do not have children, and have been employed continuously since marriage. Furthermore, while three wives earn less than their husbands, two wives earn the same and five earn more. The only common element between them lies in their words and actions: the housework is their job, they do it best, they do it all.

It is interesting, however, to speculate why one-third of the wives studied act in such traditional ways with respect to housework. Could it be that being a wife in a *cross-class* family encourages retention of traditional gender identities, or even develops them? For, of course, these women do all share at least one thing in common—their cross-class marriages. Moreover, all of these women entered marriage with educational qualifications and occupational positions which exceeded their husbands'. Jorgensen and Klein (1979) suggest that couples experiencing hypogamy (husband marrying 'up') are aware that potential marital problems exist and that they thus make a special effort to agree on household and decision-making role expectations. As a result, these authors suggest, such couples suffer less frequent and less intense marital conflict than the heterogamy theory would predict (1979: 70). We have already seen that cross-class marriages are not always free from conflict. Of the women discussed presently, Mrs Ashcroft is to divorce, Mrs Henley has separated from her husband on one occasion, Mrs Barnes and Mrs Light experience significant conflict with their husbands. Therefore, it may be that the 'special effort to agree', if undertaken, does not necessarily succeed. Whether successful or not, however, it may also be that this effort to agree on household behaviour entails enactment of traditional role behaviour on the part of the wives domestically as a way of ameliorating their very non-traditional behaviour occupationally. That is, it may be that these women are aware (consciously or unconsciously) that potential marital problems do exist in cross-class marriages, and they therefore act in ways which minimize the extent to which they deviate from traditional definitions of feminine behaviour. Thus housework becomes their way of asserting or establishing their femininity: even if they may deviate from the norm outside the home, inside they are well and truly wives, women, domestic workers. There is no way in which this research can move beyond speculation on this issue unfortunately. The right questions were not asked; the numbers interviewed are too few and too non-randomly chosen. It is hoped that this speculation is at least plausible, if not also interesting. It is certainly a matter worth further study.

Husbands who Help

Of course, not all wives refuse help with household chores, not all husbands refuse to give help. Among the couples interviewed, there are a number of quite conventional two-earner marriages: the wife assumes responsibility for and does most of the housework; the husband acts as a willing helper in the performance of this work. Two families in which the wives work part-time come into this group. Mrs White and Mrs Thompson undertake the major share of the housework; their husbands assist them in expected ways: washing up, windows, gardening and occasional tidying. Similarly, two families in which the husbands are not engaged in full-time employment share housework between spouses in this manner. Mr Norton, a disabled person and part-time worker, undertakes most of the household chores while Mrs Norton, employed full time, helps him with these tasks. Mr Stone, at home with responsibility for two small children, does a major portion of the domestic work during the day while his wife is at work. When Mrs Stone returns home, and at weekends, she participates more fully in the household chores, as does Mrs Norton. In addition, five other families fall into the category of 'helping husbands'. Of these, three are young, pre-children husbands and wives: the Astons, the Youngs and the Petersons. In these families, the wives assume responsibility for the bulk of the housework primarily, but not wholly, because of their husbands' longer working days. Mr Young and Mr Peterson work considerable amounts of overtime each day; Mr Aston is engaged in renovating the family home in his after-work hours. Where differential work involvement in the Abbot family led to a break with tradition, in these families it has acted to reinforce tradition.

Of perhaps greater interest than three couples still early in their marriages are the last two couples to be discussed in this section. The Frenches and the Millers have both been married for more than 20 years. Mrs French took 12 years out of paid employment in order to raise two sons. During this time, she undertook teacher training, enabling her to return to work in a job markedly different from her pre-marriage position as a telephonist. 18 months prior to interviews, Mr French took voluntary redundancy from his long-term job as a tanker driver; he now works as a part-time driver. Mrs Miller withdrew from teaching for only 9 years, returning to full-time employment when her youngest child was aged 6. For 10 years, while her children were young and when she taught on both a supply and full-time basis, Mrs Miller employed outside help for domestic chores. She no longer has any outside assistance. Mr Miller has been continuously employed on a full-time basis throughout his marriage.

In both of these families, the wives assume responsibility for the housework, their husbands act as helpers and contribute generously to the work needing to be done. These families are of interest because in their behaviour and attitudes they serve as counterpoint examples to both 'husbands who refuse' and 'wives who control'.

Before re-entering the labour force some 12 years ago, Ann French did virtually all of the housework in her home. Her husband was a full-time shiftworker at this time and rarely contributed his labour to domestic work. This has now changed fairly extensively, and Martin French will more often be found doing housework. He recalls earlier times:

I was a bit lazy, I guess. I used to do a bit of housework when I was on afternoon shifts, but not much . . . One learns that it [housework] is a little bit soul-destroying, but I accept that it's got to be done. So I do it with the best heart possible . . . When Ann went full-time—the housework—she was incredible. Yes, I don't know how she did it, actually. All I can think, she must—she's a damned hard worker. I certainly have realized what is involved in housework. It's certainly opened my eyes open wide. It must have been a very very hard job for her.

Martin French now cooks occasionally, and shares all chores except ironing with his wife, although not quite equally. His changed behaviour and attitude toward housework did not arrive all at once with his wife's entry into work, of course, but developed slowly over time. Mrs French talks about how these changes came about:

It didn't happen at first, and then, very gradually, as I got older, when Martin was on late duty, I'd come home and find that he'd hoovered the bedrooms for me. But apart from that, no. His mother had brought him up very Victorian and women's work was women's work . . . Since he's been redundant, he's done a great deal more. He will cook now—except when I'm on holiday. I'll come home and find the house has been cleaned from top to bottom, the carpet's been scrubbed, you know. But I can't really rely on it. But since he's been retired, he's done a lot and then, he'll do the shopping.

In spite of a 'Victorian' upbringing, then, this husband has managed to change both attiude and behaviour, even though it took withdrawal from full-time employment for him to do so. I asked Ann French why she continued to assume both the major share and responsibility for housework: 'It's half habit and half guilty conscience. I've always had—well, its the way I was brought up, the way

Martin was brought up—it's my family that comes first.' This
woman thus lies somewhere between the wives first met who share
domestic work equally with their husbands, and those just met who
refuse to do so. Her upbringing pressures her to do more than half
and to accept overall responsibility. Her work experiences, and
those of her husband, encourage her to give up a large portion of the
actual work needing to be done. Similarly, her husband moved from
virtual refusal to participate in housework to help given willingly.

The sense of guilt associated with giving up complete control of
the household chores referred to by Mrs French resurfaces in Mrs
Miller's words. I put several questions to Mrs Miller in discovering
why she receives only limited help from husband and children with
domestic tasks:

Q: Do you think they'd do more if you pushed it on to them?
Mrs Miller: Oh yes—yes.
Q: Why don't you?
Mrs Miller: I don't know. That's guilt. I don't know—guilt—yes, that's
it, a bit. It's basically my responsibility. I take it on to myself.
Q: Although you're bringing an income into the house as well?
Mrs Miller: Oh yes, I actually bring in more than the rest of them, but
that's neither here nor there. It's my responsibility. I take it on to myself. I
suppose that's guilt.

But in spite of her feelings of guilt, Mrs Miller, like Mrs French,
accepts quite a lot of help from her husband with the chores. Mr
Miller undertakes all washing and ironing of his work-related laundry and irons anything 'flat' in the process. He tidies up and hoovers
without waiting to be asked. He washes windows and participates in
the monthly food shopping trip. All outside chores are his responsibility, and he lays the table and washes up the dishes: 'I say to her,
what do you want a washing-up machine for, I'm that.' And he cooks
occasionally, but only when his wife is ill or absent. Thus, if not an
equal participant, Mr Miller is at least a generous helper. His wife,
moreover, is very willing to accept his help: 'I think you should
accept any help you're given, even if it's not done the way you would
want it. I'm not obsessed with housework. You come to know how
many corners you can cut.' Mrs Miller's words provide a clear
contrast with the wives who refuse any help with housework. Mrs
Miller's standards do not exclude others from domestic chores: she
is not the only one in her home capable of doing housework satisfac-

torily. Not entirely free of traditional ideas which associate house-work with woman's work, she experiences some guilt about the chores and thus retains ultimate responsibility. But this guilt, this identification with the housewife role, does not swamp her entirely, and so she accepts 'help' from her husband. Moreover, Mr Miller, like Mr French, does not view housework as outside his role in family life. Far from refusing to offer his labour, he gives it cheerfully. With these two families, then, we end the examination of the domestic division of labour with regard to household chores, and turn to the children of cross-class families.

Part Two: Children and Childcare

In all, seventeen of the women studied have children. At the time of interviews, six had children at home under age 13 still requiring considerable care. This section examines the way in which care has been and is provided for these children, before moving on to look at the occupations some of the children have followed once grown.

Childcare

Childcare is almost always the exclusive responsibility of mothers, and cross-class mothers are no exception:

My husband is not really involved in their care or hardly at all. Either before or after work. He does no chores, just playing with them. I feed, clothe, and wash them.

Mrs Unger

Mrs Unger works part-time and earlier described her wish to assume full responsibility for both housework and childcare. There is, however, little difference between her words and those of Mrs Allan, who has one child age 5 and who has worked continuously on a full-time basis since this child's birth: 'I am responsible for all of her care—feeding, cleaning, clothes, and so on. My husband plays with her, helps her with her homework.' Or, in fact, between either of these women and Mrs Mason who took several years out of paid employment for childcare, returning to work when her youngest child was 7 years old: 'I used to worry about no one being home after school so I tried to be home for them. I was completely responsible for their care. I did all the bringing up.' Only one mother, Mrs

Fielding, reports that her husband participated fully and equally in childcare. The Fieldings, it will be recalled, also share normative understandings which govern equal participation in the domestic chores and in paid employment. For the others, the words of the three mothers above speak most accurately.

In addition to feeding, clothing and washing their children, however, these mothers must also provide adequate care for their children during the times when they are at work. The ease with which such care is provided varies, of course, with the age of the child. Three mothers returned to work very soon after the births of their children, taking maternity leave only which varied in length from 18 to 40 weeks. Thus it was necessary for these women to provide suitable care for very young children. Mrs Henley and Mrs Parker both employ registered child minders to care for their daughters. They are the only mothers studied to do so. Mrs Allan, in contrast, found a solution more common to the others: her own mother.

Mrs Allan's daughter is now aged 5 and in school. The efforts involved in providing care for her while mother works as a teacher illustrate the difficulties which reside in combining paid employment with motherhood. Mrs Allan resumed her teaching duties when her child was 8 weeks old. Each day before work she would take her daughter to her mother's home, which was at some distance from both her own home and the school at which she teaches. After work she would retrieve her daughter from her mother's care, and child and mother would go home. This routine continued until the child was aged 3 and entered nursery school. This complicated Mrs Allan's day considerably, for now she would deliver her daughter to nursery school for the morning, pick her up at lunch-time and take her to her mother's for the afternoon, return to work and finally join up with her child once again at day's end before returning home to begin preparations for the evening meal. Now that her daughter is older and in school, Mrs Allan's schedule has eased once again, and she simply drives her to and from school each day. Although using her mother as a minder increased the amount of driving Mrs Allan was required to do in order to put her child into her mother's care, Mrs Allan much preferred this system to any other one available. She says: 'I was lucky. My mother acted as a perfect substitute for me, didn't act as a granny but as a mum.'

Other women have also turned to their mothers, or their mothers-in-law, to solve their childcare problems. Mrs Unger's mother-in-law gave up her own paid employment so that Mrs Unger could return to work on a part-time basis. Mrs Unger's son is in school; her younger daughter spends 4 days a week from 8 a.m. until 2.30 p.m. with her grandmother. Like Mrs Allan, Mrs Unger is responsible for taking her daughter to her mother-in-law's home each day and for picking her up after work. Similarly, Mrs Miller's mother was instrumental in Mrs Miller's return to paid employment: 'My mother insisted I go back to teaching full-time. She was so proud of me, and felt it was such a waste. So she said: "I will look after the children and if anything goes wrong I'll be here." ' Mrs White's mother takes Mrs White's children to school on the 2 days per week that she works full-time, and gets them ready and off to school on the morning of Mrs White's nightshift work. Mrs Everett's mother-in-law lives in the house next door. When Mrs Everett's children were small, they would return home after school to their grandparents. On school holidays, they would accompany their grandparents to the country for vacations. These mothers consider themselves very fortunate to have such good care readily available. Research indicates that 'granny' or a close friend is the preferred solution to providing care for pre-school age children (Rapoport *et al*. 1977; *Social Trends*, 9, 1979). As an alternate solution, state nurseries are few and far between (Fonda and Moss, 1976; Mackie and Pattullo, 1977), and so having a mother or mother-in-law willing and able to assume caring duties relieves these mothers of considerable worry and allows them to continue working.

Other mothers were not, for various reasons, able to look to relatives for assistance with childcare. Some, like Mrs French or Mrs Jason, delayed entering the labour force until their children were old enough to care for themselves. Others, like Mrs Creighton or Mrs Light, are teachers and were thus able to arrange their work schedules to be home at the same time that their children finished school. Mrs Smith, however, has chosen to allow her two sons, aged 10 and 11, to return home alone and assume responsibility for their own care:

The kids are on their own for three-quarters of an hour after school before their father gets home. I didn't like this when I first started working, but we thought we'd try it, see if they could manage on their own. They have our phone numbers at work. And it's worked out fairly well. They have various things they have to do—like take the dogs for a walk. There's been a few skirmishes, but on the whole it's worked out quite well. It's such a short time to have anyone in to look after them—they're not babies after all.

This is not the preferred solution, though, and mothers using it report often worrying about their children being alone.

Very few of these women report any feelings of guilt about working while also having family responsibilities however. This is very much in line with the findings of the *Women and Employment* study (Martin and Roberts, 1984) in which some 70% of the women interviewed agreed that married women have the right to work if they want to, whatever their family situation (Table 12.1, p. 170). If women feel that it is their right to have paid employment, it follows that they will be less likely to feel guilty about doing so. Mrs Unger explains how work itself militates against feelings of maternal guilt:

I don't think about them at all—honestly. I don't think: I wonder what John [her son] is doing at school. But when I'm back, I'm back. At work, it's work. There's always something interesting going on at work, you don't have time to worry, to think about them. I feel no guilt about working—none at all—I feel guilty sometimes because I haven't thought about them while I've been at work, but that's not the same thing.

While Mrs Unger works part-time, and is thus home to care for her children by early afternoon each day, her words and sentiments are echoed by two other mothers who work full time:

I think about the family very little at work. The kids at school get at you right away. You get so tied up in it, you haven't got time to worry about your own problems. Sometimes I suppose I have felt a bit guilty, but it's not so bad because I've got all the same holidays. I don't know, you can't help wondering sometimes if you've done the right thing, but I dislike being home so much. I mean, if you're here [at home], you only make it worse by losing your temper because you're so agitated.

Mrs Smith

I don't see any real disadvantages to working except missing the odd thing my daughter does at her school. I try to balance home and work, but I'm paid for my job and therefore it comes first. I'm committed to it. If my daughter is ill, then my mother takes her, not me. I feel you are a better mother and wife with a job. I intend to work as long as possible.

Mrs Allan

Overall, then, although worries often exist whether or not adequate care is being provided for their children while these women are at work, few express any strong feelings of guilt about working itself. They may suffer some remorse, but generally the benefits of employment override guilt. Such benefits also seem to outweigh the obvious extra demands on these women's schedules created by combining paid work with motherhood. These mothers are almost solely responsible for both childcare within the home and for the provision of care during working hours. Like other mothers, cross-class mothers see children as primarily their responsibility. Like other fathers, cross-class fathers restrict their participation to the pleasant side of parenting: reading to children, playing with them, helping them with their homework. With respect to childcare, there is little in cross-class family life to distinguish it from any other family life. If one had expected otherwise, one would be disappointed. Participation in paid employment, even for wives whose occupations (and often incomes as well) exceed those of their husbands, does not mean a lessening of childcare responsibilities. Fathers who do not dominate their families occupationally, also do not assume a larger role *as fathers*: in cross-class families, childcare remains women's care.

Grown Children

What becomes of the children of cross-class families? In whose footsteps do they follow? If the adage reads 'like father, like son', what becomes of the sons—and daughters—of couples who present such very different occupational models to choose from as do cross-class couples? Ten parents in this study have children who have entered or are about to enter paid employment. Table 7.1 indicates the occupations these children have chosen. Although four children who are still in full-time further education are included in this table, the other children in school below the level of university or college have been excluded. While various parents expressed preferences about the future careers of their young children, none were willing to say that their preferences would in fact be what their children were likely to end up doing. As seen in this table, the children of these cross-class couples have overwhelmingly entered non-manual employment. None have followed their fathers into the same or similar occupations. If compared with their fathers, all but three have experienced upward occupational mobility; if compared with their mothers, most have remained at an equal level.

Table 7.1. *Children's Occupations by 'Class' of Occupation*

Family	Non-manual	Manual
Creighton	Teacher (f)	
	Forester (m)	
James	Chemical	
	engineer (f)*	
Jason	Chemist (m)	
	Accounts clerk (f)	
Mason	Archaeologist (f)*	
French	Insurance underwriter (m)	Storeman (m)
Light	Catering management (f)*	
Miller	Nursery nurse (f)	
	Accountant (m)	
	Geographer (m)*	
Thompson	Police constable (f)	
Henderson	Secretary (f)	Site engineer (m)
Everett	Car designer (m)	Jaguar mechanic (m)
	Civil servant (f)	

Note: Sex of child is given in parenthesis. With the exception of Light, an asterisk denotes a child presently in university; the Lights' daughter is at a College of Further Education.

A study such as this cannot, however, make any meaningful statements about the mobility chances or otherwise of 'cross-class' children. What this study can do, though, is illustrate a few of the difficulties which may attend family life when both mother and child exceed the occupational attainments of father. That such difficulties may exist is seen in Mrs White's words below. Although her children are still young, and thus not included in Table 7.1, Mrs White's worries about the future serve well at this juncture:[4]

Life would be a lot easier if he [husband] was a teacher or I was a factory worker. You would be either one thing or another then. We do have different values and push in different directions. I'd rather see my son unemployed than work in a factory like his father. The children see that we have different jobs, different values, and this affects them—confuses them—quite a lot.

Teacher and mother of two, ages 8 and 10

Sometimes the problems suggested by Mrs White are minor, a result of interests which fathers do not share with their wives and children. The Creightons are in this situation. Their daughter followed her mother into teaching and went on to marry a teacher. While Mrs Creighton is delighted to have both daughter and son-in-law share her love of teaching, sometimes their after-dinner conversations revolve entirely around teaching and thus exclude Mr Creighton, a welder, from joining in. This was reported by Mrs Creighton as a minor difficulty, however, and one which her husband has learned to live with. More serious is when the ambition of the mother conflicts with the apathy of the father and results in children doing less well than they might. Mrs Light's eldest child has left school at age 16 to enter a College of Further Education for a catering management course. Mrs Light is quite disappointed with her daughter's decision and attributes her leaving school at this early age to her husband's negative attitude towards education:

You see, this is what bothers me academically about my daughter. He [her husband] didn't study. He didn't see any need and he says as much and the children catch on to that. But then the time comes when he's unemployed because of his lack of qualifications. I try to point this out to the kids.

Mrs Light, teacher

No, I'm not worried about my kids. But I say that because of my school days. I hated every second of school, so I can't force things on them that I couldn't understand myself. So I'm not much of a pusher as far as education. My wife is the one who pushes them a lot in that direction, and enforces certain standards and expects certain results. I'm perfectly happy to see that they're not playing truant and that their behaviour at school is good. That's probably more important to me than their education.

Mr Light, hire-car driver

The reader will recall that Mr Light has experienced downward occupational mobility in comparison with his own father, and that Mr and Mrs Light suffer considerable conflict over his inability (or unwillingness) to equal or exceed her performance in the labour market. The conflict which may potentially exist in cross-class life for this couple extends into their relations as parents as well.

Disputes which revolve around educational differences may occur in other ways. Mrs Miller reports that her three children all went through times during which they felt a gap between themselves and their father because of his lack of education and subsequent occupational position:

I think the children have all gone through a stage where they looked down on their father because he was a mere plumber. But that was only when they were teenagers. When they were grown up, they realized that the man is worth far more than the word that describes him. They know he has immense knowledge that they'll never have. Immense skills in his hands that they'll never have. And they much admire him for that. When they were younger, though, having a plumber for a father wasn't as good as a surveyor or a physicist or whatever. All three asked why he hadn't had a good education and I explained it to them.

Mr Miller was aware of his children's feelings, and in his colourful way describes how he dealt with each one in turn:

There's been no conflict really. One of my sons said to me: my earning capacity will be higher than yours. My remark to that was: well, I bloody well hope so, cause it cost us enough for you to do it [university]. And that's it. I said the same to the others as well. I suppose if we were jealous natured, we wouldn't have sent them to university.

Few other fathers or mothers report that their children experienced similar problems when growing up, although it is reasonable to assume that some may have but remained silent about their feelings. Far more parents share Mr Miller's obvious delight that his children have exceeded him occupationally. Mr Jason, a turner machinist, sums up the sentiments of the others when he speaks about his university-educated son, a chemist: 'He's done marvellous. It was my wife's dream and I was terribly pleased. He's got more brains than I have.'

Problems may exist, then, but for most of the families studied these difficulties either pass with time or are overshadowed by the parents' happiness with their child's achievement. For one family, however, it seems unlikely that these problems will be resolved easily. Mr and Mrs James are each married for the second time, and live with Mrs James's two teenaged daughters. Mrs James was previously married to a college lecturer; her present husband is a forklift driver. For Mrs James this is a change she enjoys very much:

My first husband had more responsibility with his job; more calls on his time. I felt I was running everything single-handed and I don't feel that way now. Mike's job allows him much greater freedom. His job isn't a mentally responsible one, which means he can completely forget about work. There's no carry-over from one day to the next. I feel I have more of a partner now ... I chose a man without really knowing anything about him. It was attraction, physical attraction, at first. I found out about him later. I accepted that being a car worker didn't make any difference. He's him ... He is sometimes quite conscious that I'm more educated than he is, and I get quite cross with him—after all, your education isn't you as a person. All that matters is that he's a nice person and a sensitive person and if I can spell better than him—so what?

Unlike her mother, however, Mrs James's elder daughter is unable to accept that 'being a car worker didn't make any difference'. Sara James is the only child I interviewed, thinking that a 'cross-class' stepchild–stepfather relationship might be quite interesting. I spoke with her at some length, dwelling on her plans to enter an Oxbridge college and about her relations with her stepfather. I asked her how she felt about the difference in occupations between her father and her stepfather. She replied:

I don't like it. I think I resent Mike [her stepfather] because he's not as clever academically, because I can't talk to him on the same level as I can to my father. So in that respect, I tend to despise him a little bit. I mean, it's not fair—he's the person my mum's chosen; if she can get along with him—but I can't understand why she can get on well with him and I can't. On an intellectual level they have nothing in common. I don't think we are a family—at least not as a traditional family is—there's me, mum and my sister, and then there's mum and Mike.

While at age 18 one cannot be expected to have the same under-standing as an adult about what is and is not important in marital relationships, this child's difficulty in accepting her stepfather as her equal extend beyond a teenager's immaturity. At issue for Sara James are clear intellectual and social status differences. These dif-ferences impinge upon her strongly, not only in her own home but in her outside social worlds as well:

My friends all are from similar backgrounds to me. None of them have factory workers for fathers and it puts me in an awkward position when they go on about car workers. No one says anything to me about it but I don't hide the fact that he's not my father.

Sara will be leaving home soon to enter university and so these problems will fade in severity. Although I interviewed Sara after meeting her parents and was thus unaware of the extent of her unhappiness during their interviews, both mother and father reported a certain amount of difficulty in maintaining harmonious family relations in their discussions of the 'somewhat formal' rela-tionship Mike James has with his eldest stepdaughter.

At issue for Sara James, as for the Miller children in the past, are differences in occupational prestige and social acceptance. There is a social status difference between a car worker and a university teacher; between a plumber and a physicist. People react to the incumbents of these occupations quite differently. For Sara James and the Miller children, however, it is as children that they experience such social differences. They are, in effect, one step removed from the problem. After all, one does not choose one's parents, and if children really cannot cope, eventually they can leave home and start an independent existence. If, though, a child does not choose his or her parent, an adult does choose a marriage partner. And in cross-class families, men and women have, for the most part, chosen mates with very different occupational status to their own. In order for their marriages to be successful and harmonious, they must come to terms with this differing status—both between themselves, inside the family, and between themselves and the outside world. In the next chapter, the consequences of status differences are examined. Initially, emphasis is placed on rather 'subjective' issues: how do these men and women feel about the differences in their occupational achievements, and how do they interpret or explain status differences between husband and wife. But because status does not, by definition, exist only in private worlds, the chapter turns back to more concrete issues and examines how, if at all, status differences between spouses affect their social relations with others.

Notes

1. The recent OPCS Department of Employment survey, *Women and Employment: A Lifetime Perspective*, J. Martin and C. Roberts, 1984, seems to indicate that working status affects the household division of labour quite dramatically with husbands of working wives participating equally in housework to a much greater extent than previous studies would suggest. 44% of wives employed full time and 23% employed part time reported that their husbands shared housework equally with them. At first glance these figures are very surprising, but the authors go on to explain why they feel they might not be accurate and, in doing so, illustrate the difficulties involved in conducting research into family life with survey methods: 'It is likely that these figures underestimated women's share of domestic work. At the pilot stages we asked in much greater detail about an extensive range of tasks . . . we found many women who gave long lists of what they did, and whose husbands appeared to do relatively little of this work, who nevertheless said that they shared housework equally . . . There seemed to be common feeling among many women that if the tasks were shared equally when husband and wife were both at home this constituted equal shares overall

even if she was doing added work when he was not there.' (p. 100).
That there are often differences in *reports* of behaviour and *actual*
behaviour is suggested by Araji (1977) who notes that in families where
role behaviour and role attitude incongruence exists, both married men
and women express egalitarian *attitudes* but do not generally reflect these
attitudes in egalitarian *behaviour*. Both of these studies reflect the
growing trend which says that husbands ought to do more in the home,
while confirming the fact that most continue not to. By discussing both
who does exactly which chores and who assumes overall responsibility
for chores with the participants studied here, it is hoped that the problem of behaviour–attitude incongruity is overcome.

2. In this research, six out of thirty families share tasks equally between
husband and wife (although only five are discussed in the text, see
note 3 below). This is quite a large percentage of the group taken as a
whole. It is certainly a much larger proportion than found by Paloma
and Garland (1971). In their larger study of fifty-three American dual-
career families, only one couple was reported as sharing household tasks
equally. Although it may be that times have changed and more couples
do share these chores equally, or that American husbands and wives
differ from British ones, or that cross-class families differ from dual-
career families when it comes to housework, it is beyond the scope of
this research to argue definitively for either of these alternative explanations. Moreover, it is beyond this research to state that 20% or more of
husbands in cross-class families generally will share household tasks
equally with their wives. Six husbands here were found to do so—in
other research this figure could either be larger or smaller. Only additional research will be able to tell.

3. Because of the emphasis on responsibility for housework, the Smith
family has been omitted from this discussion. Mr and Mrs Smith share
tasks in ways very similar to the Robertses or the Merediths. Unlike these
other families, however, Mrs Smith feels that the work is ultimately her
responsibility: 'I suppose I am in charge—that's where it comes to the
crunch, isn't it? Who actually organizes it, plans it, and decides.' In this
way, Mrs Smith differs from Mrs Meredith (for example), who is
reported in the text as disclaiming such responsibility, and from the
others who report that such responsibility is shared with their husbands. In actual labour put in, however, Mr Smith differs only very
slightly from the other 'sharing' husbands.

4. Barth and Watson, 1967, anticipated the difficulties which potentially
reside in cross-class families with respect to children. They suggest that
' . . . it seems likely that the presence in the same nuclear family of
parents from different occupational worlds . . . would generate dilem-
mas for all family members' (p. 227). The difficulties experienced by the
Whites give substance to Barth and Watson's suggestions.

8

Social Status and Social Worlds

At the end of Chapter 7 it is suggested that Mike James's stepdaughter, Sara, has difficulty in coping with the status of his employment as a car worker, but that she experiences this difficulty at a certain distance from the problem. That is, she did not choose her stepfather and is thus not 'responsible' for his offending status position. Husbands and wives do choose each other, however, and this chapter examines how they cope with having chosen marriage partners who had, or acquired, occupational status highly divergent from their own. In the first part of the chapter, the focus is on the relationship between husband and wife alone, on how they explain and interpret the status differences which exist between them. Emphasis here is on their private, family worlds and the consequences— if any—of status differences within these worlds. But because status does not exist solely in private worlds, the second part of this chapter turns to cross-class couples' social relations with others outside their families. In the first instance, interest is on the effects of two markedly different occupations within one family on participation in social activities at the workplace, in particular on the experience of differential treatment from work colleagues. Secondly, the nature of 'cross-class' social worlds is examined, and in this examination two tenets of sociological research are found to be in opposition. Previous investigations into the sociology of friendship point towards male dominance in the friendship choices of married couples; that is, husbands are more likely than wives to initiate friendships which become part of their shared social worlds. Such research also indicates, however, a strong tendency towards status equality between friends. Quite obviously, for cross-class couples both of these findings cannot hold. If husbands in cross-class families are dominant in the choice of shared friends, then wives in cross-class families must experience status inequality in their sociable relations. If status equality is to be maintained for wives in such families, then husbands must not only forgo dominance but must also experience status inequality themselves. For these reasons, the choices cross-class couples make with regard to friends are of interest and are, therefore, discussed in some detail.

However, before beginning an examination of the effects of differential status positions on family or social worlds, it is best to make clear exactly what is meant by the idea of status itself. Considerable literature exists in the United States regarding 'status inconsistency' between spouses. For the most part, interest in status differences between husbands and wives in the United States parallels the 'unit of analysis' debate in Britain which focuses on class differences in occupational attainments between spouses. The bulk of this American literature is not referred to here, however, for in examining these studies it quickly becomes evident that researchers in the United States confuse class and status distinctions, often failing to distinguish between them, and thus render the implications of their work uncertain (see Appendix 2 for an extended discussion of this issue). Instead, this work follows the tradition of Max Weber who makes one of the clearest statements in sociological thought separating status situation from class situation although, as he notes, these two may be closely linked:

In contrast to the purely economically determined 'class situation' we wish to designate as 'status situation' every typical component of the life fate of men that is determined by a specific, positive or negative, social estimation of honor . . . This honor . . . can be knit to a class situation: class distinctions are linked in the most varied ways with status distinctions. (1946: 186–7)

Drawing on Weber, David Lockwood reiterates the conceptual separateness of these two aspects of social stratification, and stresses Weber's notion of social honour:

Class focuses on the divisions which result from the brute facts of economic organization. Status relates to the more subtle distinctions which stem from the values that men set on each other's activities . . . prestige cannot be accorded without interpersonal judgements of worth . . . (1958: 208)

Both Weber and Lockwood emphasize the separateness of class and status as well as the links between them, in particular the link between occupational position and status. As Lockwood notes, status—or prestige, to use his word—is based largely on an individual's position in the occupational structure: 'The most widely influential criteria of prestige are, therefore, those which express the occupational achievement of the individual' (1958: 209). Subtle distinctions are made between individuals, then, on the basis of the occupations those individuals hold. These status distinctions are, moreover, reflected in differing experiences of deference, acceptance or derogation, as described by Goldthorpe and Hope:

> . . . if 'prestige' is to be understood in any way approximating to its established sense within the sociological tradition, then it must refer to the position of an individual or group within a structure of relations of deference, acceptance and derogation, which represent a distinctive 'symbolic' aspect of social stratification . . . relevant to ideas of social superiority or inferiority, which the incumbency of an occupational role . . . confers. (1974: 5)

American sociologist Talcott Parsons follows Weber in separating status distinctions from those of class. And, like Goldthorpe and Hope, Parsons was aware of the honorific, symbolic aspect of social status, basing much of his writing concerning the familial consequences of unequal employment positions between husbands and wives on this feature of the stratification system. He refers to 'invidious comparisons' being made between husband and wife (1940: 80), and to the development of 'jealousy, a sense of inferiority, etc.' (1943: 192). Moreover, he locates the source of this potential marital conflict in the family's unitary existence within a community of families:

> The family as a unit has a certain order of 'reputation' in the community. Its members share a common household and therefore the evaluation of this in terms of location, character, furnishings, etc. in the system of prestige symbolism . . . (1953: 422)

For Parsons, then, it is the traditional meaning of status differences between spouses—the sense that husband and wife by virtue of their differing occupational positions might experience differing relations of acceptance, deference or derogation—which is important. And it is this traditional, 'Parsonian', sense of status differences within family life which is at issue here.

Part One: Husbands, Wives and Status Differences

The aim of questioning cross-class husbands and wives about status differences was to discover what such differences mean to them as marriage partners. Do they in fact perceive any difference at all in status between themselves and their spouses? And if they do, what are their responses to this situation? It has been noted that Talcott Parsons's understanding of status differences between spouses informs the way in which the present study was conducted. Valerie Kincade Oppenheimer also turns to Parsons in her examination of wives' labour force participation in the United States, and agrees that 'it is reasonable to assume that the social statuses of closely associated individuals tend to rub off on each other' (1982: 262). Turning away from Parsons' insistence on functional imperatives with regard to this issue, Oppenheimer suggests the existence of various mechanisms utilized to moderate or overcome the effects of status differences between family members:

> ... where a publicly known status of one member of the family group is much below that of other members, we might expect certain social mechanisms to come into play to deal with the disadvantages resulting from such a marked status inconsistency. (1982: 263)

Oppenheimer's suggested mechanisms are not augmented by reference to specific empirical findings but are of sufficient interest to serve as a basis for organizing the data presented here. In brief, the four mechanisms outlined by Oppenheimer are: (1) the offending status is given up; (2) the negative effect of the highly discrepant status is somehow neutralized; (3) the relationship with the family member who has the much lower status is broken off; (4) the family opts out of the usual evaluative system (1982: 263). With the exception of the first of these mechanisms—that is, none of the husbands or wives have given up their employment—all others are found within the cross-class families studied as husband and wife adapt to the differences in their occupations. An analysis of these reponse mechanisms will now begin, starting first with the, as yet, least-favoured option: divorce.

The Breaking of Relations

Only one cross-class couple planning to dissolve their marriage through divorce was located for interviews, although it is reasonable to assume that other cross-class marriages have ended in this way.[1] For the Ashcrofts, marked status differences in occupations contributed to their decision to divorce:

> ... there is a social stigma about being a milkman which comes out. I'm sure he's fully aware of the gap between our different occupations. I tend to make friends with a different sort of person than he does. Ideally, in a marriage, you want to be as close as possible. This isn't a healthy differ-

ence—the differences are just too great. There's a gap in occupation, in status, in education, and just generally in ability.

Mrs Ashcroft, computer programmer

I think that in the back of my wife's mind she finds it galling that I'm a milkman. But I'm really not sure if our job differences are part of the problem. It's only in the past few weeks that I've ever thought about it. I suppose so.

Mr Ashcroft, milk roundsman

Mrs Ashcroft, who initiated the divorce, has thus broken off her relationship with the family member—her husband—who has the much lower status. At the time of interviews, no other couple was considering this response to the problem of status discrepancies between spouses, although the Henleys have endured a temporary marital separation. For the majority of the other couples, some variation of the two remaining mechanisms suggested by Oppenheimer comes into play as they respond to divergent status positions.

Status Differences Neutralized

Among the couples studied the predominant response to status differences in occupational position is to neutralize these differences in some way. In general, one of two ways is chosen: either the wife brings in some other attribute of the husband or of his job which offsets his lower status; or either husband or wife changes the expected status order of their occupations so that the wife's job is lowered in status and the husband's raised. Most of the individuals using this mechanism admit the existence of status distinctions in the minds of others which favour the wives. Their ways of responding to invidious comparisons between spouses reveal how differences which are perceived to exist in the outside world can be minimized and transformed in the inside, 'personal' world:

My job probably has more status but if you think of the machinery he uses—£30,000 machines. Thousands of pounds go into farming. It is very skilled work that he's doing. Teaching can be very repetitive too. There's a lot more to his job than meets the eye.

Mrs Parker, teacher

It's very different. Oh yes, people do think there's more status [to her job]. When I was first married—before I was married actually—I did have a few people make snide remarks. Lots of people looked down their noses and said: cor, fancy marrying a plumber! But there you are: I didn't think about the differences when I married him, and I still don't because he's the very best plumber you can get. People send for him whenever there's trouble—always. He goes for miles around the countryside. He's made himself the very best. He's really absolutely superb. He's very knowledgeable.

Mrs Miller, Deputy Head teacher

Yes, people do think that. But they don't understand what he does, how complicated and skilled his job is, how much maths he must know. Just because he's not an academic, people look down on him, but he's very clever, very skilled.

Mrs Leonard, senior secretary married to a heating and ventilating fitter

These wives acknowledge that others may assign higher status to their occupations than to their husbands', but discount such ideas on the basis of their personal knowledge of the content of their husbands' work. This emphasis on the amount of knowledge possessed by their husbands is echoed in other wives' words:

I personally don't feel my job has more status. I've seen him go to night school to get his qualifications. I know what his job involves. To me he's not a manual worker—that's someone who either digs holes or does very monotonous factory work. His job is very involved and needs a lot of knowledge, basic taken-in knowledge and flair, than mine. He amazes people with his knowledge.

Mrs Meredith, administrative officer married to a heating and ventilating fitter

Although my husband's a manual worker, his skills, the things he knows, are equal to anybody, to professional people, so that I think we are on a par.

Mrs Everett, senior records officer married to a heating and ventilating fitter

I think my job has higher status but after all he's the one who gets the bank loans, has the bank accounts, so I really don't see why it should. That's why I really do disagree on this thing about qualifications. I'm only good at my job. You ask me anything about general knowledge, anything intelligent and I couldn't say it. He does manual work but he's far more intelligent than I am. I can be good at what I'm doing but I wouldn't say I'm as intelligent as he is.

Mrs Unger, MLSO married to a roof-tiler

For the most part, then, these wives understand that status difference between their jobs and those of their husbands are thought to exist, that others may see them as having much greater occupational status than their spouses. But they mute the importance of outsiders' opinions by seeing skill and knowledge in their husbands that others might miss. The 'objective' social world which assigns differing levels of status to differing occupations is thus overcome in personal, private living. These wives value the work their husbands do, the knowledge they possess.

Perhaps not surprisingly, no husbands responded to my queries about status differences by suggesting that they were much better read or more intelligent than their wives. Two husbands referred to money as a mitigating factor (as did one wife). More usual than references to money, however, is the bringing in of some attribute of the men's occupations which offsets the possibility of higher status attaching to their wives' jobs. Mr Thompson, for example, spelt out a clear and dramatic difference between the work he does as a train driver and that of his wife, a school secretary: 'I've got more responsibility than her—in my job. In her job, she can make mistakes and erase them. If I make a mistake, I can kill people'. For Mr Thompson, the greater responsibility associated with his work entitles him to greater status. Although others might disagree, for this husband his wife's non-manual occupation presents no status threat. Other husbands express similar views. Mr Everett compares his work with the office work done by his wife, and considers his of more value:

Lots of people who work in offices think that they are better than manual workers. But I do a lot more for society than a person sitting in an office.

heating and ventilating fitter

In contrast, Mr Henderson is willing to allow equality of status to the occupations chosen by him and his wife:

There's printers and there's printers. A health visitor has more status than a nurse and a colour printer has more status than a black-and-white printer. I have high status within my trade.

Interestingly enough, however, Mr Henderson is no longer a colour printer, although his wife is indeed a health visitor. Poor eyesight forced Mr Henderson to revert to black-and-white print work some years ago. In his mind, though, he retains the status of his previous position—perhaps as a way of maintaining parity with his wife?

For these men, potential differences in status favouring their wives are thus overcome by some aspect of their work. In the Allan and

Fielding households, husband and wife agree upon this mechanism for diverting superior status away from the wives' occupations. Mrs Allan disparages the idea that teachers have higher status; her husband agrees with her estimation of teachers, and goes on to note the increased status of his own work as an electrician:

Teachers used to be high status but now they are two a penny. Basically, people are not impressed by teachers.

Mrs Allan

I think things are changing. The status of teachers is changing, getting lower. There are lots of trendy people, in blue jeans with long hair, in teaching now and I think the teaching profession has suffered because of this. And the status of electricians is higher than it used to be. And it will continue to go up with the advent of complex machinery. Electricians have already split away from other trades; we attract all the brightest kids now.

Mr Allan

The Fieldings as well are agreed upon the higher status of Mr Fielding's work as a fireman. Mrs Fielding echoes Mr Thompson's remarks when she says: 'I don't risk my life as a teacher.' She went on to note: 'Many people are prejudiced against teachers, but everyone likes firemen.' Mr Fielding was willing to allow some difference in status, but generally reflects his wife's view of firemen: 'Intellectually speaking, it is probably quite true that teachers have higher status, but people seem to have a strange liking for firemen.'

In these varying ways, then, status discrepancies which could cause difficulties between husband and wife are neutralized. In their family worlds the differences which outsiders see, differences which rank the wife's occupation above the husband's, are transformed, muted. In a later section of this chapter, we will see that this outside world still impinges upon cross-class families and makes invidious distinctions between husband and wife. But between these husbands and wives just discussed, no such distinctions are made.

There is, however, an alternative way of coping with status discrepancies between spouses and that is to 'opt out' of the evaluative system altogether. Oppenheimer suggests that this is a mechanism currently open to radical left groups in society (1982: 263). The discussion which follows indicates that Oppenheimer is perhaps too restricted in her suggestion, and that this may be a way open to others as well.

Opting Out

Understanding that an evaluative system exists in society and taking oneself out of that system is an option open to anyone. As with norms about proper behaviour for husbands and wives, an individual can decide to ignore the status distinctions outsiders make. As will be seen, such decisions do not necessarily free that individual from the consequences of invidious comparisons, but the attempt may be made none the less to say: I am not a part of all that. In Chapter 9 it will be seen that this is not an uncommon reaction to issues of social class placement. With regard to social status, however, it seems less easy to opt out. In fact, throughout many of the interviews it became clear that, for some, opting out of the class system altogether is a very much easier thing to do than opting out of status hierarchies. This may well be because status distinctions impinge more directly upon individuals' perceptions than do class divisions. On more than one occasion in interviews, questions about status brought forth short, terse responses from the participant. There was considerable reluctance to discuss this issue in any depth at all, in marked contrast to very nearly all other issues touched upon. Thus, it may be that these few individuals to be discussed here do not actually opt out of the status evaluation system but instead feel directly threatened by invidious comparisons between spouses. They say that they do, however, and at present the intention is to accept their words at face value. Soon it will be seen that regardless of their explicit desire not to be a part of 'all that', they remain so—by virtue of the simple fact that status distinctions are made by others and these distinctions impinge upon their family and social worlds.

Mr and Mrs Creighton provide examples of unwillingness to discuss status differences between spouses. After speaking at some length in friendly and detailed interviews, both husband and wife suddenly became short of words when asked to consider questions of status differences. Mrs Creighton acknowledged that such differences exist in other people's minds but insisted that 'it has nothing to do with me'. She did go on to say that teachers may get good or bad reactions from others, but feels that in regard to her husband's job: 'There is no social significance to being a welder. The person is considered, not the job.' Mr Creighton was equally reticent about discussing this issue. For him, there is no issue, no problem, no difference: 'it doesn't mean a thing to me'. In very similar ways, and using similarly few words, Mr and Mrs Smith agreed that others see teachers as having higher status than telecommunications engineers but both report, more or less identically: 'other might think so, I don't, it is not a part of my life.' The Petersons were somewhat more willing to talk about status differences between their occupations and, like the Creightons and the Smiths, agree that outsiders would attribute higher status to Mrs Peterson as a teacher than to Mr Peterson as an electrician. On a personal level, though, such comparisons are not made:

I think that teachers do have more status generally, but I don't think of my husband and I in that way at all. Really, I think it is all a matter of attitudes, and ours are very similar.

Mr Peterson used fewer words than his wife, but indicated similar views by separating her from her profession: 'I'm married to Jane, not a teacher.'

These three couples agree upon 'opting out' as the solution to outsider's impressions of status differences. Their general reluctance to discuss questions of status might mean that opting out is little more for them than an uncertain defence mechanism against the invidious comparisons which they realize are made between their diverse occupational attainments. Regardless, husband and wife agree in the attempt and through their agreement manage to deflect conflict away from their marriages. For the Patons and the Henleys, no such agreement between spouses exists. While both Mrs Henley and Mrs Paton remove themselves from any system of differential evaluation, their husbands do not employ similar mechanisms and experience difficulty over the higher status accorded their wives in their local communities. The reader will recall Mr Henley's insistence that he has now adjusted to 'being Mrs Henley's husband'. Similarly, Mr Paton resents his wife's greater public recognition within the community as a district nurse. Both wives report that status differences have caused problems in their relations with their husbands, and each attempts to cope with these problems by opting out of the evaluative system. Mrs Henley not only opts out, she brings in other characteristics of her husband in an attempt to neutralize obvious differences between them:

It used to affect us more when we were first married. My husband has a good background—he's a fish out of water at work. He reads good books, listens to good music and so on. It could be a problem but I've made it not a problem—I see people as people—I see my husband as a person.

Mrs Paton also refuses to accept status distinctions between her and her husband and would not discuss this issue in relation to herself. She did note, however, that her husband attributes higher status to her work as a district nurse: 'My husband thinks there are differences, that I've got more status because of the people I know and because he's not treated very well by my colleagues.' As a result of this differential treatment towards her husband from her work colleagues, Mrs Paton's attempts to opt out of the evaluative system are not wholly successful, and conflict with her husband over her job remains. Mrs Henley has also found her attempts to reconcile status differences between herself and her husband thwarted by social relations with others. She recalls a recent incident:

There was a crisis at a party. My husband got paranoid—everyone kept asking him what he did. Everyone else was a professional. He left the party. He probably feels inferior but he shouldn't do. At this party I thought—there's a difference here. It was the first time I saw it.

Teacher married to a printer's helper

The experiences of these two wives confirm the difficulties inherent in opting out of status comparisons within the confines of private, family worlds in the face of outsiders' actions to the contrary. If others make distinctions between husband and wife, make invidious comparisons, then consequences detrimental to marital harmony may ensue. None the less, opting out of status hierarchies is one way of coping with status differences between spouses. These few individuals attempt to remove themselves from the system of status evaluation, albeit with differing degrees of success. For the most part, they acknowledge that status comparisons are made, usually to the detriment of the husbands, but they are not themselves participants in such acts. By opting out these couples, like those who neutralize status differences between husband and wife, strive towards marital harmony.

Part Two: Cross-class Social Worlds

Status differences between spouses do not, of course, exist solely in private family worlds. In continuing this investigation into the consequences of such differences, attention now turns to cross-class couples' relations with others outside their families. In the first instance, relations with work colleagues are discussed, in particular attendance (or not) at workplace social events. Secondly, the choices cross-class husbands and wives make with respect to friends, both individually and as married couples, are examined.

Husbands, Wives and Work Colleagues

In relating the problems which have occurred as a result of status differences between their own and their husband's occupations, Mrs Henley and Mrs Paton (above) both refer to differential treatment accorded them in social activities outside the home. The experiences of these two couples are probably not unusual: the outside world does differentiate between people on the basis of the occupations they hold. For cross-class couples, however, this problem is intensified by the character of the occupational differences between husband and wife. Among the many ways in which differential treatment towards such couples might occur, two differing ways were revealed during interviewing as particularly important. Firstly, as suggested by Talcott Parsons, those in the local community or neighbourhood may make invidious comparisons between husband and wife—or at least seem to do so, as reported by Mrs Henley and Mrs Paton, and confirmed by Mrs Unger: 'Oh yes, our neighbours never speak to us. They're both teachers and, you see, he [her husband] drives a truck and that's out of their class.'

In addition, and perhaps more importantly, work colleagues may discriminate against one or other spouse because of occupational differences. Predominately this occurs when husbands come into contact with their wives' work associates, but at least two wives report suffering considerable discomfort in attending social events at the workplaces of their husbands. Mrs Light's disappointment with her husband's inability or unwillingness to equal her own occupational attainments has been discussed previously. She finds her husband's occupational position especially upsetting when confronted by his co-workers and their wives at workplace parties:

Yes, if I go to a taxi do, all the wives are shopgirls or telephonists and, because I'm a teacher, I'm immediately put to the side, I'm not one of them. I can't find anything in common with them. If people aren't professional, I find it difficult to talk with them.

The resentment Mrs Light feels towards her husband for not being a professional like herself, for not coming up to her expectations occupationally and financially is very clear. The outward manifestations of his failure—including the necessity for Mrs Light to socialize at gatherings outside her chosen occupational level—serve only to exacerbate an already troubled marriage. The resentment expressed by Mrs Light surfaces again with Mrs Ashcroft, now due to divorce. However, in breaking relations with her husband, Mrs Ashcroft has, unlike Mrs Light, freed herself from attendance at somewhat humiliating social events:

As I said, there's some social stigma about being a milkman—it's fairly far down the ladder. I felt very resentful when I went to dinners at his place of work. They seat themselves according to superiority, so I'm down there with the milkmen and I know very well I could go and converse with the managers and their wives.

Computer programmer

Neither Mrs Ashcroft nor Mrs Light employs any of the coping mechanisms discussed earlier; for them, it seems that the inability to come to terms with differences between husband and wife *within* the family leads to outside occurrences assuming disproportionate importance.

Mrs Light and Mrs Ashcroft are the only wives who report such difficulties in associating with their husband's work colleagues. Much more often the problem is reversed, and husbands are either reluctant or refuse to attend functions at their wives' places of employment. Differential treatment towards husband and wife from the wife's colleagues is responsible for their reluctance:

There are people at my wife's school who look down on me but I don't think much of them anyway. It has contributed to our not going to events at the school so much.

Mr Allan, maintenance electrician

I don't go often. I know some teachers and I don't like them as people. All they ever talk about is teaching.

Mr Peterson, electrician

My colleagues find it unusual, strange that I am married to an electrician. They treat him differently. Sometimes he finds it difficult to talk to them.

Mrs Peterson

He won't go often. He avoids large numbers of teachers together . . . When he does go, it's difficult. It's the end of the conversation when people ask him what his job is.

Mrs Aston

If I go, I seek out other non-teacher spouses to talk to.

Mr Aston, garage driver

Sometimes, no direct differential treatment is received but the husbands' perceptions that such *might* occur discourages attendance:

He won't go to social events at the school because he gets inhibited with teachers. He doesn't feel comfortable. He doesn't think he's as good as teachers.

Mrs Thompson, school secretary married to a train driver

I don't think—possibly—that academics—possibly I might feel out of my depth. They tend to talk a lot of shop. I'm not going to sit on the sidelines. I couldn't participate, so—um—I wouldn't go.

Mr French, former HGV driver

I don't think the teachers treat him differently, no, not really. Teachers come from varying backgrounds. I don't think they react badly to him. I just think he feels inadequate. I think, in a way, perhaps he has an inferiority complex because he's not as well educated as I am and he tends to have difficulty in coming.

Mrs Mason, married to a plasterboard jointer

For these men, then, and others with similar views—Mr Parker and Mr Henley—attending social functions at their wives' schools is something they prefer to avoid. Differential treatment from their wives' colleagues—either real or perceived—is at the base of their avoidance. Whatever the mechanisms used by these individuals in their private, personal worlds to dispense with status distinctions between husband and wife, they cannot control the actions of others less willing to disregard such differences. The only control they have is not to go.

The eight wives discussed so far all work in schools. It is important to note, however, that differential treatment is not restricted to teachers alone, and that it occurs in regard to teachers most predominately when they are gathered in large groups. Moreover, several of the couples who do not attend social events at school have teacher-colleagues among their mutual friends, and the husbands report enjoying many leisure activities with them. Thirteen wives studied do not work in educational institutions. Of these, seven do not have social events at work to which they could bring their husbands and so the problem of differential treatment on such occasions does not arise. Among the remaining six couples, three report problems with husbands either reluctant or refusing to attend, two report their husbands' attendance under false pretences so to speak, and one reports no difficulties at all.

Mr Stone and Mr Paton are very reluctant to attend social functions: Mr Paton goes only to the annual Christmas party; Mr Stone, not at all if he can manage it:

He feels uncomfortable, people only pay attention to me.

> Mrs Paton, district nurse married to an agricultural fitter

He doesn't like my work colleagues at all. He finds them unattractive—a large body of people with little in common with him.

Mrs Stone, architect married to a former factory worker, now househusband

While these two husbands refuse to meet with their wives' colleagues, or are very reluctant at best to do so, two others solve the problem of invidious comparisons by remaining vague about the nature of their work. Mr Harvey and Mr Ashcroft have not experienced differential treatment; Mrs Harvey and Mrs Ashcroft suggest why:

People tend to assume that he is also a professional because he's my husband. At work, people know the company he works for but they don't think he actually wires up telephone exchanges. they assume he's white-collar.

> Mrs Harvey, head librarian

People at my place of work didn't really respond badly to him at all. But then, most of them didn't know what he does. He's very extroverted, you see, and gets away with it.

> Mrs Ashcroft, computer programmer married to a milkman

The point should by now be clear: cross-class differences in occupational standing between husbands and wives can cause problems in associating with others. Differential treatment, feelings of inferiority, or a simple lack of things to talk about with spouses' work colleagues all flow from such differences. These problems are not, of course, unique to cross-class marriages, and one can think of several other situations in which they might occur—most notably, perhaps, at gatherings of dual-career couples and their work associates who are married to non-employed wives. But while housewives might, in association with professionally employed wives, suffer similar experiences to those of cross-class husbands, there is far more social approval for their role in society than for men who do not at least equal their wives' occupational accomplishments. Social gatherings which bring together cross-class husbands and husbands who fulfil the convention of male occupational dominance accentuate the gaps in status between cross-class spouses, and are thus to be avoided.

Of course not all cross-class husbands and wives report difficulties in attending social events at the women's workplaces. Some few report no problems at all in doing so, nor in attending similar events at the men's workplaces. Mrs Leonard, for example, notes that her co-workers are married to a variety of manual and non-manual workers, and so she and her husband 'fit in very well'. In addition, Mrs Meredith reports:

Maybe I'm blind to it, but because we have no problems about the differences between us, it doesn't exist as a problem between us and the outside world. Social events at his place tend to be very large events. We go and take friends from my side and go as a group. We tend to go to more events at my work. Mine are more fun. There are more people that my husband relates to from my circle than the other way round. He is drawn more into my circle.

Administrative officer married to a heating and ventilating fitter

Mrs Meredith makes an interesting point about her husband in her reply: 'He is drawn more into my circle.' The emphasis so far in this discussion of status differences has been on the differential treatment many cross-class husbands experience in socializing with their wives' colleagues. As Mrs Meredith notes, however, her husband finds her work associates more interesting than his own. In fact, among the families studied there are just as many husbands who are reluctant or refuse to participate in social events at their own places of employment as there are who avoid such gatherings at their wives' workplaces:

I find my workmates and their wives dull. We have very little in common.

Mr Fielding, fireman

No, not at all. They're all football orientated and snooker—going to pubs.

That's the main reason I don't see them. I'm not interested in these activities.

Mr Smith, telecommunications engineer

We never went. We wouldn't have fitted in. I was very much an outsider with my background and attitudes.

Mr Stone, former assembly line worker

Never, they're a funny bunch. Everyone's different but I have nothing in common with any of them.

Mr Everett, heating and ventilating fitter

The comments above are typical of the fourteen husbands who choose not to attend social functions at their own workplaces. Furthermore, of these fourteen men, only three see workmates socially away from work, while six include their wives' colleagues among their joint friends. It should be noted, though, that non-attendance at workplace social events is not uncommon among manual workers. In the *Affluent Worker* studies, it was found that only a minority of workers participate in leisure activities at the workplace. Only one in four skilled workers, and less than one in ten semi-skilled workers in Luton, took advantage of any workplace social facilities, including the workers' bar (Goldthorpe *et al.*, 1968: 90–2; 1969: 72). Cross-class husbands, however, seem to turn away from workplace social events for very different reasons from those given by affluent workers. Where the former cite different interests and different expectations, the latter exhibit active dislike of the workplace itself (1968: 92). As the next section of this chapter demonstrates that cross-class husbands live almost entirely in non-manual social worlds, their withdrawal from intimate association with their manually employed co-workers should not be surprising.

This withdrawal by husbands from social events at their own workplaces is not spread evenly across the families, however. Referring back to the typology of social origins of cross-class families presented in Chapter 3, we find that the husbands who do not attend such social events come predominately from two 'types' of family. All husbands who have been downwardly mobile, and all husbands whose wives experienced upward mobility after marriage, refrain from socializing at their own workplaces. In addition to these men, only two other husbands may be included among the nonattenders: Mr Henderson, whose social activities are dominated by his church membership, and Mr Young, whose wife was upwardly mobile occupationally prior to marriage. In regard to the husbands who have experienced downward occupational mobility, the reasons behind their non-attendance are relatively easy to adduce: these men are all from middle-class homes; all socialize with their wives in exclusively middle-class circles. The 'status gap' between their work lives and their family lives is quite marked for these men, and so workplace social activities no doubt hold few attractions for them. In regard to the other husbands (Mr Henderson apart) adducing reasons for their non-attendance is a much more speculative task. These men, and their wives, all come from working-class family backgrounds; their wives have brought them into cross-class families by virtue of upward occupational mobility. And, Mrs Young apart, they have done so after several years of marriage. One 'story' that one might tell about their unwillingness to mix socially with large groups of manually employed men (like themselves) is that these husbands look 'upwards' socially. Not having been able themselves to achieve middle-class occupations, they have supported (encouraged?) their wives' efforts to do so, and with their wives think themselves people apart from the working-class world of their workmates. Perhaps. On the other hand, given the small number of families being considered, it may just be coincidence that all of the husbands who have come to be partners in cross-class marriages in this fashion refrain from socializing with large groups of their work associates. In any event, refrain they do: work and workmates are, for them, a thing apart from family life.

Friendship Choices of Cross-class Couples

During interviews, all husbands and wives were asked about the people with whom they most often spend time socially, both as individuals apart from husband or wife, and jointly with their spouses. These friendship choices are now examined. Cross-class couples' relations with others socially are interesting for at least two related reasons. First, such couples straddle the manual/non-manual boundary and thus have opportunities to form friendships with others from two distinct occupational worlds. Previous research indicates a strong tendency towards occupational similarity in friendship choices. With cross-class couples' mutual friends, however, the question is: similar to whom, husband or wife?

That friends are chosen from among status equals is very nearly an axiom of sociological research. Study after study has demonstrated that few sociable relationships cross class boundaries.[2] Moreover, the fact of differential social association has formed the basis of many investigations, not only of family life, but of the class structure itself. Prior to undertaking the *Affluent Worker* studies, Goldthorpe and Lockwood wrote:

... we wish to draw attention to the importance of one particular issue which should, perhaps, be made the focal point of inquiry; that is, the extent to which differences in status in the occupational or work milieu carry over into community and associational contexts, and exert an influence here on the structuring of social relationships. (1963: 139)

Several years later, Stewart, Prandy and Blackburn reaffirmed the importance of friendship patterns by constructing new occupational scales based upon respondents' friendship choices: 'we believe that friends most closely reflect the stratification positions of respondents' (1980: 33). Although the aim of these authors was to reassess the stratification system of modern Britain, in the final analysis what they achieved was a restatement of the strength of differential social association:

We take our findings to be, first, a strong indication of a structuring, in stratification terms, of patterns of association on the basis of friendship, and only second, a less than entirely adequate scale of stratification arrangements. (1980: 56–7)

Stewart, Prandy and Blackburn's findings are complemented by Goldthorpe *et al.* in the Nuffield study of occupational mobility:

What we document here, as various other inquiries have done before, is the extent to which in modern Britain segregation, or at all events, highly differential association, on class lines is a dominant feature of the structure of sociability. (1980: 180)

The impetus behind such investigations, and the basis of class segregation in patterns of sociability is an inexorable pressure towards status equality between friends. Almost by definition, friends are those who are chosen freely and from among equals:

There is one demonstrable contingent criterion which is of great significance for the actual formation and persistence of friendly relationships—namely that of perceived equality of status. Why this should be so is obvious. Not only do relationships of superiority and inferiority or superordination and subordination hinder the development of a proper understanding between individuals but the very concept of hierarchical distinctions tends to subvert almost all of the contingent factors revealed by analysis to be significant in the formation of friendships. Without perceived equality there exists the suspicion of patronage or clientism; without equality the negotiation of reciprocity becomes difficult; without equality the occasions for interaction are often severely limited; without equality mutual understanding requires more work to be done. (Dixon, 1976: 6)

If status equality thus describes friends, then the friends of cross-class couples are their status equals. Examination of their friendship choices reveals, therefore, the places cross-class families occupy in the stratification hierarchy.

In addition to status equality between friends, however, previous research suggests that husbands are much more likely than wives to be the initiators of joint friendships. In their study of American middle-class couples, Babchuk and Bates (1963) found substantial support for the hypothesis that husbands initiate more joint friendships than do wives: not only are husbands' friends from before marriage more likely to remain mutual friends after marriage than wives' friends, but husbands are also more likely than wives to initiate new friendships after marriage. In Britain, support for Babchuk and Bates comes from Bell (1968) and Edgell (1980). Bell confirms male dominance in friendship choices, and goes on to note that husbands' work relationships are a major source of married couples' mutual friends. Edgell found husbands to be dominant in one-half of the middle-class couples studied, while in the remaining half husbands were more likely to initiate the couples' close friendships and wives initiate more casual ones. Allan (1979), however, offers only partial support for the pattern of male dominance in the friendship choices of his middle-class couples. He suggests, though, that his sample size was too small to show marked consistency with the expected pattern.[3] The findings of this research are quite clear, however, and in sharp contrast to these previous studies. Wives, not husbands, dominate the friendship choices of cross-class couples. This suggests that previous research which indicates male dominance in friendship choices actually indicates status dominance. It is not that husbands are more likely than wives to dominate *friendship choices*, but that husbands are more likely than wives to dominate *occupationally*. Reverse their positions in the occupational hierarchy, and their positions of dominance in initiating joint friendships reverse as well.

However, before presenting the friendship choices of the families, a brief explanation about the ways in which data were collected from respondents, and the method of data presentation, is in order. Each person interviewed was asked to provide details about three friends seen socially on a regular basis, first as individuals away from husband or wife and, secondly, jointly with husband and wife. Friends could overlap these two categories, and there was no restriction on including relatives other than spouses and children. The details provided included the occupation of the friend named and that of his or her spouse if married, the nature of meeting this friend, the types of activities undertaken together and how often these occurred. Eleven wives and eight husbands were unable to name any individual friends with whom they socialized independently of their spouses. Two additional families were unable to name any friends seen jointly. The majority of the remaining couples named between one and three friends in each category, with four husbands and four wives naming more than three joint friends. In presenting these data, the format changes somewhat from previous chapters in that the thirty families are presented as a group, with individual families discussed only when particularly interesting. In addition, as the primary concern is with the activities of husbands and wives together, greater emphasis is placed on the friends they see jointly—their mutual friends—than on their individual social relationships.

Nearly half of the husbands and 40% of the wives interviewed were unable to name any friends with whom they spend time socially away from their spouses, or see in other than single context association. In this regard, single context association refers to participation in activities in one location or for one purpose only. Table 8.1 distributes the husbands and wives according to the occupational category of friends seen individually. Clearly revealed by this table is the tendency for occupational status equality to be maintained by cross-class husbands and wives in the development of individual friendships. No wives report having chosen only others with manual occupations as their personal spare-time associates. As individuals, more than half the wives studied socialize exclusively with others employed at levels similar to their own occupations. Moreover, the

Table 8.1. *Distribution of Cross-class Husbands and Wives by Occupation of Individual Friends*

Spouse	No. friends named	Single context only	Manual only	Mixed manual and non-manual	Non-manual only
Husbands	8	4	10	3	1 *N* = 26
(%)	(46)		(38)	(12)	
Wives	11	1	0	2	16 *N* = 30
(%)	(40)			(7)	(53)

Note: The four husbands who declined interviews are not included in this table.

two women reporting 'mixed' manual and non-manual friends—Mrs Henley and Mrs Ashcroft—were in fact including social relationships more likely to become part of their past friendships than to remain so in the future. Mrs Henley referred to one manually employed woman friend, a cook who is married to the caretaker at her school She noted that she had recently begun to withdraw from association with this woman, and did not expect to maintain relations with her in the future. Mrs Ashcroft reported spending time on her own with two manually employed friends of her husband; with divorce now occurring, she does not know if she will maintain friendly relations with these two. As individuals, then, the wives socialize almost exclusively in non-manual worlds.

In contrast, the husbands reporting individual friends socialize predominately with others from the manual world. Ten of the fourteen men mentioning friends seen in other than single contexts only restrict these friendships to persons of equal occupational status to their own. The one husband reporting only non-manual friendships is Mr Norton, a former social worker now disabled and employed as a kitchen helper. The three men reporting 'mixed' friendships include Mr Stone, a university graduate, former factory worker and now househusband, who keeps contact with friends from his university days; Mr Fielding, a fireman, who named one of his wife's work colleagues, a teacher, among his individual friends; and Mr Barnes, a lorry driver, who mentioned two local villagers known to him since childhood, both of whom are employed in non-manual work. Apart from these, no other non-manually employed individuals were mentioned as individual friends by the manually employed husbands studied. This contrast between husbands and wives regarding their choices of individual friends serves to underline the strength of the pressure towards status equality among friends. By virtue of their marriages, all husbands and wives have ties to both manual and non-manual worlds; they have opportunities to choose friends from either world. And yet, as individuals, they choose from only one or the other. They choose others most like themselves.

This contrast between husbands and wives serves also to underline the importance of status rather than husband dominance in friendship choices. Although there is near equality in the likelihood of wives having non-manually employed individual friends and husbands having manually employed ones, when it comes to joint friends there is no such equality. Among the shared friends of cross-class couples non-manually employed individuals dominate. Husbands and wives do not choose equally from their occupational worlds when choosing joint friends, nor do they choose predominately from the husbands' occupational level. When choosing joint friends, they choose 'upwards' so to speak; they choose the status equals of the wives.

Table 8.2 redistributes the families in a manner similar to Table 8.1 but concerns instead the friends that husbands and wives socialize with together. Four families have been omitted from this table but will be discussed subsequently in the text. They are: the

Table 8.2. *Distribution of Cross-class Families by Occupation of Joint Friends*

Non-manual only	14*	}		Manual only	2	}	
			18				8
Non-manual plus cross-class[+]	4	}		Mixed manual and non-manual	6	}	

$N = 26$.

*This number includes one family naming a manual friendship which is enjoyed in one context only, a workers' social club.

[+]The category 'cross-class' refers to couples in which husbands are employed in manual work and wives in higher level non-manual or professional employment.

Hendersons, who referred only to others seen in single-context association at church; the Masons and the Creightons, who were unable to name any mutual friends at all; and the Whites, who socialize in quite separate circles—Mrs White in non-manual social worlds, Mr White in manual. In addition, the category cross-class has been added to the table. This category refers to families similar to the research families in which husbands are employed in manual work and wives in higher level non-manual or professional employment. In Table 8.2 the families have been divided into two groups: those who have *only* non-manually employed friends, or non manually employed *and* other cross-class couples like themselves as joint friends; and those who have manually employed individuals among their friends. Other cross-class couples are included on the non-manual side of this table as a result of the findings of this study which argue for their inclusion in non-manual social worlds.

Table 8.2 demonstrates quite convincingly the predisposition for cross-class couples to socialize with others of occupational status similar to that of the wives. Two families alone restrict their joint friendships to only manually employed individuals, whereas fourteen families have only non-manually employed mutual friends. Table 8.3 re-emphasizes the non-manual nature of cross-class social worlds by showing the occupational distribution of all joint friends mentioned in interviews. In this table 'mentioned by both' indicates that both husband and wife named the particular friends as joint friends, while 'wife only' and 'husband only' indicates joint friends referred to by only one spouse in interviews.

Table 8.3. *Occupational Distribution of Joint Friends*

	Non-manual	Cross-class	Manual
Mentioned by both	26	4	12
by wife only	24	3	5
by husband only	11	0	4
Total	61	7	21
(%)	(68.5)	(8)	(23.5)
	(76.5)		

N = 89 (couples counted as one unit).

As shown in Table 8.3, the great majority of cross-class couples' joint friends are in non-manual occupations. If one combines manually employed individuals and couples with other cross-class couples, then more than three quarters of all joint friends referred to are accounted for. Manually employed individuals, and couples without a spouse in non-manual work, account for only about one-fifth of the respondents' joint friends. It should be noted here that no instances of manually employed women married to non-manually employed men were cited as among the friends of these cross-class couples. In fact, only three women in manual employment were mentioned as friends: the cook referred to earlier in connection with Mrs Henley; a cleaner married to a car worker, with whom the Jameses socialize at the factory workers' club every fortnight; and a seamstress married to a factory worker, a friend of Mrs Jason since the days prior to her marriage some years ago. Of the remaining fourteen married couples included as manually employed, two wives are in junior white-collar jobs and twelve are full-time housewives. Similarly, among the wives included as non-manually employed friends, all are either full-time housewives or employed at levels similar to their husbands. Thus, the wives of the cross-class families studied here have virtually no social contact at all with women employed at levels substantially below their own. As individuals, they choose women friends in occupations similar to or identical with their own. As wives, they choose joint friends who may include men employed at the same or similar level as their husbands; they are unlikely, however, to include women employed at this level.

In addition to the occupational status of cross-class wives dominating the friendship choices of cross-class couples, the wives themselves dominate in initiating joint friendships. Table 8.4 redis-

Table 8.4 *Origin of Joint Friendships by Initiator and Occupation of Friend*

Initiator	Non-manual	(%)	Cross-class	Manual	(%)	Total	(%)
Wife	38	(62)	4	8	(38)	50	(56)
Husband	17	(28)	3	10	(48)	30	(34)
Jointly	6	(10)	0	3	(14)	9	(10)
Total	61	(100)	7	21	(100)	89	(100)

$N = 89$.

tributes the friends shown in Table 8.3 by originator of friendship. As might be expected, wives are more likely than husbands to initiate non-manual friendships; husbands more likely than wives to initiate manual ones. Cross-class friendships are more or less equally initiated by both spouses. Table 8.4 demonstrates the considerable dominance of cross-class wives in initiating friendships which become shared between husband and wife. It shows that more than half of these couples' mutual friends were originally introduced into their social worlds by the wives, while only just over one-third were introduced by the husbands. As noted earlier, female dominance in friendship choices among married couples is quite uncommon in sociological research findings. Among cross-class couples, though, male dominance in friendship choice quickly gives way to status equality for wives. This suggests that status similarity is of greater importance in friendship choices than is the sex of the family member occupying the highest position in the occupational hierarchy. Allow wives to dominate occupationally, and they will dominate friendship choices as well. And through this dominance, cross-class couples will come to live in predominately middle-class, non-manual social worlds.

As noted by Bell (1968), the workplace is a potential source of mutual friends for married couples. Table 8.5 below indicates the sources of friendship for cross-class couples by the initiator of these relationships. Like Bell's husbands, the workplace is the main source of friends for cross-class wives, with 22 out of 50 mutual friendships initiated by wives formed at present or past places of employment.

As this table indicates, husbands as well look to work associates for friends but to a much lesser extent than their wives.[4] For the

Table 8.5. *Origin of Joint Friendships by Initiator and Circumstances*

Initiator	Work	School	University/ College	Relative	Other	Total
Wife	22	2	5	9	12	50
Husband	9	7	1	0	13	30

$N = 80$.
Note: Nine friendships which were initiated jointly are omitted from this table.

husbands, 'other' circumstances are in fact more important sources of friends than their workplaces. These other circumstances include a variety of activities such as sports, an interest in music, church attendance, army service, mending cricket nets, and visiting the pub. In meeting people in these circumstances and expanding friendly contact with them to include wives and a variety of other activities, cross-class husbands differ considerably from other manually employed men. One consistent finding in studies of working-class sociability is the restriction of friendly activities to the original context. In other words, the friendships formed by manually employed men do not usually 'flower out' into new settings and activities (cf. Allan, 1979, especially Chapter 6). For manually employed cross-class husbands, however, such 'flowering out' of relationships is quite usual. All of the friends mentioned by the research couples are enjoyed in a variety of settings and activities, including dinners at pubs and in restaurants, dining in each others' homes, seeing concerts, films and sporting events, and just visiting. Several couples mentioned taking holidays together with their mutual friends. The activities undertaken with the thirteen friends met by husbands in 'other' circumstances—as well as with friends met at school or work—are no exception to this 'flowering out'. Given, however, that cross-class couples' sociable relations are predominately non-manual, or middle class, in occupational status, it should not be surprising to find that their pattern of activities with these friends is middle class as well.

Table 8.5 indicates one marked difference in the source of friendships between husbands and wives. Nine relatives are included among the friendships initiated by wives while none are included among those initiated by husbands. These relatives are invariably sisters or brothers of the wives, and are socialized with in the same manner as friends met in different circumstances. It should not be surmised from this difference between spouses that the relatives of cross-class wives are closer in relationship to the families than are the relatives of cross-class husbands. During interviews both husband and wife were asked about contact with their relatives. While one might have imagined potential problems between cross-class couples and their respective families of origin because of their occupational differences, no such problems were reported. There is, moreover, little pattern at all between the families, their social backgrounds, and their relations with kin. About one-third report close ties with relatives on either or both sides, another third report rather loose ties with kin, and the remaining third fall somewhere in between. As it turns out, wives' relatives are more likely than husbands' to be seen socially as friends but this should not in any way suggest disaffection with husbands' kin.[5]

This very nearly completes the examination of cross-class social worlds. However, before continuing to place cross-class families in the wider world through discussions of trade union activity, political preferences, and social class identification, the social worlds of a few interesting families will be highlighted. In the previous examination, four families were omitted from discussion: the Hendersons, Creightons, Masons, and Whites. The first three of these families report no mutual friends; the Whites, virtually separate social worlds.

For the Hendersons, the lack of mutual friends cannot be attributed to their differences in occupational attainment, nor to any consequences which might flow from such differences. Mr and Mrs Henderson are active participants in the Pentecostal Church and this membership dominates all of their social relationships. Husband and wife did cite various people seen socially for cups of tea or visits, but all of these activities were combined in some way with their duties as church members. Unlike the Hendersons, however, differences in occupational attainment between spouses impinge directly upon the social relationships of the remaining three families.

During my interview with Mrs Creighton she was very reluctant to discuss status differences between her and her husband or their consequences for her marriage. After the interview was finished, however, and Mrs Creighton and I were having a friendly cup of tea together, she began to speak more freely about such differences. Mrs Creighton said that she and her husband had never really had many friends over the years and she attributed this to the different occupations they had held (Mrs Creighton was a deputy Head teacher; Mr Creighton a welder). What friends they did have seemed to have come mainly from her husband's workplace, but Mrs Creighton had never known any of these men's wives. Furthermore, Mr Creighton used to feel 'out of place' among his wife's work colleagues, and so Mrs Creighton had 'kept her distance' from colleagues; had not been 'overly friendly' nor ever 'invited people home'. For this couple, then, cross-class life has meant a life without many friends; a life described by Mrs Creighton as 'somewhat lonely'.

Differences between husband and wife have also meant few mutual friends for Mr and Mrs Mason. Although pressures on leisure time as a result of full-time employment, two children, and home-making responsibilities were cited by Mrs Mason as partly responsible for her lack of joint social activities with her husband, she also referred to differences in intellectual ability between spouses as a contributing factor:

We're very different intellectually. I know it; it bothers me. It doesn't cause open conflict, just frustration within me. Possibly within him as well, but he tends not to show it. I find it very frustrating that he doesn't want to pick up a book; or if I suggest to him that he read something, he doesn't want to know. Socially, he doesn't know how to talk to any of my friends. I can talk to his friends but he doesn't know what to say to any of mine. I think it's easier for a person to talk *down* than to be able to talk *up*.

MLSO married to a roof-tiler

And so, although husband and wife have friends they see away from each other, they have none whom they share. The differences in ability which led this' wife into teaching and her husband into the building trade, and thus to the creation of a cross-class marriage, prevent the development of mutually satisfying joint friendships. Living herself with the consequences of such differences, Mrs Mason hopes that life will be different for her two daughters:

There is one thing I would like different for my daughters. I would like them to marry men of equal or above intelligence. Because I think it can be very frustrating when someone cannot grasp what you mean, or have the same sort of sensitivity that you have. I wouldn't want it for them.

Where intellectual differences have led to no mutual friends for the Masons, similar differences have created two quite separate, and distinct, social worlds for Mr and Mrs White. The Whites pursue completely different activities in their leisure time. Mrs White is active in a variety of 'good causes': animal welfare rights, the ecology movement, pacifism, and the anti-abortion campaign, as well as enjoying ballet, classical music, and art. Mr White is a sportsman. He spends most of his spare time in athletic activities with other men or with his children. He plays squash and football, coaches a children's football team, and spends time pubbing with his workmates. These two separate spheres of interest are reflected in both individual and joint friendships mentioned by the Whites. As individual friends, Mrs White referred to three professionally employed individuals, Mr White to three work associates. As a couple, each spoke of the 'wife's friends' and the 'husband's friends'. These two groups of people are never mixed, are thus not known to each other, and come from occupational levels which correspond to those of husband and wife. And although Mrs White will accompany her husband into 'his world' from time to time for socializing, it is more usual for Mr White to enter 'her world' and to participate in activities with Mrs White's friends. Even this, however, does not occur very often, as Mr White notes: 'There are her friends and there are my friends and they don't mix. We have very different interests, I don't usually interfere with what she's doing.'

At the base of the White's separate social worlds are perceptions of society which link occupational attainment with cultural aspirations. In discussing the various strata which she perceives as making up society, Mrs White, a teacher, referred to three distinct groups: those who naturally enjoy 'high culture', i.e. theatre, ballet, art, and museums; those who aspire toward such enjoyment but to whom this enjoyment does not come 'naturally'; and those with no aspirations in cultural directions at all. For Mrs White, these three groups loosely correspond to various occupational groups: highly educated doctors, professors, teachers and so on in the first two groups, and uneducated factory workers and the like in the third group. In her own life, Mrs White and 'her friends' fall into either the first or second group; her husband and 'his friends' fall into the third group. In discussing this same issue, Mr White, a printer, echoed his wife's view of the world. He too placed his friends in the last group—at bingo and in pubs—and went on to say that he has tried to be 'upwardly mobile culturally' but thinks it too difficult a task to do successfully. Mr White attributes his failure only partially to his own lack of interest in 'high culture', and suggests that a large part of the difficulty lies with those 'above him', so to speak, who think they have little in common with a factory worker. And among those 'above him' are, perhaps not surprisingly, his wife's friends.

In some respects, then, the Whites typify cross-class family life at its most extreme. Husband and wife see a world populated by entirely different types of people, loosely based upon the occupations these people pursue and more generally upon their cultural interests and aspirations. Occupationally husband and wife live in different parts of this world; socially, they seldom visit each other. If a cross-class family might be thought of as the bringing together of two worlds into one life, the Whites thus show that, within this one life, these two worlds may yet be very separate.

The Whites end the discussion of cross-class social worlds. It has become clear that these worlds are, for the most part, middle class in composition and character. Status differences between husband and wife which are transformed and muted in private, personal living are, in social relations with others, resolved in favour of the wife's position in society. Wives in cross-class families maintain status equality in friends chosen both individually and as marriage partners. And while men in cross-class families tend to maintain status equality with their individual friends, as husbands they enjoy upward status mobility through friendships shared jointly with their wives. In the next chapter we continue to look at cross-class families in wider social contexts, with a consideration of their political preferences, attitudes towards trade unions and social class identifications.

Notes

1. In the study of family life, locating only *intact* families for study is always a problem. Oppenheimer (1982: 263) suggests separation and divorce as one way of dealing with wife occupational superiority. Moreover, a longitudinal study of 1,089 women in dual-worker marriages lends support to Oppenheimer's suggestions. Evidence from this study shows that, in marriages where the wife's status was equal to or higher than her husband's, divorce was more likely to occur: 15% of marriages with wives of higher occupational status and 14% with wives of equal occupational status ended in divorce, compared with only 9% of marriages in which the wives had lower occupational status than their husbands. See Hiller and Philliber, 1982: 54.

2. Cf. Allan, 1979 for a review of the sociology of friendship. Among the studies discussed by Allan are Lazarfeld and Merton, 1954: William, 1956; Stacey, 1960; Klein, 1965; Goldthorpe *et al.*, 1969; and Hill, 1976.

3. Allan interviewed twenty-two female and nineteen male respondents of whom ten men and eleven women had middle-class occupations (or, in the case of the women, were married to men in middle-class occupations). He reports that among these middle-class respondents there was 'no consistent pattern' (1979: 61).

4. Cf. Goldthorpe, 1980: 186, table 7.4. Cross-class men are less likely than the manual workers surveyed by Goldthorpe to see workmates outside the workplace.

5. In regard to relations with kin, Allan, op. cit., notes: 'What appears to be the most banal feature of parent–adult/child relationships is in fact the most significant: in one form or another these relationships persist.

Notwithstanding the difficulty of interpreting them, a major corollary of the tables of contact rates produced in many studies is that where parents are alive the enormous majority of these relationships are extant. It is most unusual for them to lapse' (1979: 94). Cross-class relations with kin are no exception to this. Even in those families where relatives are seen infrequently, contact is maintained by telephone or post. No instances were discovered where relations had been broken completely.

9

Social and Political Perspectives

Before bringing this analysis of cross-class families to a close, there remain for consideration two issues of some importance. The first of these issues concerns the ways in which cross-class families see themselves as members of a class-stratified society. Does the concept 'cross-class' have meaning for the men and women of these families? Or have I, as a researcher, imposed upon them a label which has no meaning and which they would reject?[1] The answer to these questions will be sought in an examination of the class images held by the respondents, in particular where they see themselves fitting into the class structure. As with perceptions of status differences between husbands and wives, the emphasis with respect to perceptions of class differences is on locating those consequences unique to cross-class families. The aim is therefore to discover if marriage to a man or a woman with an occupation markedly different in class terms to one's own occupation has any special or particular consequences for individual class imagery and self-placement. The second issue concerns how cross-class husbands and wives orient themselves to the existence of trade unions and political parties. Outside of family life, outside the world of friends and relatives, there is a world of political partisanship and trade union activity, towards which attitudes and actions are often thought to be shaped by class position. It is a world which needs to be accommodated in some way, which cannot easily be ignored. Does cross-class marriage in any way shape the attitudes and actions of its incumbents towards these 'public' aspects of life? An examination of the perspectives which inform the respondents' participation politically and in trade unions attempts to answer this question. Drawing out the implications of cross-class marriage for the development of socio-political perspectives brings to a close the examination of cross-class families.

Part One: Class Imagery and Identification

The images individuals hold of the society in which they live have often caught the interest of sociologists. Martin Bulmer describes the foci of this interest:

In a stratified industrial society, how do members of different social strata come to form, to develop and to hold, images or mental representations of that structure? How do men perceive and evaluate a world in which marked objective inequalities of class and status exist? What is the relationship between such objective differences as exist in terms of income, wealth, life changes, labour market situation or education, and subjective perceptions of the system of social stratification in industrial society? What is the nature of industrial man's *Weltanschauung*? (1975a: 3)

And, one might well add, what becomes of industrial man's *Weltanschauung* when it is his *wife* who surpasses him in education, income, labour market situation and status?[2] What are the class images of cross-class men? Do these images vary from those held by their wives; do their marriages condition or affect these images? What are the class images of cross-class wives? What effect does cross-class marriage have on the *Weltanschauung* of industrial woman? These questions are addressed in this section. In addition, however—and more importantly perhaps—where cross-class husbands and wives place themselves in society, where they see themselves fitting into the class images they hold, is examined in order to understand how cross-class marriage acts upon or conditions the views these men and women have of themselves as members of a class stratified society.

Cross-class Images of Class

Very few of the cross-class respondents interviewed denied the existence of social classes. Only four individuals out of fifty-six refused to categorize people or groups on this basis. Two of these four, Mr and Mrs Fielding, see society as divided into layers on grounds of income and lifestyle differences, but refuse to call these layers 'classes' or to assign others (or themselves) to any particular layer:

There are different types of people—some rich, some poor. You get ignorant people all across the income spectrum, and likewise you get caring people all across.

Mrs Fielding

In addition, Mrs Aston denied the existence of classes, while acknowledging that others might disagree with her:

I think people think that there are classes but I don't. People are equal . . . If I have to say something, I'd say 'working class because I work', even though others would call me middle class because of my job and where I live.

Although Mrs Aston used conventional class terminology in our discussion, she would not describe nor define the categories 'working class' and 'middle class'. For her, they are meaningless words. In contrast, Mr Meredith sees too many classes in existence to be able to distinguish between them:

> I think there's a complete run of classes all the way up. I don't think there are just two classes—us and them—or middle, upper and lower and so on. I think there is a steady stream up which is very blurred and I don't think you can differentiate . . . I really don't have a view of separate classes.

These four apart, all other respondents were willing to stratify society into social classes; were willing to place others, if not themselves, into hierarchical divisions.

In general, few differences in class images exist between the husbands and wives studied. Like Mrs Aston, the majority of respondents used conventional class terminology in describing society; for them, society is divided into upper, middle and working or lower classes. Hoping to avoid putting images into their minds which did not previously exist, I waited for them to name the classes they perceived. This was done quite readily. Predominantly, three or more classes were referred to: the upper class (or gentry, aristocracy); a middle class often with one or more layers, e.g., upper middle, lower middle, middle middle; and a similarly layered lower or working class. Where size of class was mentioned, the respondents invariably put themselves into the largest class whether it was called the middle or the working class. Some few respondents used the words 'professional class' or 'white-collar class' or 'skilled working class'. Regardless of the terminology used, however, the meaning was much the same: society is stratified into layers which are hierarchically arranged (cf. Eichler, 1980: 100).

In discussing the determinants of class location, a few differences between husbands and wives became obvious. Wives were more likely than husbands to see multiple determinants of class position, especially occupation and education. Husbands referred to money or income somewhat more frequently than wives. However, few husbands and wives did not refer in some way to occupation as an important determining factor of class position for individuals and groups. Two-thirds of the wives and one-half of the husbands interviewed considered occupation as a determining factor. But while only one wife saw occupation alone as a sufficient cause of class position and all other wives consider that occupation acts in tandem with other variables, five husbands see occupation as acting alone. However, the most remarkable difference between spouses is the inclusion of marriage as a determinant of class position by seven wives, compared with only two husbands mentioning marriage. For the most part, marriage entered the discussion only when the individuals in question were placing themselves, or their spouses, in the class structure they had just described. In this sense, marriage was used to explain their own location or that of their spouses and, occasionally, to overcome contradictions which arose in their attempts to place themselves in a class position which contrasted with that of others in similar occupations. How this was done will be seen in the analysis which follows.

Self-placement in the Class Structure

In describing how they see society each respondent was being 'objective' in their assessment. That is, they were describing the 'outside world', the strata they believe exist, the bases for assigning others to particular levels, the ways in which individuals might move from one level to another. In asking respondents to place themselves within their personally constructed images, the realm of the 'subjective' is entered. As Martin and Fryer note:

Experience of the social structure is mediated through the individual's attitudes and expectations, based upon his own historical experience . . . Images of society are not only a product of present milieux, but of present milieux interpreted in the light of past experience and expectations for the future, individual and collective. (1975: 113)

And for cross-class husbands and wives, 'historical experience' includes marriage to someone in very different economic, educational and occupational circumstances from their own. Moreover, when asked to be subjective, to place themselves in the class system, this historical experience interferes. Cross-class marriage has clear and obvious effects on the willingness or ability of those so married to describe their own places in society. More than half of the families include one or both spouses with views of their class positions modified in some way by the fact of cross-class marriage. Uncertainty about one's place, opting out altogether from self-placement, and perceiving one's family as 'class divided' are the predominate 'cross-class effects' found. An examination of these effects will demonstrate that the label 'cross-class' is far from being misplaced, or imposed from without, but rather describes most accurately the experiences these men and women have of their family lives.

UNCERTAINTY

Although willing to describe the class structure in some detail, assigning both individuals and groups to various class positions, neither Mrs Leonard nor Mrs Abbot was able to include herself in her own construction:

I don't know what class I'm in any more. My parents are middle class; my husband is working class. I thought about the differences in our jobs before we were married—I was surprised to marry a *worker*—but now the differences don't really matter. The working and the middle classes mix now. We do come from different backgrounds though. We had a joke: in my family we eat 'grilled' fish fingers, and that's middle class; in my husband's family, they eat 'fried' fish fingers, and that's working class. I really don't know what class I am.

Mrs Leonard, senior secretary married to a heating and ventilating fitter

I'm neither fish nor fowl. Professionally I'm in the lower middle class but all my roots are in the working class and my marriage is in the working class. So it puts you in a funny feeling. Children from the working class who go into professions have made the transition for their own children, but it leaves them in a very difficult position. I found life as a young woman, as a teacher, coming from a working class family, I found there was an awful lot of prejudice against my background—from the profession—and only grudging admiration from my own class. It was a very peculiar and uncomfortable situation. Education is a very difficult thing sometimes. So I really couldn't say what class I am.

Mrs Abbot, Head Teacher married to a sawmill foreman

Because of their marriages, and for Mrs Abbot occupational mobility, neither woman feels sure of her own class location, although both had previously described a class structure based primarily upon occupational position. Uncertainty can come in ways other than an inability to name one's class location, however. Mrs Miller placed herself in both the working and middle class, and outside the class structure itself, in her attempt to reconcile her occupation with her marriage:

Yes, there are classes, very much so. People say that class has died out but it certainly hasn't. Money, occupation, and education, all of these plus a person's birth, and around here where you live, all go to make up your class . . . I work so I must be working class. But then I'm a professional, so I must be professional—but my marriage—I would say that I'm classless. Classless I would hope.

Deputy Head teacher married to a plumber

Mrs Miller's confusions are echoed and made explicit by Mrs Harvey who perceives a three-class model of stratification based mainly on occupational position:

I don't know. My husband does manual work, I have a desk job. It's hard to define classes when it comes to individual people. You think of people as people. I suppose I'm middle class but I don't like that term . . . there's a large grey area of white-collar workers.

Head librarian married to a telecommunications engineer

It seems especially hard to define classes when to do so, by your own criteria, would be to place husband and wife in differing class positions. These four wives illustrate hesitancy or unwillingness to categorize themselves in class terms. For others, 'opting out' of the class system is preferred.

OPTING OUT

As with status hierarchies, it is possible to acknowledge that class divisions exist in society, in other people's minds, but refuse to include oneself in such divisions. In subjective terms, an individual can 'opt out' of the class system. In this study, seven husbands and one wife choose to do so. However, unlike earlier discussions about status differences between spouses, talking about class differences did not bring forth terse, uneasy replies. Rather, these respondents were more than willing to describe their views of the class structure, other people's places in that structure, the basis for assigning others to one class or another, and so on. They were, however, unwilling to put themselves anywhere in their own constructions. Moreover, it is possible to trace this desire to 'opt out' to their marital situations, to the obvious differences in occupational attainment between husband

and wife. Because the views of these men and women are more interesting when seen juxtaposed to those of their spouses, each family's views are presented together.

The only wife choosing to opt out of the class system is Mrs Paton, a district nurse married to an agricultural fitter. Mrs Paton's husband described a three-class 'money' model of stratification in our interview, composed of an upper class—those with lots of money who do not need to work for a living, the aristocracy; a large middle class containing virtually everyone else, including himself. All those who must work for a living are middle class in Mr Paton's schema. At bottom is the lowest class, the 'rough' working class, composed of those who do not try to help themselves but depend for survival upon the state. Mr Paton's placement of himself in the middle class is entirely consistent with his class images, and allows for him and his wife to be in the same class position. In contrast, Mrs Paton described a class system based on occupation and income. She spoke in terms of upper, middle and working classes. In her schema class mobility can occur for individuals through the acquisition of a better occupation, leading to a higher income and 'better', i.e. non-manually employed, friends. And although quite embarrassed to do so, Mrs Paton categorized her husband according to her view of the class structure: 'I shouldn't say it but he is working class, I expect'. She refused, however, to place herself anywhere in the structure she had just described: 'People are all the same; we all come from the same place and go the same way.' Using her own schema to place herself would mean thinking of her family as class-divided: wife in the middle class, husband in the working class. Mrs Paton avoids this uncomfortable situation by being nowhere, by opting out.

A similar reaction is seen with Mr Young, a telecommunications engineer married to a librarian. Mr Young's wife considers herself to have achieved upward mobility through her occupational attainment. She sees occupation as the main determinant of class position, and considers that the 'best' job in the family determines the class position of all family members. She is middle class, as is her husband, by virtue of *her* occupational position.

I've changed from working class to middle class because of my job. I've moved up the scale. My husband is middle class also. The class of an individual family is based on the best occupation in the family, whether it is held by the husband or the wife. It doesn't matter which.

Mr Young, however, does not share his wife's views, and puts himself outside the class structure. He conceptualizes this structure in quite traditional terms, equating class position with income, attitudes and lifestyle. He discussed a three-class model with movement possible between the working and middle classes through the acquisition of a higher income. All this, though, applied only to others. For himself, Mr Young reported:

Class is a bit like religion—everyone is entitled to their own beliefs, clothes, rules, etc. In the past, I'd be working class. I come from a working class family, have a working class job, but I see myself outside the class structure. After all, no two people are alike. I don't like categorizing people.

Mr Young was willing to categorize people into social classes only until it came time to place himself.

The same reluctance to assign himself to any one class position is shared by Mr Peterson, an electrician married to a teacher. Mr Peterson, however, takes this reluctance one step further than Mr Young and refuses to assign anyone to specific class locations although he acknowledges that classes do exist and that others make class distinctions on the basis of occupation:

If you put yourself—or others put you—in one class or another, then you start having prejudices about people in other classes. I work in overalls—lots would say that I'm working class but I'm trying to buy my own house. Some working class people would say I'm a snob, but I don't care. I don't like labels. I like to think I stand outside the class system.

Mr Peterson may say that he dislikes labels when asked to place himself in the class structure but these labels enter his conversation, especially when discussing people he meets in the course of his work: 'I've met very nice upper-class people—gentry—even nicer than some working class or middle class people I've met.' Mr Peterson's wife holds views of the class structure which differ considerably from his. Mrs Peterson referred to occupational classes: upper professional, professional, skilled working class and unskilled working class. She categorizes herself as professional class because of her occupation but refuses to place her husband in her schema. Her refusal to place her husband anywhere at all is made more interesting by her belief that individuals may change class not only by changing occupation but through marriage as well. Although leaving open the question whether men as well as women may experience marital mobility, she thinks that class is generally more important to women than to men. As a result: 'If a woman marries a man from a lower social class, she must have a strong personality in order for the differences not to matter.'

Like the other husbands in this section, Mr Allan, a maintenance electrician married to a teacher, also refuses to place himself in any particular class position: 'I don't really place myself anywhere. You could say that I'm working class but I don't care—I'll talk to anyone.'

Mr Allan's refusal is, like that of the others, accompanied by a well-defined view of the class structure he prefers not to be a part of. He sees money as the primary determinant of class position; money governs how you live and what you do. Education is very important but only as a vehicle to a better job and, through this, more money. Somewhat defensive about class distinctions, he admits their existence, but only for others not for himself:

People tend to use class as a barrier to prevent others from getting ahead. No one is *born* to be in one class or another—it's just a matter of the lifestyle your parents have. People are all basically the same, but money and education makes the difference between them.

Mr Allan's inclusion of education as an important determinant of the class location of others is repeated by his wife. Although Mrs Allan is willing to place herself and others in a class schema, her efforts at redefining this schema so that she may include both husband and wife at the same level are very illuminating. For Mrs Allan, cross-class marriage means obvious contradictions in her views of the class structure. In our initial conversation about class, Mrs Allan described a three-layer model composed of the aristocracy, i.e. the very rich; a middle class made up of educated people whether white- or blue-collar workers; and a working class composed of uneducated people. In further discussion she described the working class as made up of manual, or blue-collar, workers. By either of these criteria—lack of education or manual work—Mrs Allan should categorize her husband as working class. And she does so, emphasizing the lack of educational opportunities at the time her husband was growing up and suggesting that, if he was in school today, he would most certainly be headed for white-collar employment. When asked to place herself in the class structure, however, Mrs Allan set aside all her earlier definitions of the working class, ignored her grammar school education and subsequent college degree, and placed herself in the same class as her husband—in the working class: 'I'm working class because I have to work. I have to earn my money.' Mrs Allan's rather trite—albeit common-place—characterization of membership in the working class is a contradiction of her earlier, well-thought-through descriptions of class and class mobility. This contradiction allows her, though, to be placed with her husband. Mr Allan avoids presenting a picture of a class-divided family by opting out of class distinctions; his wife accomplishes the same feat by joining her husband in a class posi-tion that he personally refuses to accept. Cross-class marriage can sometimes be quite confusing.

Uncertainty, opting out, or contradictions in one's views may thus coexist with well-defined images of the class structure. When asked to discuss this structure objectively, in the abstract, these respon-dents were able to do so. When asked, however, to place themselves in their own constructions, to enter the realm of the subjective, confusion or refusal followed. I suggest that such difficulties in sub-jective assessment of their own class locations exist for these men and women, despite their holding fairly consistent models of the class structure, because of their cross-class marriages. The wish to avoid a 'class-divided' marriage is very strong. Thinking of one's spouse as having a higher or lower class position than one's own quite clearly produces a sense of stress which must be avoided in some way. The general term for this type of stress is dissonance. Cognitive dissonance derives from an unsatisfactory resolution of conflict between ideals and behaviour, in this instance between the ideal of equality within marriage and occupational participation at markedly different levels. For cross-class couples, consistency be-tween ideals and behaviour is threatened by self-placement in the class structure. Although these men and women have well-defined models of the class structure, self-placement would bring inconsis-tency into their marriages; thus when asked to do so, their models fail.

Failure of class structure models is not, however, an unusual occurrence among research participants, as noted by Goldthorpe regarding the class imagery of affluent workers:

Some or other of the 'objective' features of social stratification impinge in some way upon the everyday lives of most individuals. Consequently, most individuals develop some set of working ideas whereby they can grasp and interpret this aspect of their social worlds. How comprehensive and systematic these ideas are will vary according to both the personal attributes of the individual and the nature of their social relationships and experience. But usually it will be organized into a model, the consistency of which will hold *up to a certain point*—so far, one would suggest, as it needs to hold in order for the individual to 'make sense' of his experience. Thus, most individuals can present a more or less consistent image of the class structure for so long as they are not confronted with issues in relation to which their models are inadequate. It is once this over-taxing of their models occurs that . . . their responses are likely to become uncertain and muddled. (1970: Appendix, p. 2)

But where the models of affluent workers failed to accommodate others, and easily accommodated themselves, for cross-class individuals the 'certain point' seems to be their own marriages. Their models hold just so long as they are not expected to include themselves, or sometimes their spouses. And when these models fail, the reactions just discussed may be observed. In addition to the men and women above, Mr Aston, a garage driver married to a teacher, places himself outside the class system although he stratifies other people into four classes on the basis of lifestyle and attitudes: 'the difference between hitting your wife and playing squash'. And Mr Roberts, downwardly mobile from his father's social class, sees movement between the various classes and describes the determinants of class position, but will not place himself:

There's definitely some sort of stratification but it is not as clear cut as classes. I'm not sure how stratification works; social class is inevitably tied to income or wealth. And occupation to a certain extent but only at the bottom end. It's more to do with how society educates people . . . It's not a rigíd structure. People move up, but people also travel down. For example, you could suggest that I have travelled down from the class into which I was born. [*Would you suggest that? What class would you put yourself in?*] I don't put myself in any class. Because to start with, it would be a completely subjective view. As I said before, there is a structure and it's based on education, income, a lot of things, marriage, and so on. Somewhere where I am, there's a very odd mix.

For Mr Roberts, both occupational downward movement and marriage to a woman in a middle class occupation (a librarian) hinder self-placement. Like the others, Mr Roberts' model fails when it must include himself.

SEPARATE PLACES

Among a few families, however, problems with stress resulting from differing perceptions of class position between husband and wife do not exist. In these families, there is instead acceptance of the fact that husband and wife have different class occupations. Unlike the husbands and wives just discussed, both spouses in these families place themselves in specific class locations, but generally in ones which differ from each other. In some families, husband and wife agree on this differential placement; in others, no such agreement is found. With one exception, however, little conflict between husband and wife arises over this issue.

Mrs Barnes used the word 'class-divided' to describe her marriage. An economics lecturer married to a lorry driver, she places herself in the upper middle class and her husband in the working class on the grounds of their disparate occupational attainments. Class mobility through marriage occurs in Mrs Barnes's class schema, but only for women and only upwards. That is, a woman with an occupation of a lower social class than her husband's may travel upwards through marriage, but a woman with an occupation of a higher social class than her husband's will not travel downwards as a result of marriage. Men, however, achieve their class locations only through their own occupations. Hence, Mrs Barnes's husband is working class. Mrs Barnes finds support for her views of class and class mobility in her own marriage, considering that she and her husband are very definitely 'different class people with different class tastes and interests'. Her husband does not share her views, though, and considers that he has been upwardly mobile through his marriage. Although he suspects that classes might actually be a myth and exist only in people's minds, he also reports that he has changed class since marriage and is now middle class. This issue seems of minor importance to the Barneses, and their differing interpretations cause little stress.

In contrast, Mrs Mason, a teacher married to a roof-tiler, reports some conflict with her husband over his wish to see his wife and daughters as working class—after all, he is:

I do think classes exist but they're not based on money. They're based on education. You can change class but I don't think that a working class person, with a genuine working class background, could move into the middle class. Someone with a genuine working class background—no education beyond age 15, plus home background, parents not interested in education—no. Without education you cannot get out of the working class unless you really fight to do so . . . Teachers are middle class. Education and occupation are very definitely linked. I'm middle class because of the education I've had. I see my husband as working class and he sees himself as working class. He says: as long as people work, they're working class. But I don't agree with him. I see him as working class because he hasn't had the education. He sees himself as working class because he hasn't got the *money* or the education and, of course, because he works. Unfortunately, he sees us [wife and daughters] as working class as well. But I generally tend to put him wise.

Mrs Mason's views of her marriage and her own class position are interesting because her education and subsequent occupational mobility came only after many years of marriage. She has been a fully qualified teacher for only 4 years, while having previously been a financially dependent housewife for 13 years. Her views of her position in the class structure are—like Mrs Barnes's—constructed exclusively upon her own educational, and thus occupational, accomplishments. Her husband has not accomplished all that she has; he has not, therefore, experienced the same upward mobility. In a sense, then, Mrs Mason's family is, like Mrs Barnes's, 'class-divided'.

In three other families, husband and wife also see themselves as occupying different social classes. Mr James, Mr Norton, and Mr Ashcroft all place themselves, by virtue of their occupations, in the working class. Mrs James, Mrs Norton, and Mrs Ashcroft all place themselves in the middle class. These husbands and wives tend to see class position as individually achieved; only the Nortons express a collective, family identity:

I'm a middle-class Labour voting deviant. My husband is in the same class, his job isn't.

Mrs Norton, social services training officer

I'm in the lowest class because of my job changes. I was lower middle class and still live at lower middle class because of my wife.

Mr Norton, kitchen helper

Even the Nortons' familial identity is, however, cross-cut with acknowledgement of differing individual accomplishments. These families, although too few in number to be of any statistical significance, challenge the assumption that husbands and wives perceive themselves as occupying a single place in the stratification system. They challenge the assumption that women derive their perceptions of class location from their husbands' occupations. With the single exception—disputed by his wife—of Mr Barnes, these men and women see their places in the class structure as *individually* created and sustained.[3]

There is one other family in which husband and wife place themselves in differing class locations. They do so, however, for reasons unlike the families above. Mr Henderson, a printer, sees himself as middle class, placing himself in the centre of a three-class 'money' model of stratification. This model is composed of the wealthy, the middle, and the poor, and is based upon a very individualistic conception of class mobility: 'poor people don't have to be poor, they could try harder to help themselves'. Mrs Henderson has a more well-defined image of the class structure than her husband, seeing five classes based upon occupational distinctions. Mrs Henderson described an upper class—owners and managers of big business, lawyers, doctors and the like; a middle class composed of nurses and teachers; a skilled working class—technicians, foremen and skilled manual workers; a semi-skilled working class; and an unskilled class of 'odds and ends'. Employed as a health visitor, Mrs Henderson ought thus to classify herself as middle class but does not. She believes that, although occupation is the main determinant of class position, marriage can confuse the issue: 'If you marry outside your class, you will meet people from both classes and move in both circles. I'm in a profession but I've got a fair percentage of friends and family who are working class and therefore I consider myself as working class.' To be exact, Mrs Henderson considers herself to be a part of the skilled working class—just where her husband would be if he used the same schema as his wife.

In these families, then, husbands and wives—in agreement with each other or not—perceive themselves as occupying different locations in the class structure. But what follows from these differing perceptions? In the discussions of status differences between spouses, conflict between husband and wife, and between them and the outside world, was observed. Reluctance to consider status differences was observed. With differences of class, however, no similar observations may be made. Perceptions of class divisions within their marriages have few consequences and are readily accommo-

dated into family life. Unlike those men and women discussed earlier who find inconsistency in class position between themselves and
their spouses difficult to accept, these few families accept inconsistency. Why is there little or no conflict over this issue? Perhaps
because, unlike status differences, differing perceptions of class location do not impinge directly upon an individual's day-to-day living.
Differences in status are tangible—how people react to you, or to
your spouse, whether they treat you with respect or derogation is
immediately felt. Moreover, status distinctions, often invidious,
separate husband and wife from each other: they are subjectively felt
on an individual basis. Class position is, in contrast, objectively
lived and these husbands and wives, regardless of their perceptions,
live at the *same* level. Perceiving differing class locations belies the
reality of their shared class location; perceiving differing status positions reflects reality. Thus, these men and women may accommodate perceptions which place husband and wife in differing class
locations without suffering stress or marital conflict. For the others,
discussed earlier, some stress seems to exist as a result of these
differing perceptions; marital conflict, however, is absent.

　　This study cannot explain why some families experience dissonance in their perceptions and others do not, for to do so would
require investigations beyond its range. What it can reveal, though,
is the validity of the concept 'cross-class'. There is something special
or unique about cross-class marital circumstances. This has been
observed in many ways in the preceding chapters and is affirmed
here. Moreover, this uniqueness is acknowledged by the incumbents
of such marriages themselves in their varying discussions of their
places in the class structure. For those capable of dealing with
inconsistency in class position between husband and wife, such acknowledgement is easily seen. These families are, to themselves as
well as to outsiders, composed of individuals with two different class
locations occupationally—they are truly 'cross-class'. For the
others, incapable of dealing with inconsistency of class position, the
difficulty they experience in locating themselves in class terms
reveals similar acknowledgement. Uncertainty, confusion, contradictions, and opting out would not exist unless there were good
reasons. Maintaining perceptions of equality, or avoiding perceptions of inequality, between husband and wife provides these good
reasons. In their efforts to avoid self-placement in the class structure, these men and women confirm their places—they too are truly

'cross-class'. Far from being a misplaced label, or an inaccurate category imposed upon them from without, 'cross-class families' is a most apt way of describing the men and women of this research.

Part Two: The World Outside

Cross-class families are able, then, to accommodate differing perceptions of class position between husband and wife without suffering undue stress or marital conflict. Class differences do not, however, exist solely in an individual's perceptions of his or her own position in the class structure. Participation in life outside the private domain is often thought to be shaped by class position. Involvement in voluntary organizations such as social or sports clubs, adult education, occupational associations, cultural activities, or hobbies is known to vary between the working and middle classes.[4] Similarly, participation in trade unions and voting for the Labour Party are more readily associated with incumbents of working-class occupations than with middle-class employees. Like other men and women, the husbands and wives of cross-class families must decide how they are to orient themselves towards this world outside their homes. Perhaps *unlike* other men and women, however, this outside world holds potential pitfalls for cross-class couples with the possibility of husbands and wives having very divergent opinions about it. This section examines the participation of cross-class men and women in the 'public' realm through an analysis of the perspectives which underlie their participation (or not) politically and in trade unions.

Political Parties and Trade Unions

Trade unions and political parties exist in British society, and although indifference to their existence is an option open to any family or family member whether cross-class or not, when that family is composed of a husband in manual work and a wife in non-manual work indifference is perhaps harder to achieve. This is the case because in British society there are expected links between occupational position and political partisanship or trade union membership. These links are not, of course, as strong today as in the past. Nonetheless, they continue to exist and so must be accommodated into cross-class family life. In keeping with the aims of the previous chapters, the focus with respect to political preferences and trade unions is to show how cross-class marriage acts upon the perspectives of husbands and wives and shapes their attitudes towards these aspects of public life. In particular, the aim is to show how, given the existence of a cross-class marriage, the courses of action pursued by these men and women 'make sense', or are intelligible with respect to sustaining harmonious marital relations.

There is, however, neither now nor in the past, a perfect association between class position and either union membership or political preferences. Trade union membership may reflect working class consciousness and solidarity with collective aims, or may simply be for instrumental reasons—for personal or legal protection or to gain wage increases. Some years ago, Lockwood argued: 'There is no inevitable connection between unionization and class consciousness' (1958: 113). And his words remain valid, as observed by Bain and his associates: 'The available evidence suggests that there is no simple or constant relationship between social position and either union growth or union character, and that neither of these, taken singly or jointly, provides an adequate indicator of the class consciousness of union members' (1973: 109). Virtually all of the wives studied and more than half of their husbands are members of trade unions. This membership is accompanied by a range of opinion, both negative and positive, and taken alone indicates little about the social perspectives of the respondents. Therefore, union membership will not be considered in isolation, but will instead be discussed in conjunction with political preferences.

But in a similar way, partisan dealignment amongst the British electorate since the 1970s has rendered a 'class–party nexus' analysis less adequate than before (Crewe *et al.*, 1977). The conventional equation of Conservative voting with middle class status and Labour voting with working class status has been confounded not only by greater variation of partisanship among the classes such that class is now a less good predictor of vote, but also by the growth of a third major party. In the 1983 general election, the Liberal/SDP Alliance commanded 27% of the vote among those employed in professional and managerial occupations *and* 27% of the vote among skilled manual workers. The remainder of the skilled working class vote was divided almost equally between the two other major parties, with 39% in favour of the Conservatives, 35% in favour of Labour. Only among the professional and managerial classes was there clear class partisanship with 62% voting Conservative and only 16% voting Labour (Crewe, 1983a: 14). Working class disenchantment with the Labour Party does not inevitably imply a denial of working class values and perspectives, however—no more, one might argue, than support for the Conservatives inevitably implies wholesale acceptance of middle class values and perspectives. For some voters at least, party support will be for instrumental reasons and not indicative of ideological beliefs. Heath (1981) makes this point in his analysis of the 1979 general election, and cautions us to look for the meanings behind voter preferences:

> We must remember (as sociologists sometimes forget) that voting is not merely a reflection of one's economic position and social affiliations but is also, and crucially, a response to the actions and ideologies of the political parties themselves . . . In short, we must look at the 'meaning' of Labour or Conservative voting. We have to interpret our findings, for the data will not speak for themselves. (1981: 229)

Fortunately in a study of this size it is possible to look at meanings, to gain some understanding of the perspectives which inform one course of action rather than another. Moreover, by looking for meanings, and by bringing together the respondents' reasons for particular political preferences with their reasons for union membership (or not), the pitfalls which exist in considering either one of these in isolation may be avoided.

Although the aim in this section is thus to gain an understanding of the perspectives which inform the respondents' participation in society politically and in trade unions, there is some interest in viewing the families initially as a group. Table 9.1 distributes the

Table 9.1. *Distribution of Husbands and Wives by Preferred Political Party*

Spouse	Conservative	Labour	Liberal/ SDP Alliance	None
Husbands	8	13	4	4
Wives	12	7	8	3
Total	20 (34)	20 (34)	12 (20)	7 (12)

Percentage of total respondents in parenthesis; $N = 59$.
Note: Of the four wives whose husbands were not interviewed, only one was unable to state which party her husband preferred. Husbands included in this table thus equal 29.

husbands and wives according to their political preferences at the time of interviewing. This table does not in all cases indicate actual voting behaviour. Research was conducted between the 1979 and 1983 general elections, and certain individuals indicated that they would be switching their votes. Mrs Henley and Mr Thompson, for example, are included among those supporting the Liberal/SDP Alliance, although in 1979 Mrs Henley voted Conservative and Mr Thompson voted Labour. They have each become disenchanted with their former parties and look to the Alliance to do better. The most interesting vote 'switcher', however, is Mr James who intended a Conservative vote in 1983 after supporting Labour since being old enough to vote. His reasons for changing allegiance will be discussed subsequently; suffice it to say here that Mrs James's pro-Conservative and anti-Labour views have had some effect. In addition, the Stones and the Smiths are included as Labour Party supporters even though they all normally vote Liberal in elections. All four are committed to the ideals of the Labour Party but reside in areas dominated by the Conservatives. They see their 'tactical' votes as the best way of defeating the Thatcher government. The emphasis upon the ideological perspectives of the respondents justifies placing these four with the party of their preferred choice.

Of primary interest in Table 9.1 is the almost complete symmetry of party preference by sex and party. Twelve wives prefer the Conservatives; thirteen husbands prefer Labour. Seven wives prefer Labour; eight husbands prefer the Conservatives. One is almost tempted to say that cross-class couples cancel each other out when it comes to political preferences, with the only party to gain by their existence being the Alliance. In fact, as this table shows, support for Conservative and Labour is equally balanced between the families, with about two-thirds of the respondents choosing one or the other of these two major parties. Among Alliance supporters, the near symmetry between the sexes disappears, with twice as many wives as husbands making this political choice. The 20% support among the families as a group is only somewhat less than that received by the Alliance on polling day 1983. Not surprisingly, there are few data available on cross-class voting preferences with which to make comparisons. Britten and Heath (1983) include a breakdown of cross-class voting by sex for married women and men, but in their report the number of 'strictly defined' cross-class respondents (that is, as cross-class is defined here) is too small to be more than sugges-tive.[5] In any event, the results of Britten and Heath's work, as well as those here, are based on too few strictly defined cross-class respondents to be of any statistical importance. The indications of this study are that cross-class political preferences are as likely to favour the Labour Party as to favour the Conservative Party. It would take a much larger number of respondents to know if this finding would hold nationally.

The various ways cross-class husbands and wives orient them-selves to the public realm are now considered. As noted earlier, the aim here is to show how their responses to trade unions and political parties make sense in light of their cross-class marriages. The first of these responses discussed brings together yet again families met earlier who share certain other characteristics in common.

SHARED LEFT-WING IDEOLOGICAL PERSPECTIVES

Among the families interviewed, there is a group of six families whose pro-socialist, pro-union perspectives distinguish them from the others. Most of these families have been met as a group before. Predominately they are the families characterized by normative agreement that it is the obligation of both husband and wife to make economic contributions to the household; the families characterized by equality of commitment to domestic chores. Their egalitarian beliefs extend into the social realm and place them on the left of the political spectrum. Included in this group are the Robertses, the Smiths, the Fieldings, the Stones, the Nortons, and the Frenches. All of these husbands and wives support the Labour Party; all are favourably disposed towards trade unions. Missing from this group are Mr and Mrs Meredith, who, although egalitarian in terms of paid work and housework, tend towards the middle of the road politically and therefore vote Liberal. Thus, despite sharing many other views with these six families, the Merediths do not join them in a commitment to socialism of the kind illustrated below:

I believe in socialism. I discovered it at age 16. Voting Labour is an ideolog-ical thing, an act of faith. The Labour Party is the one party concerned with social welfare.

Mrs Norton, social services training officer

I'm a great believer in large industries being nationalized. People say that they're inefficient. Well, I would rather see the monies go into society than into individual pockets. I'm a socialist. And my wife is definitely a socialist now. Whether she was one when we first married, I don't know, but she is now!

Mr French, former HGV driver

I ought to vote Labour, I'm left-wing Labour. But here, in this area, there's no chance of getting Labour in. It's a case of tactical voting really. I'm way to the left of Labour, but vote Liberal as the only way of beating the Conservatives.

Mr Smith, telecommunications engineer

·I have vaguely socialist principles. I vote Labour [because of] woolly, liberal, *Guardian*-reading thinking I guess. Their propaganda strikes a chord—socialist, helping the poor and so on.

Mrs Roberts, librarian

This socialism is accompanied, moreover, by collectivist orientations towards unions and union activity (cf. Rallings, 1975):

Union affiliation is in the blood. It's the natural thing to do. I joined the union before I joined the professional association. I think we are in danger of being undermined in the public sector. We shouldn't have to bear the brunt of all government cuts. The purposes of unions vary around the country and according to gender. They are there to protect our interests in the age old fight between employers and employees even though we are in the public sector. Now it's taking the form of wage repression and delay in appointments. The union is there to make sure I'm not exploited by my employer.

Mrs Stone, architect

I'm a socialist. I believe in trade unions. They are there to protect the employment rights of workers, as a collective body, pressing to see that they get a proper share of wages. I think it's a good idea for unions to be involved in politics; I'd support affiliation to the Labour Party.

Mr Norton, kitchen helper

I joined at college. I've always been a union member of some union or another simply because I've worked for very large, anonymous, faceless *masses* if you like. And as an individual, I can do nothing to further a grievance or anything. I've joined because NUT is, again, an anonymous mass and I want an anonymous mass *behind me*. We haven't had a full-scale strike since I've been teaching. Strikes are only called when all else has failed. It's the ultimate thing at the end of a long long struggle. It's when you've met with absolute stonewalling and some kind of action has to be taken. Then I'd strike.

Mrs French, teacher

Perhaps not surprisingly, the socialist, collectivist perspectives expressed by these husbands and wives generally extend into other areas of social participation. Mr French was a union steward for 25 years; Mrs French has served as a union representative in her school for the last 7 years. The Frenches met at an early CND rally in the 1960s; they continue their CND membership today. Mr and Mrs Norton are members of the Labour Party, and can usually be counted on to help with leafleting and canvassing during election campaigns. Mr Norton is also an active member of CND and spends two nights a week assisting his local branch. Mrs Norton, for her part, worked in Africa as a volunteer for the Save the Children organization prior to her marriage, and in later years was responsible for the creation of a battered wives' association. Mrs Stone actively supports the women's movement; Mr Roberts supports Greenpeace. Mrs Smith is a former governor of the local primary school and presently teaches children from problem families; Mr Smith was a union committee member for 2 years. Mrs Fielding calls herself a crusader. She wants to teach people 'to think' and is considering a further career in educational research. All of these activities suggest the existence of well-developed social consciences within these men and women. The Labour Party, with its concern for social welfare and equality of opportunity, is their natural home; trade unions their natural partners in the fight for fairness in society.

Of interest is the fact that most of the husbands and wives in this group have stronger ties to the middle class than to the working class. They are, in effect, part of the Labour middle class; the supporters of the Labour Party seen by Crewe and his associates as the Party's bright hope for the future:

In some groups—notably the young Labour middle class—the Party's future prospects look brighter, which suggests that Labour identifiers might continue to become steadily more middle class in composition (although still working class in the majority). (1977: 181)

Three of these husbands were raised in middle class homes: Mr

Stone, Mr Roberts and Mr Norton have all experienced downward occupational mobility in comparison with their fathers. Two of these three—Mr Stone and Mr Norton—have university degrees and maintain links with their university friends. Three of the wives come from middle class family backgrounds. Only the Fieldings, the Smiths and the Frenches come from predominately working class homes. These three families, however, socialize exclusively in middle class worlds. Further, when asked to place themselves in the class structure, those willing to do so chose the middle class. In line with their egalitarian ideologies, the Fieldings and Mr French refused to place themselves—or others—into social classes. The Fieldings' beliefs with respect to categorizing people in this way were noted earlier. Mr French echoes their sentiments:

I would definitely try to place myself as classless because I judge a person for what he is, how he conducts himself, his attitudes to a social conscience. I couldn't give a hoot whether he's a dustman, a road sweeper, a solicitor, a doctor or a barrister. If a dustman can converse and has a valid opinion, then I give him as much respect as I would the person at the top of the profession.

Apart from these three, and Mr Roberts whose view of himself in the class structure is confused by his downward mobility, all others see themselves as part of the middle class:

I'm middle class because I'm not very rich. I'm middle looking up because of my family background and education.

Mr Stone

I'm working class in origin and middle class in way of life—I've changed.

Mrs Smith

I'm middle class. I've got lots of middle class attitudes. It's basically the way you live—it has to be. Attitudes put you in one class or another. Books, for example, you don't have to be a company director to have books around.

Mrs French

Moreover, unlike many families discussed in part one of this chapter, no uncertainty, confusion or disagreement between spouses exists in regard to self-placement in the class structure (Mr Roberts apart). Members of the Labour middle class politically, and cross-class occupationally, they see themselves as middle class.

More important than consistent images of themselves in the class structure, however, is the existence in these families of coherent ideologies which inform both public and private life. The perspectives which guide their lives domestically, calling for equal commitment to paid work and housework, extend outwards into the political and social realm, giving to each a consistent, and left-wing, philosophical stance. These perspectives not only inform their lives both publicly and privately, they sustain those lives. These families are free from conflict related to the special nature of their marriages—to the *cross-class* nature of their marriages. This lack of conflict seems closely linked to their ideological positions. The belief in equality which underlies left-wing political and social action, underlies harmony in marital situations of occupational inequality. Perhaps not all left-wing men could cope with wives who are occupationally superior to themselves: these men can. Perhaps not all left-wing women could cope with their own occupational superiority: these women can. For these families, intelligible links exist between their private, cross-class family lives and their public, left-wing ideologies. Private and public life 'make sense' as one realm creates and sustains the other.

The six families just discussed are quite unique in comparison with the other families studied. These six share ideological perspectives between husband and wife which 'aid' them in making successful cross-class marriages. It is possible, with these six, for an outsider to see rational links between their private and public lives. The remaining families differ from these six in a variety of ways. First, agreement between spouses with respect to politics or trade union activity is often missing. Secondly, there is no clear link between political preferences, trade union activity and other forms of participation in public life. And thirdly, ideological perspectives play little or no part in sustaining their *cross-class* marriages. In many of these families, though, it is possible to see their responses to the world of politics and trade unions as shaped by the fact of their cross-class marital situations. And in many ways, these responses are a priori as expected among cross-class families as those made by the six left-wing families, despite being of quite a different order. The first of these responses discussed is perhaps as far away from the agreed perspectives of the six families presented above as it is possible to go: far from agreeing, husband and wife make opposing choices.

SEPARATE VIEWS

Mr and Mrs Allan come from very different family backgrounds: he from a mining family; she from a family of teachers and accountants with ties to the aristocracy. Mr Allan, an electrician, votes Labour; Mrs Allan, a teacher, votes Conservative. Mr and Mrs Everett come from very similar origins: both were raised in working class homes; both left school at age 14 and entered the labour force. Mr Everett, a heating and ventilating fitter, votes Labour; Mrs Everett, a senior records officer, votes Conservative. In terms of backgrounds and politics, these two families thus exemplify cross-class marriage with precision. Moreover, as earlier discussions have shown, they typify relatively happy cross-class marriages. How, then, do a husband and a wife cope with opposed political choices—surely an area with considerable potential for marital strife? Mr Allan's words suggest one solution:

She comes very much from a middle class family and automatically votes Conservative. I come very much from a working class family and automatically vote Labour. You reach a stalemate eventually and stop fighting about the same old issues.

The Allans do not discuss politics with each other; they have banished such discussions in order to cope with their obvious differences—a very reasonable response to cross-class politics.

The Everetts do talk about politics, however, and although in complete disagreement when it comes to voting, agree entirely upon the faults of the present Conservative leader:

I support the Conservatives because of what we've [her family] got. What we've got we don't want to lose. I feel that if Labour came in they might not be too kind to us. We own property. We don't know how a Labour government would affect us. But I feel we need a change from Thatcher —to make her look at her actions. I'm against Thatcher because of all the unemployment. I think there should be wage and price controls.

Mrs Everett, senior records officer

Conservatives are not for working people. They're a different race of people altogether. At present Thatcher is a complete dictator, but so was Callaghan. Governments ought to govern, not dictate. Thatcher is running the country right down into the ground. The woman has to be got out, for the sake of the country. We're fast going back to the twenties. Labour are the only ones who would look after working class people. This is the basic idea of the Labour Party. They are too extreme at times, but I'll vote for them in the next election—Thatcher has got to go . . . My wife and I agree on getting Thatcher out. She's in local government, she feels the same sense of dictatorship from the present Conservative government.

Mr Everett, heating and ventilating fitter

The Everetts, then, mute rather obvious political disagreement by mutual dislike of the Prime Minister.

In addition to these solutions to problems of potential strife, both couples share favourable attitudes towards trade unions. Mrs Allan and Mrs Everett are in fact among the few Conservative-voting respondents to demonstrate collective orientations towards union activity:

If you're going to get the benefits that the union fights for, then I think you should be prepared to join. Unions have a role to play. They speak out for individuals against the management. They've helped me in the past. I don't like the idea of striking but I wouldn't go against a union directive to strike.

Mrs Everett

Mrs Allan echoes the sentiments of Mrs Everett, and is one of the few teachers interviewed who is prepared to honour strike decisions: 'If the union called a strike, I would have to come out. It's part and parcel of being in a union.' Have these two women been influenced by their manually employed husbands in developing attitudes favourable to trade unions? It is unclear. When asked, each denied such influence but it is readily apparent that husbands and wives share common perspectives. Mr Allan reports that his father was a strong union man and that he personally never thought twice about joining. Mr Allan sees the union as the only group powerful enough to deal with management; to represent the workers as a whole above the level of the shop floor. He would support strike action, arguing: 'you are duty-bound in that you have an obligation to the whole'. Mr Everett wishes unions were more political, favours affiliation to the Labour Party (his wife, of course, disagrees with him on this) and sees trade unions not only as vehicles for workers' protection but as another way of continuing the fight against the present Prime Minister. One suspects that these husbands have influenced their wives' attitudes towards trade unions, but in the face of denial such suspicions cannot be substantiated. In any event, husband and wife do share agreement on the role of unions at least, and suffer little conflict as a result of their political disagreements.

There is another family in which in past elections one spouse has voted Conservative, the other Labour. In this family, though, it is the husband and not the wife who has preferred the party on the right of the political spectrum. Mr Young works for a nationalized industry (BT); he is against nationalization and socialism, arguing that the former 'does not work' and that the latter is unfair: 'I believe in a fair day's work for a fair day's pay. I've always had to work for what I got—others should do the same.' Mr Young's wife, however, comes from a long-time Labour-supporting family and has usually voted for the party favouring both nationalization and socialism. The Youngs avoid conflict over their political differences by keeping their opinions to themselves. They, like the Allans, do not discuss how they are going to vote; do not, in fact, know if they vote for the same or different parties. In addition, the Youngs agree upon the activities of trade unions. Their words in interviews are almost mirror reflections of each other's attitudes:

I joined because I believe in unions. They are there to represent the workers. People should pay union dues and support their unions.

> Mrs Young, librarian

I believe in unions so long as they represent the rights of the workers . . . I would honour any strike because a union's got to be a union.

> Mr Young, telecommunications engineer

Like the other 'cross-class' voters, then, this couple mutes political disagreement by agreement on union activity. Unlike either the Everetts or the Allans, moreover, political disagreement is coming to an end for the Youngs. Perhaps once both husband and wife make the same political choice they will end their self-imposed silence on this aspect of public life:

I used to be more Labour until so many infights started. The SDP offers a nice middle ground. I'm definitely not Conservative and Labour seems to be too far left. I can identify more with the middle ground.

> Mrs Young

A total capitalist society is wrong, but socialism doesn't work either, so I'm thinking of voting for the SDP. I find them interesting, so I'll probably vote for them next time.

> Mr Young

Perhaps the SDP/Liberal Alliance is the natural home for pro-union, anti-left cross-class couples? When the Youngs make this change in their individual political choices, they will be joining others of this research who find the middle way the most comfortable way (e.g., the Millers, Mrs Leonard and Mrs Ashcroft). The Merediths, for example, would be 'cross-class' voters in the same way as the Youngs were formerly, were it not for the existence of the Alliance:

> I don't like either the Conservatives or Labour. I'm not sure why. If there was no middle road, that is, no Liberal/SDP Alliance, my wife would go towards Labour, I would go towards Conservative. As it is, we both just accept that we vote Liberal.

> Mr Meredith, heating and ventilating fitter married to an administrative officer

The Merediths share the attitudes of the Youngs towards trade unions.

There is one family in which voting for the Liberal party masks profound disagreement between spouses, both with regard to trade union activity and other ideological perspectives. Mrs Parker voted Liberal in 1979 and intended to support the Alliance in 1983. In previous elections she has voted Conservative. Mrs Parker makes these political choices because she is, in her words, 'anti-Labour'. Mr Parker voted Liberal in 1979 but was uncertain how he would vote in 1983. In all previous elections he has voted Labour. Mr Parker, moreover, makes his political choices for exactly the same reasons which his wife cites as behind her anti-Labour stance. Mr Parker supports Labour because he is for socialism and against nuclear arms. He voted Liberal in 1979 because he had received no information about the Labour candidate. Mrs Parker is against Labour because she is against socialism. Not surprisingly, neither spouse thinks that the other exerts any influence on their political decisions.

The disagreements the Parkers have in these areas are matched by disputes over the role and activities of trade unions. Mrs Parker is a member of the National Union of Teachers, and sees her union as a 'common voice for teachers'. At the time of our interview, she was supporting union directives for a withdrawal of services. Mr Parker, however, disagrees with his wife's views strongly and considers unions to be unnecessary—at least for him. When I arrived to interview Mrs Parker, I interrupted a family argument about her union activities. Despite my arrival, the argument continued for a while and Mr Parker accused his wife of being 'irresponsible' and of 'setting a bad example' for the children she teaches. The sides taken by husband and wife in this argument present a striking contrast to the conventional picture of pro-union Labour voter versus anti-union Conservative voter. Mrs Parker comes from a Conservative-voting family and has only recently shifted her allegiance towards the Liberals; Mr Parker comes from a Labour-voting family and, despite voting Liberal in 1979, may yet revert to Labour support. Nonetheless, it is Mrs Parker, not her husband, who is strongly pro-union. Mr Parker is not unique in being an anti-union Labour supporter, other men in this research join him in his views. He is unique, however, in having a wife who so strongly disagrees with him. The conflicts evident in other areas of the Parkers' lives carry over into the public realm.

It is difficult with these families to draw direct links between their *cross-class* marriages and their political and union stances. Rather, these families describe a not unexpected pattern of behaviour among cross-class families. Cross-class occupationally, they cross class lines politically (although not always in the usual ways). The Parkers apart, they are able to mute these political disagreements with agreement in other areas. With such agreement, strife is avoided. In terms of politics, however, resistance to influence from one's spouse is evident. Freedom of choice electorally extends even, it seems, to husbands and wives. In the Thompson family, this freedom of choice exists not only for husband and wife, but was found in Mrs Thompson's family of origin as well. The Thompsons are former 'cross-class' voters, with Mr Thompson having given up his support for Labour because of that party's adoption of unilateralist nuclear policies; Mrs Thompson giving up support for the Conservatives because of her dislike of Mrs Thatcher. Mrs Thompson was unlikely to vote in 1983, while her husband has turned to the Liberal/SDP Alliance. These political differences cause little problem between husband and wife. Mrs Thompson accepted her husband's choice of Labour, despite her own support of the Conservatives: their differences simply reminded her of her youth: 'I used to be very Conservative—my mother always voted Conservative, my father Labour—like my husband and I. But I probably won't vote now. I just don't know. Anyone but Thatcher.' The Thompsons and the others demonstrate that marriage, and cross-class marriage as well, can accommodate considerable differences of opinion. These families have, in effect, agreed to disagree.

If separate views between husband and wife are a priori to be expected among cross-class families, then so too must be instances of domination, of families in which the views of one spouse convert the other away from long-held views. There is one family here which typifies this response to cross-class political perspectives quite dramatically. In this family, the husband has joined his wife in support for the Conservative Party; agreement on trade unions, moreover, seems not far away.

DOMINATION

Mrs James is the daughter of a coal-miner. Although she experienced considerable poverty in her working class childhood, as an adult she has long been part of the affluent middle class. Her first husband was a college lecturer, and Mrs James herself has taught on a part-time and full-time basis since 1958. Five years ago Mrs James married again, to a man employed as a forklift driver for the last 29 years. Her second marriage thus typifies the coming together of 'class opposites'—a 'pure' cross-class marriage. Her influence on her husband politically typifies one certain response to this coming together:

I'm only Conservative because I'm anti-Labour . . . I don't think Labour is organized. There are too many wings: left wing, right wing, centre wing. I think they're too influenced by trade unions. No one seems in control. They are too easily swayed by loud voices . . . I think I influence my husband more than he influences me. I think I'm converting him from Labour to Conservative. He says that he'll vote Conservative next time.

And although Mr James denies his wife's influence, he is definitely changing allegiance:

Up till now, I've always voted Labour. But I'm rather disillusioned now. Mrs Thatcher has taken my fancy. She does what she says she's going to do. They [the Conservatives] will try to help working people. The Labour party used to be the party of the working class, but there are just too many infights. All they do is run down other parties . . . I don't think my wife has influenced me. I can see it myself. She says I've just opened my eyes. I'll vote Conservative next time.

Mrs James's influence on her husband's views may also be seen in his changing attitudes towards trade unions. Mrs James gave up her union membership in 1963; Mr James is unable to do the same but during a recent dispute at work voted with a tiny minority opposed to strike action. He has experienced considerable discomfort at work as a result of his open disagreement with the union's activities:

. . . to be honest, I don't really think the union is for the worker so much as for themselves. When trouble brews, first the union protects themselves, not the workers. They won't risk their necks like in the old days. I'm not so keen as I was in the old days. I voted against the last strike—I was personally threatened for doing so . . . My wife and I really don't talk about it because we would disagree. She totally disagrees with unions. I've said to her: well, you've accepted the pay rises and all that the unions do for you. She says she can't help what unions do . . . my attitudes have changed definitely. I was very keen 10 years ago. Now you stand there and listen to them. I think they're demented, have got a screw loose. They get so carried away with themselves.

Although Mr James reports that he and his wife 'don't talk about' trade unions, her words contradict his report and give substance to the suggestion of domination:

Mike's a union member, he doesn't have any choice, it's a closed shop. I always say to him: I couldn't have someone that I know is less intelligent than me telling me how to act and think in a given situation. I fervently believe that trade unions are no longer representing the true working man. They are representing themselves. They are after *power*—big brother—they are not truly representative of the working man. My husband *wants* to agree with me, but he's been a trade union man for so long, he finds it hard to agree with me. We have had good old discussions, rousing discussions—not rows—but quite lively.

Mr James's acquiescence to his wife's views politically, as well as to her management of finances and the running of the household, leads one to believe that acquiescence to her views of trade unions is not far away.

The Jameses illustrate the domination of one spouse's views very aptly. In two other families it is possible to infer similar dominance; these two, however, serve less well as examples of this expected response. Mrs Creighton, a Deputy Head teacher, is very strongly pro-Conservative. She supports this party because she feels they have the best people and best leader, and are more likely than any other party to put concern for the country ahead of concern for its own good name. Mrs Creighton is a union member, but joined for personal legal protection only. She is against strikes and has crossed picket lines. Mr Creighton, a welder, shares his wife's attitude towards unions and joined only when threatened with redundancy. He would strike only with considerable reluctance and thinks 'unions get away with too much'. In our discussion on politics, however, Mr Creighton was less than forthcoming. He claims to be uninterested in politics, and to vote as the mood takes him. He did, though, add the following comment to his rather sparse discussion: 'My wife votes Conservative, and I usually vote the same way as my wife.' Does he do so because his wife influences him? Possibly.

In the White family, similar hints of influence from wife to husband may be observed. Both Mr and Mrs White are union members, joining because 'everyone else did':

I joined because everyone else in the school is in the union. If I'd been in another school I might not have joined . . . I did strike but because everyone else did, to be honest.

Mrs White, teacher

Management preferred you to be in a union originally. Now it doesn't matter if you join or not. I joined because everyone else did.

Mr White, printer

Politically, husband and wife both come from strongly pro-Conservative families; however, neither has chosen to follow their parents' political allegiances. Instead, husband and wife both vote Liberal. In the Whites' complementary behaviour, there seems to exist little reason to suspect dominance of views from one to the other. Mrs White, though, feels that she does influence her husband to a marked degree, saying: 'I don't know why I'm so against Labour—it's a family thing. My husband would be more likely to vote Labour if I didn't argue with him.' Is she correct in her estimation? Again, *possibly* remains the only answer. With the Jameses the presence of influence is clear. One would expect that some husbands or wives would be susceptible to influence from their spouses, but the Allans, the Everetts, and the Youngs show that resistance to such influence is also quite feasible. Moreover, when asked if they thought they were influenced in any way by their spouses, virtually every respondent answered no, not at all. Political autonomy is as important, it seems, as political independence. In any event, as the

Jameses most aptly demonstrate, dominance of one spouse's views over the other's can exist and is, in its way, as reasonable a response to cross-class family life as keeping one's views private.

COMPLEMENTARY VIEWS

Among the husbands studied, there are three men whose work experiences and/or family backgrounds have engendered attitudes towards trade unions and political parties which would—in the absence of their cross-class marriages—warrant them the label 'working class Tory'. Their Conservative leanings, moreover, find their complement in the views of their wives. Mr Peterson is one of these men. Now employed in private industry as an electrician, Mr Peterson previously spent six years on the assembly line at BL. This work experience has left him strongly opposed to nationalization and resolutely anti-union:

> I see no personal benefit at all in joining another union. I was a member for 6 years. There's no difference between union and management: they both treat you like cattle. Most union members just use it as a way of avoiding work . . . I vote Conservative. I'd have more to lose as an individual if the Labour Party was to get power. A Labour government would probably spend money on things I don't approve of—like reducing bus fares: I don't use the bus. Or raising the rates for schools—I don't have any kids in school. . .

Mrs Peterson shares her husband's dislike of unions although a member of the National Union of Teachers for legal protection against possible complaints from parents about her actions as a teacher. And like her husband, Mrs Peterson votes Conservative, echoing his extreme individualism: 'I am opposed to socialism.' For the Petersons, cross-class family life brings no conflict of ideologies. Husband's and wife's views complement each other.

A similar congruence of perspectives is found in the Abbot family. Like Mr Peterson, Mr Abbot works in a nationalized industry and, as with Mr Peterson, this fact has turned him against both nationalization and the Labour Party:

> I've always voted. I think if you have a vote you should use it. I don't vote Labour because I'm opposed to nationalization, even though I work for a nationalized industry myself. I know how inefficient it can be. The Labour candidate in this area is to the left of Labour so I wouldn't vote for him

anyway, even if I didn't like the Conservative man. I've voted for the same man for the last four or five elections. Not just because he's Conservative, but because he's good—he takes an interest in the area.

Mr Abbot, sawmill foreman

Mr Abbot's reasons for preferring the Conservatives are mirrored by his wife's:

I'm not highly motivated but I always vote. I think one should. I voted Conservative last time mainly as a reaction to the previous Labour government. In this area, the person is very good. I voted for him as a person, not just because he happened to be Conservative.

Mrs Abbot, Head teacher

The Abbots also share generally indifferent, but somewhat negative, attitudes towards trade unions although Mr Abbot tends to be slightly more hostile towards their political activities than is his wife.

For the Abbots and the Petersons, then, cross-class marriage presents no problems of cross-class political or ideological stances. The Conservatism of the husband finds an ally in the Conservatism of the wife. In the Jason family, a man from a working class Tory home married a woman from a middle class Tory home. Not surprisingly, both continue to vote Conservative:

I vote Conservative first because I'm opposed to the Labour Party, and second because the Conservatives are more for the individual, not for the masses. I've a great admiration for Mrs Thatcher and Mr Edwardes [former head of BL].

Mrs Jason, MLSO

I voted Conservative. I always have. Father was a Tory. It was taught into us as children not to have a Labour government.

Mr Jason, turner machinist

In addition, however, Mr Jason's work experiences have contributed significantly to the growth of anti-union feelings in his wife:

I hate unions. I've had to deal with them all my married life and I just hate them. I agree with the principle but they've got so beyond themselves. It's like having two bosses. My husband doesn't have a choice, so he belongs. But he's quite passive, not militant at all. As I have a choice, I choose not to belong.

Mr Jason is not only 'passive' in his trade union activities, he disagrees with strike action: 'Membership is compulsory so I must belong. At the last strike, though, I crossed picket lines and worked. I didn't agree with what they were doing, so I worked.' Both husband and wife noted in their interviews that most of their co-workers favour both trade unions and the Labour Party, hence political discussions at work are avoided if at all possible.

These three families demonstrate a perhaps *unexpected* cross-class response to the public realm of politics and trade unions. The manual employment of the husbands in nationalized industries has generated (or confirmed) anti-Labour, anti-trade union views which find support in the complementary views of their non-manually employed wives. Far from experiencing conflict in their social perspectives as a result of their differing positions in the occupational structure, these men and women have found natural allies.

In the last group of families to be discussed one spouse does not vote. Thus, the other spouse enjoys his or her political preferences in isolation so to speak. Like the families met earlier who make opposing political choices, however, these families too share considerable agreement with respect to the activities of unions.

ISOLATION

In the various ways cross-class couples respond to trade unions and political choices seen so far both husband and wife have exercised their right to vote. Thus, agreement between spouses has been achieved either through complementary political choices or by accord in other areas despite opposing political choices. In the families now to be discussed no problem of divergent political choices exists by virtue of one spouse declining to vote. Mr Mason, for example, does not participate politically, believing that all parties are the same; thus it does not matter to him who is elected. Mrs Mason, in contrast, votes Conservative: 'My family has always voted Conservative. And I continue because Labour and unions tend to go hand in hand. I don't know—the Conservatives appeal to me, but mostly because of unions and their effects on Labour.' Mrs Mason is, clearly, anti-trade union. Her husband, moreover, shares her opinions and is not a union member. In a similar way, the Patons are agreed upon their anti-trade union beliefs and neither has chosen to join. In the Paton home, though, it is Mrs Paton who declines to vote: 'I've never voted. I'm not interested. I never intend to vote. We [she and her husband] don't discuss politics at all. I think he votes Labour or Liberal, but I've never asked.' In fact, Mr Paton has voted Labour in the past and is considering supporting the SDP in the future. His support for Labour came from being raised in a Labour-voting family; they have probably now lost his vote as a result of all the public quarrels among the party members. In very like manner, Mr Barnes is also an anti-trade union Labour voter:

My family always voted Labour and I do because I've been a labourer all my life. But I'm not really strongly in favour of them . . . I used to be a union member, but not any more. I got pissed off with all their moaning and groaning. Unions just don't do any good.

And like Mrs Paton, Mrs Barnes does not vote and chooses not to join a union. These husbands and wives, then, avoid the need to seek political agreement by one spouse 'opting out' of participation and avoid conflict over union activity through mutual dislike of unions. There is, however, no rational link between their behaviour and the fact of their cross-class marriages. Many people do not vote, and many more dislike trade unions. For these cross-class couples, political isolation for one spouse eliminates a possible area of marital discord but cannot really be attributed to their marital circumstances.

However, for three other families in which the husbands choose not to vote, there may well be a link between cross-class marital situations and opting out of political participation. These three men are all occupationally downwardly mobile. All three were born in middle class homes, live now in cross-class homes. All three, in addition to not voting, are anti-trade union. Two, therefore, refrain from membership: Mr Light, a hire-car driver, and Mr Aston, a garage driver. The third, however, was requested to join the union by his boss at work. Mr Henley's wife reports that her husband 'was shocked' at having to do so. Mr Henley continues as a union member, but does not support strike action. His reasons are quite interesting:

I stayed in during the last strike. I didn't want to disturb management—to rub them up the wrong way.

Printer's helper

Mr Henley clearly does not identify with working class ideals of collective action.

The wives of these three men have in the past all voted in accordance with their family backgrounds and 'notional' class interests: Conservative. Their support for this party is quite mixed, however, with Mrs Aston unlikely to vote Conservative again, having done so because the Prime Minister was to be a woman but now reporting: 'I dislike extremes in any party'. Similarly, Mrs Henley's support for the Conservatives has waned considerably as she has come up against government restrictions on funding for education. A teacher, Mrs Henley planned to vote for the SDP in 1983. Mrs Light, though, is a strong Conservative supporter. Her dislike of communism is keenly felt, and is shared by her husband:

I voted Conservative last time because I didn't like what Labour had to offer and I think they're more and more towards communism and I'm dead against that. I would never vote communist. So I voted Conservative, and partly because it would be a woman who would be PM. I was thrilled when Maggie got in, because she's a woman, and I think she's done a damn good job.

Mrs Light, Deputy Head teacher

I'm a political atheist, but if the alternative was communism, I'd fight that—don't get me wrong. I suppose I'm more of a Conservative than anything else. But I don't vote. I haven't voted ever since the first year I could . . . Thatcher is about right, but I can't abide the carrying-on. To me it's laughable. But if the alternative was communism, I'd fight that. There's no way I'd live under that particular regime.

Mr Light, hire-car driver

Mr Light does not vote because he cannot abide the 'carrying-on', Mr Henley because he is 'not interested', and Mr Aston because he did not know who to vote for: 'Labour is too extreme left and the Conservatives are too extreme right'. With only three cases, it is hard to know if their occupational 'dislocation'—that is, their downward mobility, contributes to their political apathy or indecision. But the possibility exists that it does. And if it is the case that it does, then their cross-class marriages are partly linked to their withdrawal from political participation.

Unlike the other responses in this section, 'isolation' is not really a response at all. Rather, it describes life in these particular cross-class families. Husband and wife avoid political disputes by one spouse withdrawing from political participation. They avoid disputes over trade unions through mutual dislike of unions. In very different ways, then, these families achieve the same ends sought by the others: harmonious relations within areas of life which might be expected to have potential for cross-class marital conflict. But in fact, as we have seen, political disagreement seldom does cause conflict between these husbands and wives. Couples who disagree either 'agree to disagree', or keep their opinions to themselves. Many are simply indifferent—both to their spouses' views and to the world of political parties and trade unions in general. This is, perhaps, to be expected. Political parties and trade unions do not 'fight back' so to speak: if someone chooses to ignore their existence, they are left to their indifference. The status order does 'fight back', however, and impinges directly upon the lives of cross-class husbands and wives. Thus we observe many more difficulties between spouses with regard to status differences than we do with regard to political differences. Political isolation or political differences are seemingly much less costly psychologically than are social isolation or social differences. And as such, much less threatening to cross-class marital stability.

This discussion of the families and their various social and political perspectives, their responses to cross-class life in the 'public' realm, brings the study to a close. It is hoped that a clear and informed understanding of cross-class family life has been gained. In the chapter which follows, a brief discussion of the place of cross-class families in sociology is offered, and the main findings are summarized.

Notes

1. Although it is important to ask if the concept 'cross-class' makes sense to those to whom one would wish to apply such a label, this label would not necessarily be misplaced in the absence of their concurrence. It is, of course, the aim of sociology to understand social action from the perspective of the social actor. In addition to this, however, is the need for sociological inquiry to go beyond the perceptions and understandings of the individual actor, and to interpret his or her acts in light of the specialized knowledge available to the investigator. Thus, although I suspect that most of the respondents would agree with, and understand, others calling them 'cross-class families', their denial of the appropriateness of this term would not, in itself, constitute sufficient reason for its abandonment.

2. Bulmer himself asks a similar question: 'All the papers refer to the images of society of men; when is someone going to do research on women's images of society?' (1975b: 177).
3. Predominately the literature on differing class perceptions between husbands and wives has come from the United States. The findings of these studies are quite mixed, for example: Van Velso and Beeghley (1979), who report that an employed married woman uses a combination of her own, her husband's and her father's characteristics in assessing her own position. Also, Ritter and Hargens (1975), whose results suggest that traditional assumptions concerning working women deriving their class positions and identifications solely from their husband's occupations do not hold. In contrast, however, Mahoney and Richardson (1979) argue that it is the husband's occupational status alone which is the determinant of both his and his wife's general social status. Appendix 2 discusses the problems of class and status analysis in American sociology and thus these problems need not be repeated here. As far as the cross-class couples studied here, husband's occupation is much less important as a determinant of both class position and status position than wife's occupation.
4. Compared with other manual workers, the cross-class husbands of this study participate more often and in more social organizations. Only five of the husbands (18%) do not participate in any formal organization; seventeen (61%) participate in one or two such organizations; and six (21%) participate in three or more. For a national comparison, see Goldthorpe, 1980: 187–8, Tables 7.5 and 7.6. The wives of this study tended to participate in more formal organizations than their husbands.
5. Britten and Heath analyse results from the 1979 British Election Survey; as 'strictly defined' cross-class voters they include twelve women and seventeen men. See p. 58, Table 4.3.

10

Summary of the Main Findings

In this chapter the main findings of the study are summarized. Initially, however, two points must be made. First, it is important to emphasize that this is primarily an investigation into the lives of thirty married couples, and concentrates on intra- and extra-familial relations. It is thus a study in micro-sociology. In Chapter 1 reference is made to the continuing debate over the place of married women in the analysis of class stratification. Although this debate is of central importance in that it provides the intellectual framework for the 'discovery' of cross-class families, this study cannot and does not purport to make any contribution towards its resolution. Such resolution, if and when it occurs, will come only from studies much wider in scope than the present one. Furthermore, in Chapters 1 and 2 arguments are offered which suggest that the category 'cross-class family' should be reserved for marriages of the type studied here, and that marriages between women employed in junior non-manual work and men employed in manual work should not be so categorized. Strictly speaking, though, I can only defend the *inclusion* of marriages between men in manual occupations and women in higher level non-manual or professional work in the category cross-class, and cannot justifiably defend the *exclusion* of other types of marriages. Arguments are presented which, if correct, do suggest that other marriages might well be misrepresented by the label 'cross-class'; that is, there are persuasive theoretical reasons for limiting application of this concept to the very special kinds of families studied here, but these theoretical reasons cannot stand alone. It remains possible that future empirical work will demonstrate that other families too warrant being called 'cross-class families'. In the absence of such research, however, there is some basis for regarding the families studied here as among the very few *genuine* cross-class families to be found in British society.

Secondly, it is important to comment upon the number of families located for study and upon the methods employed in finding these families. As noted in Chapter 1, it is not unusual for studies of family life to comprise only a small number of families, and this study is no exception. However, the preceding chapters have shown that the families gathered here, although few in number, represent a wide variety of marital situations, stages in the family life cycle and—most importantly—responses to cross-class occupational circumstances. Perhaps the thirty families of this book do not encompass all variations of cross-class family life; they do, however, encompass a considerable diversity of such families. Some question might exist about the suitability of the present study for sociological investigations of family life, however, because of the way in which the families studied here were located. These thirty families are not a random sample of cross-class families; they cannot, therefore, be spoken of as 'representative' of some wider universe of cross-class families in the population as a whole. Cross-class families are, almost by definition, 'deviant' families and, as such, widely dispersed geographically. Locating and interviewing such families through simple random sampling techniques—should a sampling frame exist from which one could proceed—would entail financial resources beyond the reach of most researchers. However, no sampling frame does exist. Therefore, obtaining a random sample of cross-class families would require selecting an enormous number of families from some other source, and filtering through these until the desired number of cross-class families were found. This would be an extremely expensive undertaking. And so, cross-class families must be located for investigation in the best way possible within realistic financial and geographical constraints. The approach taken here yielded a reasonable number of families, and families who, as has been noted, present a diversity of situations. The inability to locate cross-class families by more rigorous methods does not, however, lessen the importance of such families for sociological investigations. While it may not be possible to state with certainty that this or that proportion of cross-class families in general will exhibit this or that trait, it is possible through these thirty families to see norms and modes of behaviour which exist on a very wide scale. Furthermore, by being *deviant* families, cross-class families throw into sharp relief the underlying assumptions which generally guide men and women in marriage. Through cross-class families it is possible to see the strength and perseverance of cultural norms governing marriage; to see the harm such norms can do if accepted unexamined, if broken without understanding. And here, perhaps, lies the ultimate importance of the study of cross-class families—by deviating from cultural norms, they render explicit the enduring nature of those norms.

Normative Agreement

In this study considerable emphasis is placed on the existence of normative agreement between spouses. It has been argued that, without such agreement between husband and wife, marital harmony may be threatened. That is, the existence of a common value-system between spouses such that husband and wife are in general agreement over the norms which govern their marriage has been seen to be an important condition of marital stability. And through this emphasis on normative agreement, it has been revealed that there is no *one* Cross-class Family, but rather several different ways of responding to a similar position in society. Talcott Parsons argued that occupational linkages of the type found between spouses in cross-class families would be injurious to marital solidarity, with feelings of jealousy, competition, etc. arising between husbands and wives. This work shows, however, that in some cross-class families unequal attachments to the labour force when wives are in superior positions to their husbands can be accommodated into family life without destructive competition between spouses. It has also been seen, though, that in other cross-class families such competition does indeed arise, together with feelings of disappointment, inferiority, and anger. What seems, then, to be of primary importance is not simply the fact of wives' occupational superiority, not simply the nature of the outward attachment to the labour force *per se*, but the extent and kind of normative agreement between spouses governing their participation in both family and occupational worlds. When husbands and wives are able to accommodate the superior labour force position of women into their common value-system little difficulty between spouses arises, either in regard to the extrinsic rewards which flow from the wives' employment, i.e. higher job security, higher pay, greater opportunity for promotion; or in regard to the intrinsic demands which attend such employment, i.e. extra work, late hours, tiredness, and mental preoccupation with work matters. And, conversely, when husbands and wives are unable to accommodate occupational differences which favour wives, stress between spouses arises most often at the very point of deviance itself—over money in families where wives are the higher earners or in the more secure job, and over work involvement as wives pursue their career interests beyond the hours their husbands set aside for earning a living. At the point at which cross-class couples differ—from each other and from the couples who surround them—lies the centre of marital discord. Without normative agreement allowing and explaining deviation from the norm of male occupational dominance, cross-class occupational linkages do place considerable strains upon the marriage bond.

The ways in which cross-class husbands and wives come to accommodate the superior occupational position of the wives has been seen to vary among the families, giving further weight to the suggestion that there is no one Cross-class Family. This is clearly illustrated in Chapter 6 where we saw both normative agreement based upon equality between spouses, and normative agreement allowing female superiority in the household as well as occupationally. In the first group of families, the normative agreement between husband and wife which demands joint occupational participation and joint contributions to the family financially prevents marital competition; that is, prevents disruptions to marital solidarity of the nature suggested by Talcott Parsons. With these families, we saw that, rather than competition between spouses straining family solidarity, solidarity itself dispenses with competition. In the second group of families, also characterized by lack of marital discord over the divergent occupational positions of husband and wife, we saw the coming together of normative agreement and economic reality, resulting in acceptance by both spouses of the occupational superiority of the wife. Wives in these families accept responsibility for long-term financial security; accept that they provide more material benefits to their families than do their husbands. Husbands in these families are often relieved at not being asked to fulfil the conventional position of 'breadwinner'; often feel considerable personal security as a result of their wives' high incomes. Like the families who share norms of equality, these families too share normative agreement between husband and wife, and this agreement allows for relatively harmonious cross-class family lives.

However, just as agreement between spouses may occur in more than one way, failure to agree also takes diverse forms. In Chapter 6 we met two further groups of families in which husbands and wives live somewhat troubled existences as a result of the occupational positions held by them. Here we saw wives who are disappointed with their husbands' occupational attainments; wives who came to marriage with certain traditional expectations which have not been fulfilled. Deviation from tradition, from male occupational dominance has, in these families, led to conflict between husband and wife, resulting, in one family, in divorce. Here also we saw certain mechanisms adopted by the wives to subvert reality, to maintain a façade of male dominance in spite of workplace accomplishments which argue otherwise. Thus, we met one wife who plays the 'helpless female', and another who lets her husband 'think he's boss'. Similarly, we met husbands who are unable to come to terms with their wives' labour force superiority, both inside the family and outside in relations with others in the local community. Wives in these families as well adopt mechanisms designed to overcome their husband's failure to fulfil the convention of male occupational dominance. Thus, we saw partial withdrawal from labour force participation by one wife, and total withdrawal from financial matters by a second. These attempts were seen to be only moderately successful, though, and conflict between spouses over the wives' commitment to careers remains. All of these families lack agreement between husband and wife allowing and explaining their deviation from the normal pattern of married life. As a result, cross-class married life brings contradiction between belief and reality into their lives, and with this contradiction, varying degrees of marital conflict.

However, there is no *intrinsic* reason why such conflict should arise from wives' occupational superiority, and, perhaps, in a world without specific beliefs about the correct and proper behaviour of husbands and wives, no such conflict would arise. These particular cross-class families show, though, that in this world—a world most certainly with specific beliefs—the realities of cross-class family life can only be accommodated harmoniously between husband and wife through some form of normative agreement which explains each spouse's place in family life.

The Household Division of Labour

In discussing the division of household chores between husbands and wives, it was noted that the internalization by women of feelings of personal responsibility for housework coexists with very nearly every level of labour force participation. Whether women work part time, full time, or not at all; whether they earn more or less than their husbands, they invariably do the housework. They invariably feel it is their responsibility. And, by and large, cross-class wives were seen to be no exception to this normal pattern. With many cross-class wives, in fact, we saw that neither career commitment, occupational superiority, nor financial power was sufficient to offset traditional beliefs about what is their responsibility in the home, what is their husbands' responsibility.

In a few families, though, this traditional division of labour between spouses is not adhered to. The same families who share normative agreement demanding joint labour force participation by husband and wife also share housework between husband and wife. Among these families generally there was seen to be a 'trade-off' of equal financial obligations for equal household obligations. The egalitarian notion of 'fairness' which was observed to underlie harmonious dual linkages to the occupational structure was further seen to underlie egalitarian divisions of domestic labour. But these families were also seen to be the minority pattern of those studied. Far more predominant were wives who willingly retained responsibility for, and did, the bulk of the housework. In regard to these 'wives who control', it was suggested that the fact of their *cross-class* marriages contributed to their unwillingness to relinquish control of household work. It was suggested that being a wife in a cross-class family may actually encourage or develop behaviour associated with traditional female roles, in this instance the performance of housework. This was suggested as a means of compensating for cross-class wives' non-traditional behaviour outside the home; that is, as a means of compensating for such wives' occupational participation at levels superior to their husbands. Control of the housework is one way at least for cross-class wives to assert their femininity in the face of occupational achievements which might suggest otherwise. This explanation is, however, based primarily on speculation. Although gender identity is presented in the study as an important variable for assessing participation (or not) in household tasks, as well as other aspects of cross-class marital life, no specific questions were put to the respondents concerning such identity. Without direct investigation of this issue, inference is all that is possible. I suggest that the explanation offered is a plausible one, though, and that future research into the lives of cross-class families would benefit by the addition of this issue more directly. Speculation aside, however, it remains clear that for most cross-class wives, like most other wives, housework is 'women's work'.

Children

From a study of this size, very little may be said about children. The children of the families studied here have predominately entered non-manual occupations, have predominately followed in their mothers', and not their fathers', footsteps. However, there are too few children from too few families to suggest that this might be the pattern found in other cross-class families. What is shown with some degree of certainty is that problems between parents, and between parents and children, may arise as a result of cross-class occupational linkages. Mothers and fathers may have different values, different standards, different expectations for their children. These differences may not only cause confusion in the minds of children, but also conflict between parents. Moreover, status differences between fathers and children may give rise to difficulties. This was observed especially with regard to the stepchild–stepfather relationship found in the Jameses' home, but was also seen to have existed in lesser degree in other families. For most children, however, feelings of status differences pass with time and, in general, discussions with these cross-class parents revealed, above all, parental delight with their children's occupational accomplishments.

Social Status

One of the more important subjects discussed concerned differences of status between cross-class husbands and wives, both in their family worlds and in their outside social worlds. In this discussion, status was understood to refer to differing relations of acceptance, deference and derogation—status as it is traditionally conceived in sociological literature. Here we observed that most cross-class couples are able to overcome differences of status between themselves within the confines of family life through some mechanism designed to divert superior status away from the wife's occupational position. Such couples either upgrade the husband's accomplishments through focusing upon some aspect of his job or of his personality, i.e., his intelligence, his skills, his interests in life, which offsets his

lower status, or downgrade the wife's accomplishments so that husband and wife enjoy equal status. Other couples attempt to 'opt out'
of status distinctions altogether, but here it was seen that the actions
of others outside family life interfere. If others make distinctions
between husbands and wives—make invidious comparisons on the
basis of their diverse occupational attainments—then consequences
detrimental to marital harmony may ensue. That others do make
such comparisons became clear in the discussion of cross-class couples' relations with work colleagues. Many cross-class husbands
were observed to be very reluctant to attend social events held at
their wives' workplaces. Differential treatment—either real or perceived—from their wives' colleagues was seen to lie behind their
reluctance. In large, formal social gatherings where cross-class husbands meet husbands who fulfil the convention of male occupational
dominance, the differences in occupational attainment between
husband and wife are accentuated; are perceived by others as 'odd'
or 'unusual'. Although able to mute status differences between
spouses in the confines of family living, cross-class couples cannot
control the actions of others outside their families who seem less
willing to disregard such differences. Workplace social gatherings
are thus, for many, to be avoided.

However, very nearly as many cross-class husbands studied were
reluctant to attend social events at their *own* workplaces as were
reluctant to attend similar events at their wives' workplaces.
Although a disinclination to socialize with workmates was noted as
not uncommon among manually employed men in general, the
reluctance to do so on the part of cross-class men in particular was
attributed largely to the nature of the social worlds these men enjoy
with their wives. Cross-class couples live predominately in middle-
class social worlds. Wives, not husbands, dominate the friendship
choices of cross-class couples. Through their dominance, moreover,
the majority of friends are chosen from status levels equal or similar
to that of the wives. More than three-quarters of these cross-class
couples' joint friends are employed in non-manual occupations; just
over a fifth in manual occupations. Furthermore, these friends are
socialized with in a variety of settings and activities, for the most
part far removed from the original context in which they were first
met—a pattern of sociability more often found in middle-class
families than in working class ones. Thus, it was not surprising to
find that many cross-class husbands choose not to mix socially with

their own workmates. Work, and workmates, were frequently seen to be a thing apart from cross-class husbands' family lives. The participation of these men in predominately middle class, or non-manual, social worlds also suggests that the experience of differential treatment is often restricted to contexts in which such men are only casually known. In the formation of personal friendships, differential treatment as a result of their manual occupations is missing, and the men socialize as equals among the status equals of their wives.

Study of the friendship choices of cross-class couples has allowed a contribution to the analysis of social stratification to be made. In various studies of middle class sociability it has been found that men dominate the friendship choices of married couples; that is, the status equals of husbands become the friends of husbands and wives. The friendship choices of cross-class couples indicate that it is not husbands *per se*—that is, not the *sex* of the family member *per se*—but rather the higher occupational status of husbands which dominates the choice of friends. When wives have superior occupational status to their husbands, i.e., when husband and wife reverse their positions in the occupational hierarchy, then wives, not husbands, dominate friendship choice. In other words, it is status dominance and not male dominance which governs patterns of sociability. This suggestion is given credence not only by the choices cross-class couples make jointly with regard to friends, but also by the fact that as individuals cross-class husbands and wives maintain status similarity with their respective occupational groups. That is, the majority of wives reporting individual friends chose others in non-manual occupations; the majority of husbands reporting individual friends chose others in manual employment. This tendency towards status similarity in the choice of individual friends underlines the importance of status dominance in the formation of joint friendships. In cross-class families, male dominance over friendship choice quickly yields to status equality for wives.

Self-placement in the Class Structure

Partnership in a cross-class marriage has clear effects on an individual's perceptions of his or her place in the class structure. More than half of the families studied included one or both spouses with views of their own class position which were affected in some way by the fact of their cross-class marriages. Virtually all of the respondents were able to describe fairly well-defined models of the class structure. When asked to place themselves in their own constructions, however, their models failed and uncertainty, contradiction, or refusal ensued. For a few families, cross-class marriage was seen to engender perceptions of a 'class-divided' family, with husband and wife occupying different class locations by virtue of their different occupational positions. Unlike differences of status between husband and wife, though, differences in class perceptions caused little marital conflict or stress. It was suggested that this might be the case because differences in status are palpable, and separate husband and wife from each other. How people react to you, or to your spouse, is immediately felt; such feelings, moreover, reflect the reality of cross-class couples' differing status positions. Perceptions of class differences, in contrast, belie the reality of the shared class position the respondents enjoy as married couples. Despite the lack of conflict between cross-class couples as a result of their differing perceptions, however, the reactions of the respondents to the issue of self-placement in the class structure reaffirmed the validity of the concept 'cross-class'. Confusion, contradictions, or uncertainty about their *own places* in the class structure, or 'opting out' altogether would not exist in the minds of cross-class husbands and wives without good reason. The fact of their cross-class marriages provides such good reason. The stressful reactions of the respondents to questions of class differences between spouses demonstrated most clearly their awareness of the 'cross-class' aspect of their marriages. Such men and women truly are 'cross-class' husbands and wives.

Political and Social Perspectives

From a study composed of only thirty families, one can say regrettably little about the voting behaviour or political preferences of the individuals involved. Among the families here, support for the Conservative Party was equally balanced by support for the Labour Party. Cross-class wives were seen to be more likely than their husbands to favour the Conservatives; cross-class husbands seen to be more likely than their wives to favour Labour. A much larger number of families selected from a much wider geographical area would be needed to discover if the choices made by these particular cross-class families reflect those of other similar families. Because of the limitations presented by the type of study undertaken, attention was focused primarily on the husbands' and wives' attitudes towards the 'public' realm of political parties and trade unions. In the first instance, an attempt was made to trace intelligible links between the fact of cross-class marriage and responses to this 'public' realm. The most interesting of these links was found to exist in those families characterized by normative agreement obliging each spouse to make financial contributions to the home and to participate equally in the domestic work of the home. For these families, it was suggested that the belief in equality which finds expression in left-wing political ideologies and favourable attitudes towards trade unions is a reflection of the belief in equality which sustains their harmonious *cross-class* marriages. For these families, private and public life 'make sense' in that one area creates and sustains the other.

For the remaining families, an attempt was made to view their responses to political parties and trade unions as logical responses to cross-class marital circumstances. Here we saw situations of dominance, of complementarity, of isolation, and of husbands and wives with quite separate, and opposing, political views. Like differences of class perceptions, differing political perspectives were seen to cause little difficulty between cross-class spouses. Political autonomy and independence were observed to exist in otherwise harmonious marriages. This was suggested to be the case because, unlike the status order, political parties and trade unions do not 'fight back', so to speak. If someone chooses to ignore their existence, they are left to their indifference. If husband and wife choose to favour opposing parties, they can remain silent about their choices—or find agreement in other areas. Political differences, although interesting, are seemingly much less costly psychologically than are status differences, and as such, much less injurious to cross-class marital stability.

This ends the review of the main findings. Other areas of investigation could well have been included in this summary such as the propensity for cross-class couples to follow the wives' career opportunities in questions of geographical relocation, or the willingness of cross-class husbands to modify their attachments to the labour force to suit the demands of their wives' employment. However, it is perhaps best to end with a brief mention of the typology presented in

Chapter 3 which demonstrates the several social origins from which cross-class families arise. In many respects revealing these social origins has been one of the more important tasks undertaken. And it is in the accomplishment of this task that a further contribution to the analysis of class stratification has been achieved. The most numerous cross-class families located for study became cross-class through the upward mobility of the wives. This is an important fact, for it means that cross-class families are likely to remain a feature of British society. If, for example, cross-class families came into being predominately through the downward mobility of husbands, they might be of lesser importance since much downward mobility among men is reversed. Under these conditions, most cross-class families would eventually move out of cross-class circumstances, living as such for only a transitory period. But in fact, cross-class families formed as a result of husbands' downward mobility are a minority of those located for study. The majority were formed instead through the occupational achievements of the wives. And should women from working-class origins continue to enter higher education, and from there enter paid employment at levels above junior non-manual work, it is likely that cross-class families will not only remain a feature of our society but will increase in number. With such an increase, a new stratum in the class structure will indeed exist, and the conventional equation of husband's occupation with family class position be inappropriate for this stratum. All this, however, lies in the future. For the present, the primary importance of cross-class families comes in the study of family life itself.

Appendix 1

Locating Cross-class Families

As noted in the text, 2,155 introductory questionnaires were distributed among women employed in higher level white-collar and professional occupations. 603 responses to this introductory questionnaire were ultimately received. Table A1 details these responses by socio-economic group (SEG) of both husband and wife. As may be seen, the overwhelming response was from couples employed at the same level. Of the Class II respondents only, 81% of replies were received from women and men in the same social class; only twenty-four replies, or 4.2%, came from women in the strictly defined

Table A1. *Introductory Questionnaire: Respondents by Wife's SEG and Husband's SEG, all Respondents by Social Class of Wife*

Husband's SEG	Wife's SEG							
	Social Classes I and II					Class IIINM		
	1, 2	3, 4	5.1	Total	(%)	5.2	6	Total
1, 2	14	12	138	164	(29.1)	1	5	6
3, 4	6	14	154	174	(30.8)	1	9	10
5.1	5	7	107	119	(21.1)	–	2	2
5.2	3	–	22	25	(4.4)	2	1	3
6	1	–	28	29	(5.1)	–	2	2
7	1	–	–	1	(0.2)	–	–	–
8	–	–	6	6	(1.1)	–	2	2
9	1	3	13	17	(3.0)	4	7	11
10	–	–	3	3	(0.5)	–	2	2
11	1	–	1	2	(0.4)	–	–	–
12	–	1	9	10	(1.8)	–	1	1
13, 14	–	–	–	–		–	–	–
15	–	–	2	2	(0.4)	–	–	–
16	–	–	6	6	(1.1)	–	–	–
Unemployed	2	–	4	6	(1.1)	–	–	–
Total	34	36	494	564	(100.0)	8	31	39

N = 603 (percentages in parenthesis); each social class = 100%.

Table A2. *Distribution of Introductory Questionnaires and Responses by Occupational Category of Wives, Class II Respondents only*

Employer or Occupation	Number sent out	Responses	Occupation response rate (%)	Cross-class respondents
Teachers	895	268	29.9	14
Health workers	449	73	16.3	4
City/County Council workers	320	41	12.8	2
Social services workers	491	182	37.0	4
Total	2155	564		24

Notes: 1. Occupations included in Health Workers are primarily District Nurses and Health Visitors (389); in addition, 60 questionnaires were distributed through the Association of Scientific, Technical, and Managerial Staff (ASTMS) to various laboratory officers, medical technicians, psychologists, therapists.

2. Questionnaires distributed through City and County councils were meant only for higher level employees; however, some thirty-nine responses were received from women in lower level occupations; these responses are not included in this table.

3. Occupations included in Social Services are librarians, social workers, and related.

category of cross-class families. The distribution of both responses and cross-class respondents was not evenly spread across all of the occupations surveyed. Table A2 shows the occupational response rate and number of cross-class respondents by occupational category. As indicated, the response rate of the various occupational groups varied from a high of 37% for social service employees to a low of 12.8% for city and county council workers. Teachers, however, proved to be the best source of cross-class respondents, with fourteen out of twenty-four respondents coming from this occupational category. This table indicates that a disproportionate number of introductory questionnaires were in fact distributed among teachers. This is, in part, a reflection of the success I found I was having in locating cross-class families in this way, but only in part. For in fact, all female, married social workers, librarians, district nurses and health visitors in Oxfordshire were sent introductory questionnaires. All social workers, librarians and related workers in Berkshire received questionnaires. All city and council workers in Oxford, Reading and Oxfordshire in the appropriate level occupations received questionnaires. There were few other sources to which I could turn besides teachers, and so after an original 'sweep' of the schools in Oxfordshire, I made an additional foray into the schools surrounding Reading.[1] This action accounts for the disproportionate number of questionnaires distributed to teachers, and for the fact that the final group of families is over-represented by wives in such jobs.

However, the difficulties experienced in locating suitable families for research actually aided the interview process. The selection procedure took a considerable length of time. Therefore, I began interviewing some families several months prior to locating others. These delays between interviews allowed ample time to reflect on the quality of the questions being asked. Thus, the nature of some of these questions changed over time. In this, I feel that I learned first hand the meaning of Bott's words: 'The achievement of the research consists not so much in finding complete answers as in finding interesting questions to ask' (1957: 5). Each interview was undertaken with a set number of questions I wanted to ask, and did ask, but through the course of the interviews it became clear that some of these questions were more important, or more revealing, than others. The core of questions remained stable throughout all interviews; thus it is possible to compare early sessions with later ones, but the development of certain issues improved through time such that the later interviews are more complete as pictures of life in cross-class families.

Note

1. I could possibly have found more cross-class families in which the wives are employed as nurses. To do so, however, was beyond my resources and control. In regard to women employed as nurses rather than as district nurses or health visitors, it was financially impossible to locate any cross-class families. The John Radcliffe Hospital falls within my geographical location and employs several thousand nurses. Their computer facilities do not distinguish marital status on personnel records, however, and thus I would have had to send countless introductory questionnaires to unmarried nurses (by far the majority according to hospital authorities) in order to find the very few married nurses with manually employed husbands. All district nurses and health visitors in Oxfordshire were approached. In Berkshire, though, only half of the available district nurses and health visitors received introductory questionnaires as the West Berkshire Health Authority was unable to assist me owing to internal reorganization. Further, the idea of locating suitable families through ASTMS came to me very late in my search. By this time, my finances were stretched to their limits and so I was unable to use this source to its maximum potential.

Appendix 2

Social Status

In Chapter 8, it is noted that 'status inconsistency' between husbands and wives is often investigated by sociologists in the United States, but that, because of conceptual differences in the use of the term 'status' between American and British sociologists, the American literature is largely omitted from consideration. The reasoning behind this omission is now given, first by a theoretical examination of the way in which it is possible for class and status to be sufficiently confused so that it becomes unclear exactly what is to be studied; and secondly, by looking at three empirical studies which purport to examine the consequences of status differences within marriage.

Luther Otto is an American sociologist of the family intent on convincing other family researchers to incorporate the theoretical advances of stratification analysis into investigations of family life. His paper 'Class and Status in Family Research' (*Journal of Marriage and the Family*, May 1975), serves the present purposes very well as its aim is to join together family and stratification research. Moreover, as a family sociologist concerned with issues of class and status stratification, Otto appears at first to understand the conceptual importance and distinctiveness of both class and status for family life:

> At issue in discussing the relevance of class and status variables in family theory and research is the fundamental recognition that *whereas classes arise out of common economic interests, statuses are rooted in family experience*. Before an individual reaches maturity, he (*sic*) participates in the family's claim to prestige, the family's occupational subculture, and the family's general educational level. These are the bases of shared life styles, values, and attitudes which figure so prominently in family theory and research. (1975: 324) (Italics in original.)

Otto goes on, however, to exhort family researchers to leave aside issues of class and to concentrate instead on 'multi-dimensional status indicators', in particular occupational prestige (p. 326). Otto suggests this course of action because of 'certain invalidating challenges to [the] conceptual integrity' of the variable social class (p. 329), but in doing so confuses class and status distinctions with the result that it is not clear quite what is to be investigated.

Under the heading 'Occupational Prestige as an Indicator of Family Social Status', Otto specifies occupational prestige in three ways. First, it is the most commonly and widely used 'status indicator'. Secondly, as such it is 'a summary measure of a family's social standing within society'. And thirdly, it refers to 'the phenomenon of differential social evaluation of occupations according to their social standing' (p. 326). 'Social standing' is, of course, a vague term. It could, however, be taken to mean relations of deference, acceptance and derogation—that is, status as it is traditionally understood in sociological thought. If this was in fact Otto's meaning, then little difficulty would arise. But when this family researcher moves on from theoretical exhortations to instructions to other researchers for the collection and interpretation of data, it becomes apparent that this is not his meaning.

Under the heading 'Measuring Occupational Prestige in Family Research', Otto poses the following question: 'Assuming that a family theorist–researcher would choose to employ occupational prestige as his best indicator of socio-economic status, how best might he proceed?' (p. 327). From being an indicator of status, of social standing, of differential social evaluation, occupational prestige has moved to become, then, socio-economic status. In shifting his meaning in this way, Otto makes an error predicted by Goldthorpe and Hope in their evaluation of occupational prestige scales:

> . . . one finds that often the meanings given to occupational prestige and thus the interpretations of occupational prestige scales, are left uncertain if not confused . . . Perhaps the most frequent source of confusion lies in shifts made from a 'strong' usage of 'prestige'—i.e., in its established sociological sense—to some much weaker one, equating it with, say, 'socio-economic status' . . . [occupational prestige scales] are quite probably *invalid* in that they measure prestige only to the degree that they measure attributes of occupations which are correlated with prestige. (1974: 5–6)

According to Goldthorpe and Hope, this shift in meaning frequently occurs when writers move from substantive issues to questions of data interpretation (1974: 6). Otto is no exception to this conceptual slight of hand. In order for researchers to comply with his instructions, they must simply gather data on respondents' occupation, industry and employment status (salaried or self-employed). Once data are collected in this form, they can then easily be coded and assigned 'explicit SEI and prestige scale scores' (p. 327), thus completing the researcher's task. Explicit SEI scores refer, of course, to Duncan's (1961a; 1961b) Socio-economic Index based upon weighted measures of the income and education distribution of detailed occupational groups. Otto's loss of any 'strong' meaning of the concept status is clear in his equation, finally, of social standing with education and income—not prestige but rather, as Goldthorpe and Hope point out, the *correlates* of prestige. Otto's confusion of class with status is made clear with the realization that his discussion of Duncan's Index comes, not in regard to status as one might expect from his eventual instructions to researchers interested in status differences in families, but much earlier during his 'exposure' of the conceptual limitations of the variable social class. Duncan's SEI is discussed not as an indicator of status, but under the heading 'Objective Indicators of Class'.

In using Duncan's scale of occupational prestige as a tool for investigating the consequences of status differences within family life, Otto falls into difficulties not uncommon in sociology. Duncan himself gave warning to researchers about the limitations of his scale:

> The index of occupational SES was constructed to predict the prestige ratings of occupations. It was not designed to secure optimal prediction of the prestige standings of individuals in their local communities or other group contexts . . . (1961a: 145) . . . It would seem strategic . . . to approach an explanation of the influence of occupation on such phenomena as migration, marriage, and family dissolution by first taking account of the occupational SES and then looking for other circumstances that may affect these variables independently of socio-economic level. (1961b: 161)

Hatt gives similarly cautionary advice to those using the NORC scale constructed by him and North:

> To apply a classification to a totally different problem from the one for which it was intended is always a dangerous and unhappy undertaking all too often found in the use of occupational indexes in stratification studies . . . (1961: 239) . . . a fully accurate index should approximate total societal position and thus reflect both prestige and esteem. It should thus be some sort of summarizing measure of those prestige and esteem values attached to an individual by virtue of his status within each of the social structures in which he participates. Occupation, by definition, cannot possibly be taken as describing esteem . . . (1961: 241)

Otto provides a theoretical example of failure to observe the warnings given by these two authors; the following three empirical studies will demonstrate why the use (misuse?) of such scales in American sociology renders comparisons with such reports on status differences between spouses incompatible with the findings reported here.

In his article 'Wife Occupational Superiority and Marital Troubles: An Examination of the Hypothesis' (*Journal of Marriage and the Family*, 1979), Richardson tests the hypothesis 'that marital discord and/or dissatisfaction may arise from conditions of status inequality within marriage' (p. 64). And he suggests that prior awareness of husbands and wives of the potential pitfalls of 'status discrepant' marriages would forestall subsequent conflict.[1] As his criterion of status discrepancies between spouses, Richardson employs NORC occupational prestige scores—an instrument which does not, however, incorporate the 'symbolic' aspect of social stratification traditionally understood by the concept status; does not measure 'esteem'. With similar interests, Jorgensen and Klein investigate the consequences of sociocultural heterogamy for marital conflict in their article 'Sociocultural Heterogamy, Dissensus and Conflict in Marriage' (*Pacific Sociological Review*, 1979). These authors are interested in the consequences of both status and class heterogamy, but in their analysis measure both variables with the same instrument—Duncan's SEI. Status differences between spouses are obtained from differences in individual SEI scores at the time of marriage (p. 58) while class differences are obtained from differences in SEI scores attributable to husband's and wife's respective families of origin (p. 57). The authors offer no explanation for their methodology.

A similar confusion of class and status distinctions is found in Pearlin whose aim is to 'observe the effects of status differences on marital relations that have the potential to evoke stress' (1979: 344). Moreover, he suggests that status heterogamy alone is a 'trivial feature' of marriage which assumes importance only in conjunction with other values (p. 344). Pearlin does not use any of the scales of occupational prestige available to him within the sociological lexicon. Rather, he constructs his own scale of occupations. He compares the relative status origins of husbands and wives by observing whether respondents married a person whose father was lower, higher or equal to their own father according to where these fathers fall into his seven category schema. This *status* schema is, however, remarkably similar to Goldthorpe's seven social classes, thus leaving open the question of whether it is in fact *status* differences between spouses which are captured by Pearlin's research.[2]

I have considered this issue in some depth because at first glance it would seem appropriate to relate the findings of this study to investigations such as those above. I do not wish to suggest that the studies discussed are entirely without value for the examination of the effects of wives' labour force superiority. They are not, however, appropriate to an examination of status differences between spouses—at least in so far as one understands status in its traditional sociological sense of differing relations of deference, acceptance or derogation.

Notes

1. Richardson writes:

   It is clear that occupational equality or superiority would neither arise accidentally nor instantaneously . . . If indeed wife occupational superiority would engender marital troubles, it would seem reasonable to assume that prospective partners would avoid marriage at the outset. (1979: 70)

Quite apart from the rather optimistic view this author takes of men's and women's abilities to foresee what will cause future problems within marriage, the findings reported here point out that wife occupational superiority can arise, if not accidentally, then at least some years after marriage when wives increase their educational qualifications and re-enter the job market in positions markedly different to those held at the time of marriage. In these situations it is difficult to know how marriage partners would have sufficient foresight to avoid potentially stressful marriages.

2. Pearlin's (1979) seven occupational categories are as follows:

   1. Professionals, higher executives, proprietors of large concerns.
   2. Business managers in large concerns, proprietors of medium businesses and lesser professionals.
   3. Administrative personnel, small independent business proprietors and minor professionals.
   4. Clerical and sales workers, technicians and owners of limited, one-man businesses.
   5. Foremen and skilled manual employees.
   6. Machine operators and semi-skilled employees.
   7. Unskilled employees.

With some few exceptions, this categorization of occupations is remarkably similar to Goldthorpe's social class schema (see Goldthorpe, 1980: 39–41).

Appendix 3

The Questionnaire

(Final version: the range and form of questions at the end of the interviews.)

Background Information

1. Place and date of birth.
2. Residence, date and occupation when married.
3. Previous marriages, if any.
4. Names and ages of children, if any.
5. Other members of household, if any.
6. Family of orientation—occupations and locations.
7. Educational background.
8. Work history.
9. Periods of unemployment.

Present Occupation

1. Job description and length of time in present position.
2. Could you tell me in as much detail as possible just exactly what you do?
3. How closely are you supervised?/How free are you to disagree with work procedures?/Do you supervise any others? If so, who and how many?
4. Do you ever work any overtime? Who decides if you do? Can you refuse?
5. Do you ever work directly with anyone else, as a team? How often?
6. How free do you feel to innovate, to change your daily routine at work?
7. Have you any form of job protection? For example, do you have: seniority rights; contract guarantees; tenure; union support; or some other form of job protection?
8. Is there a formal grievance procedure that you could use if you felt that you are or have been unfairly treated?
9. As things look now, how likely is it that you could be made redundant from your job in the next year or so because of cutbacks?
10. How many paid weeks holiday do you receive? Does your job provide for your being paid while sick? For how long?

11. Do you belong to a company pension plan? (If not, why not?)
12. Are you a member of a union?

Union Members Only

1. Name of union.
2. Did you have to join the union to get or to keep your job? If no: Why did you join? If yes: Is that the only reason why you joined?
3. Do you participate in your union in any way? For example, do you: attend workplace/branch meetings; vote; serve on committees; serve as an officer or steward; engage in social activities?
4. Do you discuss union affairs with your fellow workers? If so, how often and what kinds of issues?
5. If your union called a strike, would you come out? Probe to find reasons why or why not.
6. What do you see as the proper function or purpose of a union?
7. Is your spouse a union member? Do you discuss union matters with your spouse? Do you and your spouse agree in your attitudes towards unions?

Non-union members only

1. Is there a union where you work, one that you could join if you wanted? If yes: Why have you chosen not to join?
2. Have you ever belonged to a union? If yes: Why did you leave?
3. What do you see as the proper function or purpose of a union?
4. Does your spouse belong to a union? Did he/she discuss the decision to join/not to join with you? Do you and your spouse agree on your attitudes towards unions?

Social Activities

Clubs, organizations, and hobbies

1. Do you belong to any clubs or organizations at all? (list given including: sports/hobby club; parent/teacher association; residents/tenants association; church/church group; adult education; political party; professional association; social club; any other not listed).
2. If member: In what year did you join? How much time do you spend on activities connected with the club/association/etc.? Have you ever ór do you now hold any official position, or serve on any committees?
3. If non-member: Is there any particular reason why you do not participate in any clubs or organizations—is it a matter of time, personal preference or some other reason?
4. Do you have any activities that you would call hobbies? What are they? How much time do you spend on them?

Friends

1. Turning now to the people *you*, as an individual, most often spend your spare time with. I don't need to know their names, but I wonder if you could tell me about the people you most often see socially, away from your spouse (and children)? You may include couples, individuals, or families. How did you meet? How long have you known them (him/her)? Occupation and spouse's occupation. How often do you meet each other? What sorts of activities do you do together?

2. Again, I don't need to know their full names, but I would like now to talk about the people *you and your spouse* most often spend spare time with as a couple. They may, of course, be some of the same people you have just mentioned (same information collected).

3. Of the people you work with, are there any you see outside of work fairly often on a social basis, but did not mention in the last two questions? If yes: occupation, spouse's occupation and frequency of contact.

4. Does your spouse know any of the people with whom you work? How well?

5. Does your spouse come to any social events at your place of work? If not, why not? If yes, what sorts of occasions?

6. Do you know any of the people who work with your spouse? How well? Would you know this person's spouse as well?

7. Do you ever go to any social events at your spouse's workplace? If not, why not? If yes, what sorts of occasions?

Family Life and Kin Contact

I would like to turn now to your family life and ask you some questions about children, relatives, the running of your household, and so on.

Wives with children

1. Turning first to children, could you tell me what type of childcare arrangements you use now/have used in the past?

2. How do/did you organize your children's daily lives? That is, there are many things to be done such as getting them up in the mornings, seeing them off to school, disciplining them, and so on. How do/did all these things get done in your family?

3. How involved is/was your husband in the lives/upbringing of the children?

4. Who decides/decided if the children are ill; are sick enough to see a doctor?

5. If one of your children was ill, who would stay/stayed at home with them? If they became ill at school, who would/did the school contact?

Wives and husbands with school age or younger children

1. How much education would you like your son/daughter to have?
   What type of education?
2. Do you discuss your child's education with your spouse?
3. Have you ever given any thought to what type of occupation you
   would like your son/daughter to enter?

Wives and husbands with adult children

1. How old was your son/daughter when he/she left school? Did he/she
   take any exams before leaving school? Has he/she had any further
   education or training since leaving school?
2. Are you satisfied with the education your son/daughter received? Or
   did you hope for something different for him/her?
3. Is your son/daughter in employment now? What does he/she do?
4. Is this the type of job that you hope he/she will settle in? What type of
   work would you like him/her to do?

All parents

1. Is there anything about your life that you would like to be different for
   your son/daughter?

Childless wives

1. Do you plan on having any children?
2. Will you continue to work if you do have children? Probe for reasons.
3. If withdrawing from work: What effect will this have on your family
   financially? How long do you intend to remain out of the labour force?
   Can you re-enter without penalty? Would you or your husband ever
   consider your husband staying home with the children instead of you?
4. What will you do about childcare arrangements?
5. If planning to remain childless: Why have you decided not to have
   children?

I would like now to ask you some questions about your contact with relatives.

1. Which relatives would you usually meet once a week? Which have you
   met in the last month? And in the last year?
2. Do you usually see these relatives with your spouse or alone? Why?
   Which ones do you see together, which alone? Why?
3. Are there any other relatives, such as grandparents or cousins, whom
   you have met in the last year? How often? .

I would like to talk now about the running of the household: how the chores
get done, how you organize your finances, and so on.

1. First, speaking quite generally, how does the housework get done in
   your house? Do you have any outside help?

2. For example, who usually does the: daily cooking; laying the table; washing up; general tidying around the house; hoovering; food shopping; meal planning; laundry; ironing; gardening; decorating; washing windows; repair jobs; cares for the car.
3. Who would you say is 'in charge' of the household chores? Do you feel that you are? That is, that seeing they get done is your responsibility?

All Women

1. Do you ever feel you are being called upon to perform two jobs: housewife and worker?
2. Do you wish your husband took more responsibility in the house for housework? Have you ever discussed this with him?
3. If applicable: Why do you think that your husband does so few chores—given that you both work full time?

All Men

1. Do you ever feel that you ought to be doing more around the house?

Could you now tell me about how you manage your household budget?

1. Seeing that you have two incomes coming into the house, how do you set aside money for bills, food, clothes, and the like? What is your system?
2. How are you paid? Your spouse paid? Does this affect how you decide to manage your budget?
3. Do you have separate or joint bank accounts?
4. How do you decide what is to be spent for day-to-day living?
5. Would you say that your income is used for anything in particular?
6. Do you reserve any money from your own paycheque for your own private spending?
7. What about major expenses such as holidays, a car, children's education—how do you allow for these?
8. How do you and your spouse decide it is time to make a major purchase such as a new car, suite, refrigerator or the like? What happens if you disagree? Would you say that one of you has more say about things than the other?
9. How did you come to live here, in this house. That is, how did you choose this particular house in this particular neighbourhood?

The Relationship between Work and Family Life

1. Have you ever had to move from city to city or area to area because of your job, or because of your spouse's job?
2. If yes: How was the decision to move reached? Did either one have to quit a job in order to move?

3. If no: Why is that—is it because the opportunity has never come up, or for other reasons?

4. Do you think that your family would move if *you* were offered a better position in another city?

5. And if *your spouse* was offered a better position in another city, would the family move then?

6. Thinking back to your own job now, what are you looking forward to with respect to your work?

7. Do you think of your work as a career? Do you want a career?

8. Are there any promotion possibilities? Do you want promotion? What types of promotion might be available?

9. How would you say that the fact you work outside the home affects your family life? Do you think that there is any particular or special way that it does?

10. Do you bring work home with you at night—either mentally or physically?

11. Do you discuss your work with your spouse?

12. Do you think work and family ought to be kept separate?

13. Thinking about the *type* of work that you do now, rather than just the fact that you do work—do you think that your job affects the family, family life, in any ways at all which differ from the ways in which your spouse's job affects the family?

14. Bringing work home is one possible difference—are there any others? Does your spouse, for example, get tired from his/her job? Do you? Does your spouse recognize that you get tired?

15. How does bringing work home affect your relations with your spouse? (if applicable)

16. I would think that having two incomes does raise you family's standard of living, but I wonder how you think of your own income with repect to the long-term financial security and prospects of your family? Do you feel that your job contributes to the long-term economic circumstances of your family?

17. What about financial security—do you see your job as more secure than your spouse's job? Is your job the source of the family's financial security?

18. And what about the future—do you intend to work until retirement?

19. Thinking of your present income, how likely is it that it will continue to rise over the years? Will it level off at any point?

20. If you were to lose your job for any reason, what effect would this have on your family financially?

21. Have you or do you ever think of not working? Do you see working or not working as something about which you have a choice?

22. If you did not need to financially—say you were independently wealthy—would you continue to work? Why/why not?
23. How did you come to be a (present occupation)?

Politics and Class

I would like to change now to some different types of questions, in order to
get a more rounded picture of the way you look at things. Thinking first of
the political parties . . .

1. Do you, generally speaking, usually consider yourself as a Conservative, Labour, Liberal, Social Democrat or what?
2. How strongly do you favour that party?
3. Why do you support that party?
4. Thinking now of the last general election, the one in 1979 when the
Conservatives were led by Mrs Thatcher and Labour by Mr Callaghan, do you remember for certain whether you voted? Which party
did you vote for? Will you vote for that party in the future?
5. Do you discuss how you are going to vote with anyone in particular?
6. Do you think that you and your spouse influence each other when it
comes to voting? Do you and your spouse discuss elections? Do you
vote for the same party?
7. How about the people you work with, do you know how they vote?

Turning away from politics now, I'd like to know what you think about
social classes. People often talk about there being different classes in society,
what do you think?

1. Do you think that it is possible to move from one class to another? How
might this happen?
2. What do you think is (are) the major factor(s) determining the class
position of individuals, of families?
3. How many classes do you think there are in our society today? How
would you name them? Who would you include in each class?
4. Where would you place yourself? Why?
5. Do class differences mean anything to your family or friends?

Social Status

I'd like to ask you a few last questions about the kinds of jobs you and your
spouse have.

1. You are employed as a (occupation) and your spouse as a (occupation). Some people might say that being a (occupation) has more (less)
status/prestige than being a (occupation). What do you think?

2. Do you see any difference at all between these two types of jobs with respect to position in society, or acceptance by other people?
3. Have you ever been made to feel that there are differences?
4. Do you think that the differences in the types of jobs affect your marriage/your family life in any way at all?
5. How did you meet your spouse?

One last question, would you mind telling me how much your income is? And without telling me the amount, could you tell me if you know how much your spouse makes each year?

Bibliography

Acker, J. (1973). 'Women and Social Stratification: A Case of Intellectual Sexism', *American Journal of Sociology*, 78. 4: 936–45.

Acker, J. (1980). 'Women and Stratification: A Review of Recent Literature', *Contemporary Sociology*, 9, January: 25–39.

Allan, G. A. (1979). *A Sociology of Friendship and Kinship*, London: George Allen and Unwin.

Allen, S. (1982). 'Gender Inequality and Class Formation', pp. 137–47 in A. Giddens and G. Mackenzie (eds.), *Social Class and The Division of Labour*, Cambridge: Cambridge University Press.

Araji, S. (1977). 'Husbands' and Wives' Attitude–Behavior Congruence', *Journal of Marriage and the Family*, 39, May: 309–20.

Babchuk, N., and A. Bates (1963). 'The primary relations of middle class couples', *American Sociological Review*, 28: 377–91.

Bahr, J. (1974). 'Effects on power and the division of labour within the family', in L. W. Hoffman and F. I. Nye (eds.), *Working Mothers*, San Francisco: Jossey-Bass.

Bain, G. (1970). *The Growth of White-Collar Trade Unionism in Great Britain*, Oxford: Clarendon Press.

——, D. Coates, and V. Ellis (1973). *Social Stratification and Trade Unionism*, London: Heinemann.

Barth, E. A. and W. B. Watson (1967). 'Social Stratification and The Family in Mass Society', *Social Forces*, 45, 3: 392–401.

Bell, C. R. (1968). *Middle Class Families*, London: Routledge and Kegan Paul.

Bernard, J. (1973). *The Future of Marriage*, London: Souvenir Press.

Blackburn, R. M. (1967). *Union Character and Social Class*, London: Batsford.

Bott, E. (1957). *Family and Social Network*, London: Tavistock.

Boulding, E. (1976). 'Familial Constraints on Women's Work Roles', *Signs*, 1, 3, Spring: 95–117.

Braverman, H. (1974). *Labor and Monopoly Capital: The Degradation of Work in the Twentieth Century*, New York: Monthly Review Books.

Britten, N. and A. Heath (1983). 'Women, Men and Social Class', pp. 46–60 in E. Gamarnikow *et al.* (eds.), *Gender, Class and Work*, London: Heinemann.

Bulmer, M., (ed.) (1975). *Working-Class Images of Society*, London: Routledge and Kegan Paul.

Burke, P. J., and J. C. Tully (1977). 'The measurement of role identity', *Social Forces*, 55: 881–97.

Burman, S. (ed.) (1979). *Fit Work for Women*, London: Croom Helm.

Clark, S., and A. S. Harvey (1976). 'The Sexual Division of Labour: The Use of Time', *Atlantis*, 2, Fall: 46–66.

Crewe, I., B. Sarlvik, and J. Alt (1977). 'Partisan Dealignment in Britain 1964–1974', *British Journal of Political Science*, 7, July: 129–91.

—— (1983a). 'The disturbing truth behind Labour's rout', *The Guardian*, 13 June, p. 14.

—— (1983b). 'How Labour was trounced all round', *The Guardian*, 14 June, p. 5.

Crompton, R., and G. Jones (1984). *White-Collar Proletariat: Deskilling and Gender in Clerical Work*, London: Macmillan.

Department of Employment (1982). *New Earnings Survey 1981*, London: HMSO.

—— (1983). *Employment Gazette*, 91. 2, February.

Dickens, Charles (1864). *Dombey and Son*, London: Collins.

Dixon, K. (1976). 'Friendship and the Stability of Structural Inequality', mimeo, Simon Fraser University.

Duncan, O. D. (1961a). 'A socioeconomic index for all occupations', pp. 109–38 in A. J. Reiss *et al.*. (eds.), *Occupations and Social Status*, New York, The Free Press.

—— (1961b). 'Properties and characteristics of the SEI', pp. 139–61 in A. J. Reiss *et al.*. (eds.), *Occupations and Social Status*.

Durkheim, E. (1982). *Rules of The Sociological Method, etc.*, S. Lukes (ed.), London: Macmillan.

Edgell, S. (1980). *Middle Class Couples: A Study of Segregation, Domination and Inequality in Marriage*, London: George Allen and Unwin.

Eichler, M. (1980). *The Double Standard: A Feminist Critique of Feminist Social Science*, London: Croom Helm.

Elias, P., and B. Main (1982). *Women's Working Lives: Evidence from the National Training Survey*, University of Warwick, Institute for Employment Research.

Fogarty, M. P., R. Rapoport, and R. Rapoport (1971). *Sex, Career and Family*, London: George Allen and Unwin.

Fonda, N., and P. Moss (eds.) (1976). *Mothers in Employment*, Brunel University Management Programme.

Fox, A. (1974). *Beyond Contract: Work, Power and Trust Relations*, London: Faber and Faber.

—— (1976). 'The Meaning of Work' pp. 9–59 in Open University, *Occupational Categories and Cultures 1, People and Work*, Milton Keynes.

Garnsey, E. (1978). 'Women's Work and Theories of Class Stratification', *Sociology*, 12: 223–43.

General Household Survey 1979 (1981). London: HMSO.

Giddens, A. (1973). *The Class Structure of Advanced Societies*, London: Hutchinson.

Goldthorpe, J. H. (1970). 'Images of Class Among Affluent Manual Workers', University of Cambridge, Dept. of Applied Economics Working Paper, n.d. Subsequently published as 'L'Image des classes chez les travailleurs manuels aisés', *Revue française de sociologie*, 11: 311–38.

—— (in collaboration with C. Llewellyn and C. Payne) (1980). *Social Mobility and The Class Structure in Modern Britain*, Oxford: Clarendon Press.

—— (1982). 'On the Service Class, its formation and future', pp. 162–85 in A. Giddens and G. Mackenzie (eds.), *Social Class and the Division of Labour*, Cambridge: Cambridge University Press.

—— (1983). 'Women and Class Analysis: In Defense of the Conventional View', *Sociology*, 17. 4: 465–88.

——, and K. Hope (1974). *The Social Grading of Occupations*, Oxford: Clarendon Press.

——, and D. Lockwood (1963). 'Affluence and The British Class Structure', *Sociological Review*, 11. 2, July: 133–63.

——, D. Lockwood, F. Bechhofer, and J. Platt (1968). *The Affluent Worker: Political Attitudes and Behaviour*, Cambridge: Cambridge University Press.

——, ——, ——, —— (1969). *The Affluent Worker in the Class Structure*, Cambridge: Cambridge University Press.

Gowler, D., and K. Legge (1982). 'Dual Worker Families', pp. 138–58 in Rapoport *et al.* (eds.), *Families in Britain*, London: Routledge and Kegan Paul.

Gronsëth, E. (1975). 'Work-Sharing Families: Adaptations of Pioneering Families with Husband and Wife in Part-time Employment', *Acta Sociologica*, 18. 2–3: 202–21.

Hakim, C. (1979). *Occupational Segregation*, Research Paper No. 9, Dept. of Employment, London: HMSO.

Hardy, Thomas (1926). *The Woodlanders*, London: Macmillan.

Hatt, P. (1961). 'Occupations and Social Stratification', pp. 239–58 in A. J. Reiss *et al.*. (eds.), *Occupations and Social Status*, New York: The Free Press.

Haug, M. (1973). 'Social Class Measurement and Women's Occupational Roles', *Social Forces*, 52: 86–98.

Heath, A. (1981). *Social Mobility*, London: Fontana.

——, and N. Britten (1984). 'Women's jobs do make a difference: A reply to Goldthorpe', *Sociology*, 18. 4, November: 475–90.

Hill, S. (1976). *The Dockers*, London: Heinemann.

Hiller, D., and W. W. Philliber (1982). 'Predicting Marital and Career Success in Dual-Worker Families', *Journal of Marriage and the Family*, 44, February: 53–62.

Hunt, P. (1980). *Gender and Class Consciousness*, London: Macmillan.

James, Henry (n.d.). *The Princess Casamassima*, London: Heron Books.

Jorgensen, S., and D. Klein (1979). 'Sociocultural Heterogamy, Dissensus and Conflict in Marriage', *Pacific Sociological Review*, 22. 1: 51–75.

Joshi, H., R. Layard, and S. Owen (1983). '*Why are more women working in Britain?*', Centre for Labour Economics, London School of Economics, Discussion Paper No. 162, June.

Joseph, G. (1983). *Women at Work*, Oxford: Phillip Alan Publishers.

Klein, J. (1965). *Samples from English Culture*, London: Routledge and Kegan Paul.

Lawrence, D. H. (1929). *Sons and Lovers*, London: Martin Secker.

Lazarfeld, P., and R. Merton (1954). 'Friendship as social process' pp. 18–66 in M. Berger, T. Abel, and C. H. Page (eds.), *Freedom and Control in Modern Society*, Princeton, NJ: Van Nostrand.

Lockwood, D. (1958). *The Blackcoated Worker*, London: Unwin University Books.

McIntosh, A. (1980). 'Women at Work: A Survey of Employers', *Employment Gazette*, November, Department of Employment, London.

McNally, F. (1979). *Women for Hire*, London: Macmillan.

Mackie, L., and P. Pattullo (1977). *Women at Work*, London: Tavistock.

Mahoney, E. R., and J. G. Richardson (1979). 'Perceived Social Status of Husbands and Wives: The Effects of Labor Force Participation and Occupational Prestige', *Sociology and Social Research*, 63. 2: 364–74.

Martin, J., and C. Roberts (1984). *Women and Employment: A Lifetime Perspective*, OPCS, Department of Employment, London: HMSO.

Martin, R., and R. H. Fryer (1975). 'The Deferential Worker?', in M. Bulmer (ed.), *Working Class Images of Society*, London: Routledge and Kegan Paul.

Model, S. (1981). 'Housework by Husbands', pp. 193–205 in J. Aldous (ed.), *Two Paychecks: Life in Dual-Earner Families*.

Mumford, E., and O. Banks (1967). *The Computer and the Clerk*, London: Batsford.

Murgatroyd, L. (1982). 'Gender and Occupational Stratification', *Sociological Review*, 30. 4: 574–602.

Oakley, A. (1974). *The Sociology of Housework*, New York: Pantheon Books.

OPCS (1982). *Labour Force Survey 1981*, London: HMSO.

Oppenheimer, V. K. (1982). *Work and The Family: A study in social demography*, New York: Academic Press.

Otto, L. (1975). 'Class and Status in Family Research', *Journal of Marriage and the Family*, 37, May: 315–31.

Pahl, J., and R. Pahl (1971). *Managers and Their Wives*, London: Penguin Books.

Paloma, M., and N. Garland (1971). 'The Myth of the Egalitarian Family', pp. 741–61 in A. Theodore (ed.), *The Professional Woman*, Cambridge, MA: Schenkman.

Parkin, F. (1972). *Class Inequality and Political Order*, London: Granada Publishing, Paladin Books.

—— (1979). *Marxism and Class Theory: A Bourgeois Critique*, New York: Columbia University Press.

Parsons, T. (1940). 'An Analytical Approach to The Study of Social Stratification', *American Journal of Sociology*, 45, May: 841–62.

—— (1942). 'Age and Sex in the Social Structure of the United States', *American Sociological Review*, 7, October: 604–16.

—— (1943). 'The Kinship System of the United States', pp. 177–96 in T. Parsons, *Essays in Sociological Theory*, Revised edn., London: Collier–Macmillan.

—— (1953). 'A Revised Analytical Approach to the Theory of Social Stratification', pp. 386–439 in T. Parsons, *Essays in Sociological Theory*.

Pearlin, L. (1975). 'Status Inequality and Stress in Marriage', *American Sociological Review*, 40: 344–57.

Pleck, J. (1977). 'The work-family role system', *Social Problems*, 24, April: 417–27.

Prandy, K., A. Stewart, and R. M. Blackburn (1982). *White-Collar Work*, London: Macmillan.

Rainwater, Lee, M. Rein, and J. Schwartz (1986). *Income Packaging and The Welfare State: A Comparative Study of Family Income*, Oxford University Press, 1986.

Rallings, C. (1975). 'Two Types of Middle-class Votes?', *British Journal of Political Science*, 5, January: 107–28.

Rapoport, R., and R. N. Rapoport (1976). *Dual-Career Families Re-Examined*, 2nd edn. London: Martin Robertson. [1st edn. 1971.]

——, R. N. Rapoport, S. Strelitz, with S. Kew (1977). *Fathers, Mothers and Others*, New York: Basic Books.

Reid, I. (1981). *Social Class Differences in Britain*, 2nd edn., London: Grant McIntyre.

Rhee, H. (1968). *Office Automation in Social Perspective*, Oxford: Basil Blackwell.

Richardson, J. G. (1979). 'Wife Occupational Superiority and Marital Troubles: An examination of the hypothesis', *Journal of Marriage and the Family*, 41: 63–72.

Rimmer, L., and J. Popay (1982). *Employment Trends and The Family*, London: Study Commission on The Family, Occasional Paper No. 10.

Ritter, L., and L. Hargens (1975). 'Occupational Positions and Class Identifications of Married Working Women: A test of the asymmetry hypothesis', *American Journal of Sociology*, 80. 4: 934–48.

Routh, G. (1980). *Occupations and Pay in Great Britain*, London: Macmillan.

Safilios-Rothschild, C. (1975). 'Family and Stratification: Some Macrosociological Observations and Hypotheses', *Journal of Marriage and the Family*, 37, November: 855–60.

—— (1976). 'Dual Linkages between the Occupational and Family Systems: A Macrosociological Analysis', *Signs*, 1. 3, Spring: 51–60.

Scanzoni, J. (1978). *Sex Roles, Women's Work and Marital Conflict*, Lexington, MA: D. C. Heath.

Sennett, R., and J. Cobb (1973). *The Hidden Injuries of Class*, New York: Vintage Books.

Silverman, D. (1968). 'Clerical Ideologies: A Research Note', *British Journal of Sociology*, 19: 326–33.

Sinfield, A. (1981). 'Unemployment in an Unequal Society', pp. 122–66 in B. Showler and A. Sinfield (eds.), *The Workless State: Studies in Unemployment*, London: Martin Robertson.

Social Trends, 9, HMSO, 1979.

Social Trends, 13, HMSO, 1983.

Stacey, M. (1960). *Tradition and Change*, London: Oxford University Press.

Stewart, A., K. Prandy, and R. M. Blackburn (1980). *Social Stratification and Occupations*, London: Macmillan.

Thomas, W. I. (1966). *On Social Organization and Social Personality*, Chicago: University of Chicago Press.

Tresemer, D. (1975). 'Assumptions made about gender roles', pp. 308–39 in M. Millman and R. Kantor (eds.), *Another Voice: Feminist Perspectives on Social Life and Social Science*, New York: Anchor Books.

Tydeman, P. (1981). 'Will you take a cheque?', *Employment Gazette*, Department of Employment, October.

Vannemann, R., and F. Pampel (1977). 'The American Perception of Class and Status', *American Sociological Review*, 42. 3: 422–37.

Van Velso, E., and L. Beeghley (1979). 'The Process of Class Identification among Employed Married Women', *Journal of Marriage and the Family*, 41: 771–91.

Watson, W. B., and E. A. Barth (1964). 'Questionable Assumptions in the Theory of Social Stratification', *Pacific Sociological Review*, 7, Spring: 10–16.

Weber, Max (1946). *Selected Essays in Sociology*, H. H. Gerth and C. W. Mills (eds.), *From Max Weber*, New York: Oxford University Press, 1978.

Westergaard, J., and H. Resler (1975). *Class in a Capitalist Society*, Harmondsworth: Penguin Books.

William, W. M. (1956). *The Sociology of an English Village: Gosforth*, London: Routledge and Kegan Paul.

Willis, P. E. (1977). *Learning to Labour: How working class kids get working class jobs*, Farnborough: Saxon House.

Yankelovich, D. (1974). 'The Meaning of Work', pp. 19–48 in J. M. Rosow (ed.), *The Worker and The Job*, Englewood Cliffs, NJ: Prentice Hall.

Young, M., and P. Willmott (1957). *Family and Kinship in East London*, London: Routledge and Kegan Paul.

—— and —— (1973). *The Symmetrical Family*, London: Routledge and Kegan Paul.

Index